T0283302

THE
WALTHAM
MURDERS

ONE WOMAN'S PURSUIT TO EXPOSE THE TRUTH BEHIND A MURDER AND A NATIONAL TRAGEDY

Susan Clare Zalkind

Little
a

Published by Little A, New York

www.apub.com

Amazon, the Amazon logo, and Little A are trademarks of Amazon.com, Inc., or its affiliates.

ISBN-13: 9781503903715 (hardcover)
ISBN-13: 9781503903708 (paperback)
ISBN-13: 9781503958708 (digital)

Cover design by David Drummond
Cover image: © SV Production, © Dolores M. Harvey / Shutterstock

Printed in the United States of America

First edition

For my sister

The question remains: Does the illness give birth to the crime itself, or is the crime, somehow by its own nature, always accompanied by something like an illness?

—Fyodor Dostoyevsky, *Crime and Punishment.* Translated by
Michael Katz.

Contents

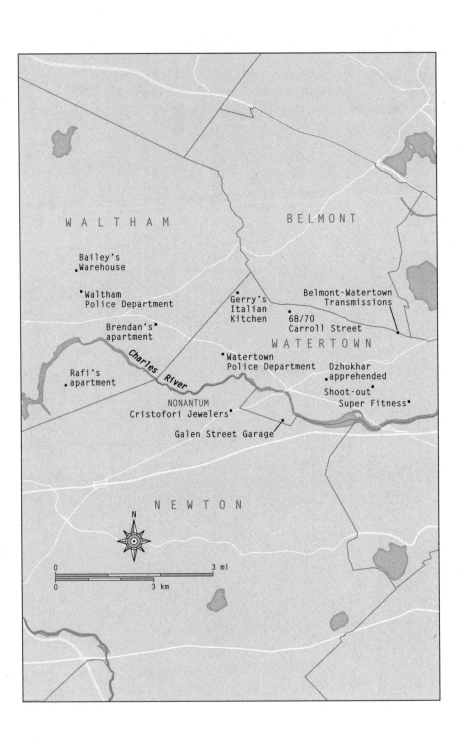

W A L T H A M

BELMONT

Bailey's
▪Warehouse

▪Waltham
Police Department

Gerry's
Italian
Kitchen

Belmont-Watertown
Transmissions

68/70
Carroll Street

Brendan's▪
apartment

W A T E R T O W N

▪Watertown
Police Department

Dzhokhar
▪apprehended

Rafi's
▪apartment

Shoot-out▪
Super Fitness▪

NONANTUM
Cristofori Jewelers▪

Galen Street Garage

N E W T O N

N

0   3 mi

0   3 km

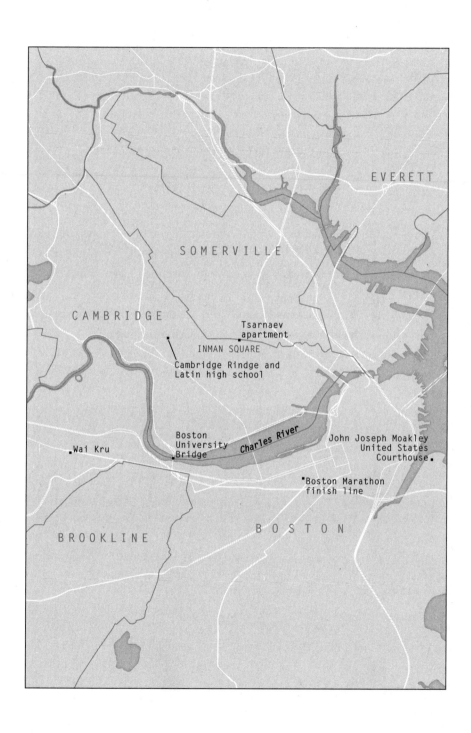

EVERETT

SOMERVILLE

CAMBRIDGE

Tsarnaev
apartment

INMAN SQUARE

Cambridge Rindge and
Latin high school

Boston
University
Bridge

Charles River

John Joseph Moakley
United States
Courthouse

Wai Kru

Boston Marathon
finish line

BROOKLINE

BOSTON

CONTENT ADVISORY

This book includes detailed reporting on suicide. If you or someone you know needs support, the Suicide & Crisis Lifeline and the Crisis Text Line are free, available 24/7, and confidential. To speak with a trained listener, dial 988 or text HOME to 741741.

In addition to specific details about the Waltham homicides, this book includes graphic descriptions and allegations of domestic violence.

PREFACE

On Sunday, September 11, 2011, three men were murdered in a second-floor apartment on a dead-end street in Waltham, Massachusetts. The killers slit the victims' throats, dumped a pound and a half of marijuana on two of the bodies, and left $5,000 cash at the scene of the crime.

One of the victims, Brendan Mess, 25, had been friends and sparring part-ners with Tamerlan Tsarnaev, a local boxer with a thick Slavic accent. Another one of the victims, Erik Weissman, 31, had been a friend of mine. The third victim, Raphael Teken, 37, was the son of a prominent Jewish spiritual leader. Hibatalla K. Eltilib, who had been Brendan's girlfriend, found the bodies.

Eighteen months later, Tamerlan bombed the Boston Marathon with his younger brother, Dzhokhar, murdered four people, mutilated and maimed doz-ens of others, and inspired a new era of domestic terrorism and fear. The bomb-ing raised dark questions about Tamerlan and the 9/11/11 killing. One month after the bombing, law enforcement questioned one of Tamerlan's associates, a Chechen MMA fighter named Ibragim Todashev, about the murder and shot him seven times in his Florida home.

Dzhokhar Tsarnaev was tried and sentenced to death in Boston's federal courthouse. Federal prosecutors fought to keep any mention of the state mur-der case out of the capital trial, and federal agencies have publicly distanced themselves from the Waltham murders. The triple homicide falls under the jurisdiction of state investigators at the Middlesex County District Attorney's Office. The murder case is still open.

This story has haunted my thoughts for more than a dozen years. I have reported on this case for almost as long. I began investigating because I felt like I had to. In lieu of facts, people spun theories. Mistruths about the murders were tossed around in court hearings, all the way up to the United States Supreme Court. I saw firsthand how the lack of answers and accountability led to a profound disillusion—a breakdown in trust in systems of governance and in truth itself. Meanwhile, similar patterns of dangerous conspiratorial thinking began to proliferate around the world.

Murder has a strange way of marking place and time. My goal has always been to seek the truth, separate fact from speculation, and tell this story as thoroughly and accurately as I am able. In doing so, I had to reconcile my own history with crime. This is also a story about my home.

Over the course of my investigation, I worked with various news outlets. I reported my earlier findings for *Boston* magazine and *This American Life*, I covered the bombing trial for *The Daily Beast*, and I wrote and produced the 2022 Hulu docuseries *The Murders before the Marathon*. These partnerships were crucial. But I never felt any sense of relief when the work was over.

I suppose, all this while, I have been searching for a feeling, or an escape from one. Some might call it closure. I simply never felt finished. In early 2022, when I turned a manuscript in to my publisher, I felt the same unsettling feeling that has followed me all these years. Then I had a few lucky breaks. I won a Freedom of Information Act dispute, got some more interviews and records, called my ever-patient publisher, and rewrote the book. For the first time, I felt lighter. I had gone as far as I could go.

There is more to this story. There are people who are dead or won't speak to me, agencies that won't answer my questions, and recorded interviews that remain under seal. Perhaps someone reading this book has a crucial missing clue. But for now, I am done. I am at the end of the road, and this is the whole truth, as best I can tell.

BOOK ONE

PART I

Life of Crime

CHAPTER ONE

The Meeting

When I first met Erik Weissman, he was sitting on a beanbag chair, pulling glass jars of marijuana out of a duffel bag, pausing to name each strain as he went: Blue Dream, Grand Daddy, Sensi Star, Sour Diesel, Black Widow, Alaskan Thunderfuck. It was 2006, the summer after my freshman year in college, and I'd recently taken scissors to my long hair. That evening, I had walked down the hill from my parents' Newton, Massachusetts, home in a green thrift store dress to meet friends I had known since elementary school, three guys who sold weed. Outside, the peonies were in bloom; inside the attic bedroom, it reeked of skunky cannabis.

Every year, personal finance and security firms churn out lists of America's safest cities, and back then Newton usually found itself somewhere around the top. The year we graduated from high school, we were number one. "Safest city in America," we'd laugh in between bong rips. We were lucky. We missed the wave of cocaine that swept Newton North High School the year after we left. Sure, our class had dabbled, and a few of us tried OxyContin back when you could still peel the time-release seal off the pills, or played around with acid and mushrooms, but mostly we smoked weed. Lots and lots of weed. We smoked from joints, carved-out apples, bubblers filled with black sticky water, and gravity bongs. So much weed that for a brief period I convinced myself I had a genuine interest in the band Phish. I have my regrets. But it could have been worse.

Boston is known for its regionality. People are fascinated by our accents, the Brahmin boat shoe version, with our *ahs* and *aws*; the Irish and Italian strains, with our misplaced *Rs*. We pepper our sentences with words like *kid*, *dude*, *weird*, and *ripshit*, a specific type of rage. We are notorious for our terrible fashion: pairing brown and navy in the winter, embroidered salmon slacks in the summer, and Bruins jerseys and cargo shorts (accessorized with Dunkin' Donuts iced coffees) at any given time of year. Newton is about a twenty-minute drive from the city. We share some of the accents, and some of the aesthetic, but it's not a fitting backdrop to your favorite crime movie, a place where tales of geriatric gangsters are extolled. The history here is less well known.

The Charles River, like the Boston Marathon, begins in Hopkinton. The municipalities of Waltham, Watertown, and Newton meet where the river narrows. Settlers from the Massachusetts Bay Colony established the district of Watertown near this narrow in 1630. Back then, the district included all of modern-day Watertown, parts of Newton, Cambridge, and all of Waltham.

Before the river was dammed in 1908, the Charles was a tidal estuary, heaving in and out like a lung. This narrow was where the salt water lapped at the river basin and where travelers going upstream had to get out of their boats to ford. Here the colonists found access to the harbor but with protection from potential invaders by sea. New England is known for its dense forests and rocky soil, but the land around the narrow was fertile and clear. Freshwater springs ran through the district like veins.

John Winthrop, the Puritan lawyer and early leader of the Massachusetts Bay Colony, initially considered founding the capital in Watertown. But it seems Governor Winthrop was really hung up on this whole "city upon a hill" idea. He established Boston on a windy moraine overlooking the harbor instead.

Boston grew into a bustling commercial capital. Meanwhile, the people around the narrow favored a more bucolic lifestyle. Away from the river, people built estates and maintained small farms, enjoying the hilly landscapes and wooded recreational parks. They took pride in their chestnut and oak trees. From the beginning, residents—especially in Newton—romanticized rural life. The three towns fought to preserve their small-town charm and refused to be absorbed into the capital.

Later, private entrepreneurs built factories near the narrow on the Charles, but the limited power of the slow-moving Charles kept large scale factories in check. After the war of 1812, the federal government built an arsenal along the narrow in Watertown where people assembled arms and ammunition through

World War II. The factories have since been replaced by tech companies and skyrocketing housing prices have changed the fabric of almost every community in the Northeast. But before all that, for century after century, these towns were a postcard picture of the American dream where the people thrived and the factories dumped an unfathomable about of pollution into the Charles. At least that's the story we tell ourselves—the one I absorbed, living around here for almost my whole life and going through the public schools.

Actually, according to archeological records, by the time Winthrop and his fleet pulled into the harbor, indigenous people in Southern New England had been congregating around this narrow, and stewarding the landscape continuously, for almost 6,000 years. The Wampanoag, Massachusett, Nipmuc, Pocumtuc, Mohegan, Schaghticoke, Paugussett, Niantic, Pequot and Narragansett nations spoke variations of the Algonquin language, formed alliances, married, and navigated disputes.

This was Massachusett land. Their Nipmuc neighbors lived to the west. For thousands of years native people lived here continuously, keeping the banks of the estuary thick with oysters and clams. The river teemed with bass and they built weirs to catch Alewife herring when they went upstream to breed. They used controlled burning to encourage growth of berries, create habitable land for game, and make room for oak and chestnut trees to grow.

Before they sailed over, Winthrop and the other colonists, wrote up a plan. The plan was: just take the land without asking. If the locals "pretend right of inheritance" then they would "endeavor to purchase" to avoid the "scruple of intrusion." Winthrop wrote that all of this was morally okay because the locals did not use fences, raise enclosed livestock, and the communities thought in terms of communal rather than individual land ownership. "That which is common to all is proper to none," Winthrop wrote in his diary. The settlers would rely on the Indians for food, then let their animals wreak havoc on their oyster beds and unfenced fields.

There is a myth that has been reiterated over and over again in local history books here for hundreds of years, and that's that the District of Watertown did not buy land from the Indians. But, according to the colony records, it appears the District of Watertown paid a "Captain Gibbons" for arranging to buy land from the Indians for Watertown in 1640, to make up for any damage done to them. Gibbons was paid about £14 by the District of Watertown for setting up the arrangement. It's unclear who the Indians were or what they received. Similar arrangements orchestrated by Gibbons on behalf of the colony involved exchanges of wampum and promises of winter coats and corn. In 1671, Indians tried to buy the right to fish by the estuary. (There is no record that Indians ever sold this right, that I found.) The people of Watertown pooled their money together to keep them away.

The first settler to own land in Waltham was a violent sea captain named John Oldham, also known as Mad Jack. Oldham was murdered off the coast of Block Island in 1636. Winthrop would use the mystery surrounding Oldham's death to justify a brutal war against Pequot nation. Prior to the war (which the Pequot people tried to advert) the Pequot nation asked the English to confirm that the colonists would not attack women or children—the colonists would not agree to these terms.

In 1641, Massachusetts became the first colony to write slavery in the legal code. Massachusetts colonists enslaved thousands of people, made them work in their fields and homes, and sold them for profit to plantations in the Caribbean. A few years later, a group of local Indian people, led by a man named Waban, gathered in Newton, under a large tree at the edge of what is now the Chestnut Hill golf club. A Puritan colonist named John Eliot had been trying to mission-ize native people, and he learned Algonquin and translated a Bible. Under the tree in an area called Nonantum, Eliot gave a sermon that is depicted in a lot of paintings and statues. But basically, what happened was this. Eliot crossed over the river from Watertown and preached for three hours in Algonquin. When he was done, Waban asked about securing land and protection for his people. Native people had lived on Chestnut Hill for a long time. Waban and his people wanted to stay in the area. Eliot moved them to the town of Natick, which was, at the time, essentially a missionized reservation. Later, during another war, they were marched to an internment camp on Deer Island. Afterwards, survivors returned to Nonantum and Cowate, despite new laws that tried to restrict them to reservations and take their children away.

Newton and Waltham are now technically cities, but they feel like towns. This is by design. Waltham has only two active central cross streets. Newton is divided into thirteen villages, which sounds sinister, considering our history. Nonantum is still the name of the village closest to the Charles River and the Watertown and Waltham municipal lines. Today, people from Nonantum call this place "the Lake" because of a dried-up pond where children used to ice-skate and mothers washed their clothes.

Growing up in Newton, my friends and I had a few sayings they don't use in Boston. Lake Talk is a cant, or a code. No one is certain where it comes from, who began using it, or when. It's not a written language. People make up new words every year.

All I know is that, on occasion, my friends and I call each other "mush," an insider term for someone from the Lake. *Mush* is used in the same way that Bostonians say *kid* or *dude*. But the point is that we are not from Boston. We are from here, and when someone says, "mush," we understand.

~

When I was nineteen, nothing could be more tedious than New England suburbia, the parks, pristine lawns, ice cream parlors, and baseball fields. Erik came into my life by way of a friend I'd known since nursery school. Back then, everyone called Daniel Adler-Golden DAG, and before he became a student of cannabis, carrying Jason King's photobook *The Cannabible* around in his backpack, he'd studied classical music and magic tricks. He'd walk down the halls of our high school burning sheets of flash paper.

The summer of 2006, DAG had a job as a caddy at the Chestnut Hill golf club. Erik was a golfer, and, along with a tip and his number, Erik gave DAG a bud of marijuana. The most beautiful nugget DAG had ever seen. After a few follow-up meetings, in which cash and plastic baggies were passed through car windows, the two became business associates. That evening in DAG's bedroom, Erik passed around jars and extolled the virtues of crystals, the pungent aromas. It felt more like a wine tasting than a drug deal.

Erik was from across the river in Cambridge, Boston's more liberal and academic sister city, but he fit right in with our suburban Newton crew. He was scrappy, with a quick sense of humor, and he was Jewish, like about half of my friends, which to me just meant he got our jokes. Erik talked the way we did, interrupting and speaking over each other when we got excited. *L'chaim*, we'd say as we passed the blunt around. Erik was loyal too, in that way that seems like a trope from a Boston crime movie but is actually true. People around here aren't quick to make new friends, but when they do, the relationships tend to last.

That night, the boys were in awe of Erik and his crystallized weed. I'd never seen them so impressed. I thought it was silly, and Erik was pretending to be a bigger drug dealer than he was, with his duffel bag of glass jars and his new sneakers. So I teased him for talking game. He told me he'd take me out and prove he wasn't bluffing.

CHAPTER TWO

Sour Diesel

That summer, I was restless. Erik met me outside of a jazz club in Inman Square, a quiet neighborhood of Cambridge. I had a job collecting cash at the door, but mostly I sat in the stairwell, smoked cigarettes, and people-watched while the music vibrated through the old wooden floorboards. Later, with Erik's encouragement, I would get a weekly gig singing at the Irish bar next door.

Erik, then 26, pulled up in his blue Audi, rolled down the tinted window, and greeted me with a big grin and a head of mousy brown curls. I had my fingers wrapped around an unfiltered Lucky Strike and a wad of door fees in my dress pocket. He had a joint of his Sour Diesel rolled into a neat, clear paper cone and a bottle of Smartwater waiting for me in the car. He told me he was driving me someplace special.

We passed the joint between us as he drove, protected by his tinted windows.

It was good weed. Like, really good weed. Everyone I shared it with at the club would lose their goddamn minds. Expert growers tell me that even with the legal dispensaries open these days, it's hard to find weed with such distinct properties. A lot of what is sold in stores today is mass-produced and comparatively bland. Cultivating and preserving high-quality cannabis plants was even more challenging during criminalization. The better the bud, the greater the risk for growers. Weed had to be grown in secret, and law enforcement could destroy entire crops at a moment's notice, lock you up, and seize your home. Some of the best weed, like Sour Diesel, takes a longer time to grow. One grower I spoke to said Erik had a connection to Diesel—not Sour Diesel—through a group of men in Montecito, Santa Barbara. DAG says Sour Diesel is a controversial strain. In 2017 he founded Node Labs, where they preserve elite "old-school" and modern weed genetics. He credits Erik for launching his career. The original Sour Diesel was cultivated in the early nineties. It was the "loudest, stinkiest weed" you could find, and there was constant debate over "who had a fake cut." DAG believes Erik most likely had a Sweet and Sour Diesel phenotype. In any case, back then, if you had a steady Sour Diesel connection, "you were the man." Especially on the East Coast. It was just that much better than everything else around, and having it meant guaranteed business for the boutique dealers Erik sold to, like DAG.

Erik had unique variants in part because he sponsored artisan growers by giving them advance payments, and he worked with them to cultivate a variety of rare strains—in addition to supporting musicians and artists.

That night, when we were driving around in Erik's car, felt momentous. The Sour Diesel warped my perception of time and added meaning to every movement and otherwise casual statement. I was drawn to Erik, and it scared me a little.

Erik drew on the joint and handed it back to me. I took another hit and slid down the leather seat of his Audi. We whizzed through the Williams Tunnel. The streetlights blurred until they looked like rings, and I imagined we were collecting them in some sort of virtual video game. He was driving me to Boston Harbor, where there was an Italian seafood restaurant beneath the federal court-house. After Erik was murdered, I would go through these courthouse doors looking for answers, while construction workers hammered together a shiny new neighborhood. In 2006, there were no tech companies or luxury apartments. The Daily Catch was one of the only decent places to eat. Erik was friends with several of the owners' seven sons. He parked in an illegal spot outside of the restaurant, walked me to the raw bar, and told me to dig in. I laughed. He was showing off. Point made. He was a big-time weed dealer. Business was good. But I was too young to appreciate oysters and too high to eat at a restaurant. The restaurant lights were playing tricks on me, and the grand gesture made me nervous. I wanted to go back to the car and talk. And so we did.

CHAPTER THREE

The Referral

After that first ride, we would get together every few weeks or so and swap stories. I asked a lot of questions about his business. Marijuana trafficking had always been a particular interest of mine, and Erik felt exciting and familiar. My father is a criminal defense attorney. I've been collecting tales about crime and criminals for as long as I can remember.

~

"You can't say why you love something, right?" my father told me one evening after I asked him to articulate his passion for trying criminal cases. Norman Zalkind grew up in Brookline, a city next to Newton. He put himself through college selling magazines door to door and launched his career during the Civil Rights Movement representing protestors in Mississippi. He talks like a cross between Bernie Sanders and Robert Kennedy. "It's like a dancer wants to dance all the time," he went on. We were sitting in a booth at a Chinese restaurant where he recently got a waiter off on an armed robbery charge. His fedora was on the seat beside us, and he was wearing a pin-striped suit, geometric red tie, and gold cuff links. Together we were inhaling a plate of lobster with ginger and scallion sauce.

Guilt and innocence are not matters my father dwells on. The way he sees it, it's not his job to decide. If his client is in trouble, then he is there to help, same as a doctor or a priest, he tells me. It makes no difference if he is appointed by the state or hired by an individual and paid more handsomely. He will fight with all he's got.

Some defense lawyers claim they only take on clients if they truly believe their client is wrongfully accused. There are a handful of attorneys who actually operate this way. But for the most part, my father says that's bullshit. "They're lying!" he yells at the newspaper or the television or wherever the latest smooth-talking lawyer is making this claim. "You can't make believe you're being moral about it," he says. "It's not the way it works. Society hasn't developed it that way." Not that he agrees with the system as it stands. That's why he does what he does. "There is no redemption in our society," he complains. The prison system is inhumane. He tells me this all the time. "If they were just giving fair sentences, I wouldn't be able to do it as easily. But they aren't."

~

Murder is one of my father's specialties. Homicide cases are his heroin, he says. They have the highest stakes. He's taken on about seventy-five state murder cases and a few federal homicides. My earliest childhood memories were marked by stories of his infamous clients, like Richard Rosenthal, the financial analyst charged with impaling his wife's heart on a wooden stake after she yelled at him for burning the ziti, and Lonnie Gilchrist, the stockbroker who was charged with shooting his former boss in the chest. My father's trials set the rhythm of our life, dictating everything from dinnertime conversations to family vacations. We would celebrate each acquittal and mourn every conviction.

Of all his trials, the one that left the greatest impression was Sean Ellis's. In 1993, Ellis, a Black nineteen-year-old, was charged with murdering Boston police officer John Mulligan as he slept in his cruiser outside a Walgreens. I was six years old, learning to read, searching for the Zalkind name in the newspapers that covered the kitchen table. At night I fell asleep to the sound of my father pacing around the house as he practiced his cross-examinations. My father had a growing suspicion that the detectives investigating Mulligan's murder were crooked. Later, in a separate incident, Kenneth Acerra and Walter Robinson, the detectives who allegedly found Ellis's wallet in Mulligan's cruiser, confessed to stealing from drug dealers and pimps. My father tried the case three times and got two hung juries before state prosecutors finally convinced a jury to convict. He grieved that loss for a long time. We all did.

Ellis would spend twenty-two years behind bars before another attorney, Rosemary Scapicchio, found that evidence of the officers' corruption had been withheld from my father, which earned Ellis a retrial. Justice Carol S. Ball found that because the dead cop and the two detectives investigating his murder had been stealing from drug dealers together, weeks before the homicide, the detectives had a motive to cut the investigation short and frame an innocent man.

Murder investigations are revealing. If they are done well, all parts of the decedent's life, and those who knew them, are upturned and made subject for scrutiny. It didn't matter why the cop was killed. So long as the investigation was open and active, the victim's cohorts stood to be exposed. The judge ruled that the detectives had motive to fear a thorough investigation into the murder because it might dig up dirt on them. "They, therefore, had a powerful incentive to prevent a prolonged or comprehensive investigation," Ball wrote in her ruling. Ellis's murder charges were overturned and ultimately dismissed.

~

My dad also likes flashy career criminals who pay him well. *True criminals*, he calls them, people who live their whole lives on the other side of the law. He would tell me stories about busts. But the criminals I was most intrigued by were the ones who got away. My family took regular trips to rural Jamaica, where I absorbed stories of the drug trade and met a bona fide drug lord. I watched police helicopters chasing smugglers whipping across the horizon in a speedboat and other scenes I probably should not mention. There are people my father doesn't want me to write about. "They're dangerous, Susan," he tells me.

Because of these experiences, when it came to narco-trafficking, I considered myself a bit of an expert among my peers in Newton. My closest confidants were always my girlfriends, but I also remained close to that same group of guys I knew from elementary school. As I got older, I found that my girlfriends and I did a lot more watching—watching the boys skateboard, watching them play video games, watching their bands practice, and watching their shows. But when it came to drugs, the boys listened to me. Took me seriously. I liked that. Even more than I liked the drugs, I think.

Erik took me seriously too. Cruising around Boston and the suburbs, I told him the stories about the criminals and smugglers I knew growing up—the secrets I'd stored away. Erik referred to his Sour Diesel source as "hippies" and said he'd been buying from them for over a decade. He said he only worked with "friends," and the "hippies" were totally safe. No one to be afraid of, he assured me.

One night Erik drove me past a dead-end street in Brighton, where he said wanted to buy a house. A dead-end street is a perfect home for a weed dealer, he told me—less foot traffic. We cruised like that, on and off for about a year, meeting up to get stoned off his Sour Diesel and share stories every time I came home from college in Portland, Oregon.

A high school acquaintance of Erik's once told me it seemed like Erik went straight from trading Magic: The Gathering cards to selling weed, which made me laugh, thinking about him and those glass jars, collecting all the exotic strains. Erik had been picked on when he was a child; he was scrappy and wore glasses. When he wasn't showing off, Erik was awkward, shy, and trusting. Too trusting, maybe.

It didn't matter that weed should have been legal. It wasn't. Operating in an economy without the protection of the law, where bad people can take advantage of your secrets, is dangerous. Of course, for me, the secrets and the risk were part of the allure.

My habit of hanging out with weed dealers proved to be unsustainable. Roughly a year and a half after I'd met Erik, my then-boyfriend—a marijuana dealer from a political family in Philadelphia—called me to say he was running away from a murder scene. He had been picking up an ounce and chatting with a couple outside a Philly stash house when he said he saw two men jump out of a car, gun down the couple, and drive off. My boyfriend was calling to ask for advice: What should he do with his . . . *onion*? He meant an ounce of cannabis. I told him to throw it out and to stop selling weed until things cooled down. He didn't listen to me. I gave him an ultimatum that didn't end well.

The following week he arranged to receive "a package" on loan from Sam, a notoriously temperamental drug dealer who went by Saddam for effect. My ex received the package and was almost immediately robbed, possibly by people working for Saddam. He still owed Saddam money for the drugs, and since he had no product to sell, Saddam and his crew were after him. By that point, I had dropped out of college, moved to Cambridge, and was working as a nanny. For the next six months, when I wasn't babysitting, I was buying dirt weed, picking out the seeds, and chain-smoking spliffs. I was paranoid. My ex called me from pay phones at odd hours. There was a possibility, he said, that Saddam might come after me too. In retrospect, this was extremely unlikely. But it felt pretty real at the time. When my ex finally called to say that the Saddam ordeal had been resolved, he proudly proclaimed that he'd learned something from the ordeal and had come up with a new motto: "Don't be surprised if, when you consort with criminals, they commit crimes." He went back to selling drugs, before eventually making a failed bid for office, but I took his lesson to heart.

I stopped smoking pot and enrolled at Boston University. When I saw Erik again, I told him about my ex and tried to convince him to get a new job. My father's clients no longer appeared so intriguing; the ones I knew best had made it out okay, but there were many who hadn't, and I told Erik all the cautionary tales I could think of on our last car ride. There was the man who found two dead bodies in his driveway, left there by a rival dealer. The guy who did fifteen years after his electricity bill tipped the feds off to his grow operation. There were smugglers I knew who never got caught, wore ascots, and lived in large homes. They might have been rich, but they were also sad, lonely, and in constant fear of their past. Two young men I had been briefly acquainted with as children in Jamaica had become boat drivers for the Colombians trafficking cocaine. On my last trip to Jamaica, I had learned they had been called to court, only to have their throats slit in the middle of the night. I was haunted by that story as well. Erik didn't have to live like those boys had, with that kind of risk.

Erik didn't believe he was. This was New England, not machete country. He wasn't driving a speedboat into the mangroves. He had an Audi with leather seats. He told me he was investing in a glass bong company and weed café in California called Hitman Glass. (Hitman as in *Take a hit, man.*) He said that he would, eventually, get out of the game; marijuana would be legal soon, he was sure of it. But he was going to continue doing what he was doing until then. He claimed he wasn't like those dealers who got in trouble. He didn't make rash moves. He only worked with friends. He just sold weed. He was a healer. It was medicinal. I didn't care. I wanted him to stop. He listened quietly. We were parked in my parents' circular driveway, my hand was on the door, and I was looking out at the row of dark green rhododendrons that separated the house from the road. After a brief silence, Erik asked me to connect him to the smugglers I had just taken great lengths to explain were actually creeps. I remember he said something like "I hear you, but what I'm saying is: I want you to introduce me to them." And that's when we stopped talking for a while. He invited me to his birthday twice, lavish seafood dinners at The Daily Catch for a dozen of his closest friends. I declined his invitations both times.

The last time we spoke was in early 2011. Erik called me asking for my father's number. The police had raided his apartment. He sounded scared. I told him everything would be okay.

CHAPTER FOUR

The Bust

I want to scream into the past.

Time travel fantasies are traps, but it is difficult for me to think about December 2010, the weeks before Erik's arrest, without being seduced by a hopeless, delusional daydream. It could have been so easily avoided. A text would have sufficed. One text, sent backward in time. "Do not leave for Cancún without paying next month's rent," I'd write. "Please, do not forget. Make sure the payment goes through." That's all it would take, and Erik would be in California right now, at his weed café, watching a Lakers game. Safe.

Instead, that December, Erik went to Mexico with Brendan Mess to ring in the New Year.

Weeks passed, and Erik had not paid his rent, nor answered any of his landlord's emails or calls. The landlord could not legally enter the apartment without Erik's permission, so he called on the Boston Police for a welfare check. When the police opened the door, they found $8,000 cash on Erik's coffee table and three bags of weed on the living room floor. The nature of their visit quickly changed. They searched Erik's whole apartment. They allegedly seized $21,500 cash, twenty-three bags of marijuana, several bags of hashish, a small bag of cocaine, a few painkillers, and a scale.

This was not Erik's first arrest. The trip to Mexico coincided with the conclusion of a two-year probation sentence, which had prohibited him from leaving the state. Erik had been pulled over for a traffic violation in May 2008 in Allston. "I knew you would smell it," Erik said after the officer commented on the aroma emanating from his window, according to the police report. Erik was charged with possession with intent to distribute. He pleaded guilty and, along with the probation sentence, was ordered to take regular drug tests.

Erik was arrested again the next year, in May. He was hanging out with the Newton guys in an apartment in Brighton. They threw a lot of parties. After one such event, a police officer came across Erik and one of my childhood friends hanging out by the back of Erik's car. They were holding balloons to their faces. The officer reported hearing a hissing sound.

I always thought nitrous was ridiculous. The boys had to go through all this effort to secure a big metal tank just so they could huddle around in circles and get dizzy off balloons. It looked like a children's birthday party. But nitrous does not show up on most drug tests, which might explain the appeal to Erik at the time. Erik told the officer the nitrous was his. He protected my friends and took all the blame himself. Erik had been fighting to get his probation sentence reduced, but after the nitrous incident he gave up on that effort. His probation sentence ended in November 2010. When he left for Mexico the next month, it was in part to celebrate the end of his legal worries. Taking the trip without first paying his rent would of course spark a much bigger issue.

My father liked Erik. Erik reminded him of weed smugglers from back in the day. He took me out to dinner at Harvest in Harvard Square for rib eye steak and oysters to thank me for the referral. (I had developed a taste for oysters by then.) He was optimistic about Erik's case. He thought he could get the court to drop all the charges. The police did not have a search warrant, he explained. None of the evidence they seized from his apartment was admissible in court.

But Erik was still in a jam. As it turned out, the hippies were not as friendly and understanding as Erik had described them to me on our car rides. Before his apartment was raided, Erik owed the hippies $50K. But when police seized his weed and his cash, he had no way to pay them back.

Erik's arrest was not the hippies' concern. They wanted their $50K. They would not give Erik any more weed until he paid. Meanwhile Erik had invested all his savings in Hitman Glass. He could not take the money out without dissolving the business and abandoning his dreams for the future. He thought he could figure out another way. At least, he tried to put a positive spin on his predicament. Though Erik also confided in at least one person that his situation was so desperate he had contemplated suicide.

Erik's father, Nikki Weissman, would tell me that in the last months of his life, Erik was in "distress." After his son's murder, Nikki suffered from time travel fantasies as well. If only Nikki had been there that night in Waltham, he could have fought the assailants off. "They killed Erik, but they killed me at the same time. Because I can't forgive myself for not being able to protect him," he told me at a ceremony honoring Massachusetts homicide victims. Tamerlan was a "jihadnik," he said under his breath.

The raid put Erik out of an apartment as well. For several months, he crashed on DAG's couch. The hippies checked up on him there. One came to visit, and Erik showed him the couch. He wasn't playing games or ripping them off. He was broke. In the summer of 2011, six weeks before the murders, Erik drove DAG to the airport. During the course of that car ride, Erik asked DAG if he knew anyone who could sell him a large amount of weed. Erik said he had a new set of customers in mind. This caught DAG off guard. Erik had always disclosed his sources and his customers to him in the past. More to the point, DAG had always bought weed from Erik, not the other way around. That's how DAG knew: Erik was desperate.

CHAPTER FIVE

Three Bodies

When I dropped out of college and became a nanny, I moved into an apartment in Cambridge with two guys I'd met on Craigslist, tech dudes who moonlit as musicians, DJ Die Young and the bassist for a local heavy metal band, Eyes Sewn Shut. I lived there for seven years, the Wendy of the home for lost club boys. There was a rotating cast of DJs, musicians, and promoters who crashed on our couch. Our kitchen table was a still life of Narragansett cans. Our front porch was occupied by my potted plants and clamshells overflowing with cigarette butts.

Eventually, I transferred to Boston University, a short walk across the river, and began working toward a history degree. I studied environmental history and slavery, and this time around I put my all into school. I geeked out over primary source material, thumbing through old diaries and archives and building databases of my own. My days were spent in libraries and lecture halls. At night, I went out dancing at clubs in Cambridge's Central Square, sheltering behind the DJ booth with my roommates when strangers came too near. Even when the club scene spilled into my kitchen a few days a week, I stayed away from drug dealers. I was no longer seeking that kind of kindred spirit. But I couldn't stay away from crime.

In an effort to assimilate to my new university, I joined the student paper, *The Daily Free Press.* I started as a photographer, but it wasn't long before the crime beat called me. All it took was one story—an underage drinking bust—and I was hooked. I was home. To my surprise, I found I was adept at making connections in law enforcement. Talking to cops felt more risky than talking to drug dealers ever did, and I found I genuinely enjoyed these conversations, at least with those who seemed to share my curiosity and gallows humor.

Charming my fellow students did not come as easy. I was no longer getting stoned, and when I was around my academic peers, unlike when I was around cops and dealers, flaunting my drug trafficking know-how did not seem to win me interest or admiration. I felt awkward on campus and at parties, other than the ones my roommates threw. Outside of Cambridge, I had about a half dozen girlfriends within walking distance in Central Square. But I was most at ease in moments of intensity, interviewing students facing expulsion or talking to the frazzled witnesses of a hit-and-run. I wasn't just a stoner party girl anymore. I had a calling. I was going to be an investigative reporter.

~

After I graduated from BU, I got a job as an overnight production assistant at New England Cable News, a local NBC affiliate covering all of New England. At NECN, I wrote the chyrons, the headings beneath the stories, and regurgitated script for the anchors to read. I was working freelance, my shifts started at 1:30 a.m. or 2:30 a.m., and I made something like $13.50 an hour, with no job security and no benefits. I would wake up right around the time my roommates came home from the clubs, dance with them in my bathrobe, sip some orange juice, and leave. The work itself was boring, and I was dangerously sleep deprived. But I was in a newsroom, and that was all that mattered to me at the time. On those rare days when my sources came through and I was able to tip off the camera crews and get our station a first shot of a murder scene, I felt high, like it was all worth it. I was on my way.

I did not go to college with plans to become a journalist. But, in retrospect, it is surprising that I did not aspire to be a legal reporter years earlier. The O. J. Simpson trial is the granddaddy of modern TV news, and I was seven years old when Simpson set off on that infamous ride in his white Bronco. That afternoon, my parents were throwing a surprise party for their dear friend Ken Hartnett, a newspaperman with a crown of curly white hair who did stints at the Associated Press, the *Boston Globe,* and the *Boston Herald* and was then an editor at the *New Bedford Standard Times.*

June 17, 1994, was Ken's sixtieth birthday, and we had dozens of his journalist friends over for the occasion. Ken was led to our front door with a blindfold
just moments after news helicopters in California started tracking aerial shots
of the ex–running back absconding down the highway, in an attempt to shake
charges for his wife's murder. *Surprise!* The reporters went ballistic. I'd never seen
grown-ups so excited. I wove in and out of the party guests, waist high, in white
socks with lace trim, clicking my patent leather shoes on the wood floor and
mimicking their laughter and cheers. My mother sat Ken down in front of the
TV in the green velvet living room chair, and the journalists gathered around
like courtiers—jokers, all of them—housing great big mouthfuls of vanilla cake
with rainbow sprinkles.

Nicole Simpson's murder was the first case I followed, arrest to verdict,
discussing witnesses and legal strategy with my father, fixated on each turn of
courtroom drama with the rest of the world.

When I stopped smoking weed I started smoking cigarettes like a wheezy
old man; I sucked down rollies and Winstons before breakfast and late into the
night. I tried to stop as soon as I started. My attempts never lasted more than a
couple of days. At NECN there was a new deadline to hit at the start of every
news hour. I hardly had time to leave my seat and go to the bathroom. These
nicotine cravings would, I realized, be a distraction. So I swapped out the nicotine fix for bubblegum and breaking news. The thought that I might one day
land a case as thrilling as Nicole Simpson's homicide was so powerful a lure that
it got me to quit smoking and pulled me out of bed in the middle of the night
and through the newsroom doors.

On Sunday, September 11, 2011, the tenth anniversary of the most
devastating attack on American soil since Pearl Harbor, I was bored. NECN
ran a weekend-long memorial program. For three days, the station was slated
to cover all 9/11 stories all the time. All of upper management was there,
and we had reporters in New York City. Meanwhile, I was tasked with the
monotonous duty of turning the prompter in the dark production room.
I watched as the anchors read the neon script and guided viewers through
somber memorials and interviews with grieving family members. I had to
shake my head during commercial breaks to keep from falling asleep. Stories
about the survivors and the first responders moved me, of course. But I was
relieved when it was over.

The next day, September 12, 2011, I came into work a couple of hours after midnight. We spent most of the Monday morning shows recapping the events of the weekend. When I went to work in the early hours of Tuesday morning, I thought I was free. The tenth anniversary had been thoroughly commemorated, and we could get back to the action.

I got into the station, poured myself a cup of stale coffee, and bought a cinnamon raisin bagel from the vending machine, gnawed at the rubbery bread, and scrolled through social media—part of a mindless routine that for better or worse I still adhere to today. Back then, I primarily used Facebook. Usually my feed was pretty straightforward: new love, new breakups, links to music, invitations to parties. But that morning my friends were posting cryptic messages and I was struggling to make sense of them. When I saw a high school friend post *RIP Heady E*, I thought he broke a bong or something and closed the browser window. I didn't have time for stoner sagas. I had important work to do.

The big story that day concerned a thirteen-month-old boy found dead in a day care van. The driver had abandoned a toddler in the late summer heat for more than six hours. The Boston Police Department was in instant agreement with the press in regards to the gravity of the case. Commissioner Ed Davis promptly released information about the investigation into the driver, the child's identity, and plans to probe conditions at the day care center further. The tragedy and the aftermath would become the focus of local TV news stations for weeks to come. But while the rest of Boston media was chasing down that story, I was looking for something new, something that would pull me out of my production assistant gig to a job at the assignment desk, or even as a reporter. There was a report on the blotter about a woman who fell through a sky roof. I was trying to determine if it was fatal. Stories about fatal porch collapses had been big that summer. *BARBECUE GONE WRONG*, I'd write in the chyron. Or *TRAGEDY ON A TRIPLE-DECKER*.

A story in Waltham seemed more promising. It began with three dead bodies and an address: 12 Harding Avenue. That's how it crossed the wire, with the names, ages, gender, and cause of death unknown. Three bodies in a second-floor apartment on a dead-end street in Waltham. Police were called to the scene at 2:25 p.m. on Monday afternoon, September 12, 2011.

For the last six months, I'd been monitoring every car crash, fire, and suspicious death in New England. I'd look for these stories in our news subscription services. The alerts would run alongside the program where I was supposed to write the anchors' scripts and fill in the chyrons. New stories would begin with a line or two—fire, four alarm; crash, three vehicles, shots fired—followed by a time and an address. It wasn't my job to decipher these messages. Assignment editors at the news desk were supposed to look through these alerts, figure out which ones amounted to news, and if they did, send cameras and reporters to the scene. I probably shouldn't have spent so much time pursuing this additional duty; my chyron headings were riddled with typos, and my recaps of last night's hockey games made it evident that I possessed a loose understanding of the rules at best. (Erik, to his credit, had messaged me with a list of sports lingo to use when I first got the gig.) To the dismay of my producers, I followed the news alerts obsessively, deciphering the memos and sending my findings to the news director with tips from my growing cache of sources. I couldn't spell or write about sports. I struggled with the hourly writing deadlines. But when it came to crime stories, my instincts were good.

One body could mean anything—a heart attack, a stroke. You don't want to send out a camera crew if you only have one body and no inkling of foul play or an arrest. Two dead bodies is a story. It's never a car crash. When it's a vehicular death you learn about the cars first and the carnage later. If there are two dead bodies in a building it might be a freak accident, maybe. You can't report two dead bodies as a homicide until you know for sure. But it almost always is murder. I would write in 2XMX for the production slug, MX being shorthand for murder. What kind of murder is hard to say. But up until then, every alert I saw about two dead bodies in a suburban town like Waltham, without any word of shots fired, a suspect, or an arrest, turned out to be a domestic murder-suicide. Murder-suicides don't make for great TV. They don't have "legs." There is no arrest or court date to look forward to. We covered them, usually, but not at the top of the show. Three dead bodies was bound to be interesting. A-block material, almost certainly. So even though there was no information about foul play, a manhunt, arrest, or suspect at large, reporters had to go.

CHAPTER SIX

Drug Related

Journalists arrived at 12 Harding Avenue, a modest two-family home on a crumbling dead-end road, and were met with neighbors' whispers. A woman had run out of the house screaming. The victims were three young men, they'd been stabbed, and there was marijuana on the bodies. But the only information journalists could confirm on record came from Middlesex County District Attorney Gerald Leone. We had video of Leone dressed in a dark suit and American flag pin, speaking to a scrum of reporters outside the apartment on Monday evening. I studied Leone's broad shoulders, thick brown hair, and authoritative, furrowed brow, as I wrote up a chyron for his name and location.

Leone peppers his press statements with sports references and punches his fist into his hand for emphasis. Years later, I'd examine all the video of Leone I could find. He boxed for Harvard, won two fights in the New England Golden Gloves championship in 1984, and refereed Golden Gloves tournament games at Lowell Memorial Auditorium throughout his years as a prosecutor.

Leone sticks to the script with reporters. He's not one to be heckled. He states the facts and steps out of the way, in a manner that must have also served him well flagging low blows and backhanded jabs in a crowded arena. That evening in Waltham was no different. He would not release the victims' names, genders, or cause of death for another three days. *This could be my big break,*

I thought. A case that might finally launch my career, and pull me out of my freelance, overnight, assistant producer gig for good.

~

The Middlesex office was once a launchpad for Massachusetts prosecutors with political dreams. Middlesex is the largest county in Massachusetts, covering more than fifty cities and towns, and has a population of more than 1.5 million. The district is big enough and close enough to the capital to be relevant, but it also has one of the lowest crime rates in the state. The office has name-brand recognition in key districts, while facing fewer challenges and less scrutiny than the Suffolk office, which includes Boston.

Leone was elected Middlesex district attorney in 2006, in an unopposed election, following an endorsement from his predecessor, Martha Coakley. Coakley quit her job as a district attorney to run for Massachusetts attorney general, a position she held from 2007 to 2015, overseeing the district attorney offices across the state, including Middlesex.

Coakley's rise to fame began in 1997 in the infamous nanny trial: the most publicized murder case in Newton's history. Together Coakley and Leone charged Louise Woodward, an eighteen-year-old au pair from Cheshire, England, with shaking to death eight-month-old Matthew Eappen. The case touched a nerve about childcare, yuppies, and shaken baby syndrome, it made national headlines and incited feverish tabloid coverage. My father was a regular commentator on the trial and was briefly hired by Woodward in a civil suit.

Coakley and Leone convinced a jury to convict Woodward of second-degree murder. But they were also publicly chastised for taking the case too far. There were questions about whether a murder was committed at all. In a highly unusual rebuke of the state's case, the judge reduced the conviction to manslaughter and sentenced Woodward to time served. The state's own expert witness would later cast doubt on the forensic evidence.

After the trial, Leone went on to spark name recognition on his own in federal court, acting as first Assistant US Attorney in the prosecution of Richard C. Reid, the "Shoe Bomber." Reid is the one who boarded a flight from Paris to Miami a couple of months after 9/11 with a pair of handmade explosives hidden in his sneakers. His attempt to blow up the plane was unsuccessful. But Reid is why you have to take off your shoes at airport security today, and his guilty plea was considered the crown jewel of Leone's prosecutorial career.

～

NECN's video footage of Leone outside 12 Harding Avenue was drab. This was not a Bronco chase nor a celebrity crime. There were no dead infants. But it was the most unusual murder case I'd ever heard of, and not only because of the incredible violence; it was the contradictions that intrigued me.

That evening the square-jawed Leone stood outside the Waltham apartment.

It was a "graphic crime scene," Leone said, but the murders did "not appear to be a random act." There were no signs of a break-in. Though investigators had been called to the apartment only a few hours earlier, he said one thing was evidentially clear: the victims and the assailants were known to one another.

The neighbors were naturally upset that a violent crime had taken place so close to home. "Just knowing that who's done it is still on the loose. So that makes it frightening," Jackie Delaire told *Waltham Newswatch*. But local officials and law enforcement continued to assure the public there was nothing to fear.

Then law enforcement peddled a narrative about why the victims had been targeted. The murders were "drug related," police told the neighbors as they removed bags of weed from the apartment, according to a report a few days later in the *Boston Globe*. The suggestion being that so long as the neighbors themselves were not involved in drugs, they had no need to fear.

"I'm very happy the district attorney said it did not appear to be random," Mayor Jeanette McCarthy told the *Waltham Patch* shortly after the homicides. "Naturally, it's disturbing. But the DA is working with the police and they have it under control as far as I can see."

"I don't think people need to worry about their safety or their children's safety," City Councilor and State Representative Tom Stanley told *Waltham Newswatch*.

But the *Boston Globe* noted that police "provided no details in their search for one or more assailants." When the *Boston Globe* noted that the triple murder was "the most violent crime officials could recall in this small city," Waltham police declined to comment on record but seemed to suggest, on background, that actually, gruesome murders happen here all the time. "There have been two other homicides in this city of 60,000 residents in the past twelve months," police informed the *Globe*. It is extremely unusual for police to brag about having a high murder rate. Yes, there was a fatal shooting over some Percocet in Waltham in September 2010, and it was big news simply because it happened in Waltham. Prior to the Percocet shooting, there was a murder-suicide in Waltham. The Percocet shooting was an attempted robbery gone wrong. It was a quick, stupid, unplanned killing. Even then, there was hand-wringing about a drug murder like that happening in a place like this, more hand-wringing than for the triple murder, it seemed. And neither that shooting nor the domestic murder shared any of the bizarre characteristics of what happened on September 11th.

Although the early news reports did not mention the September 11, 2011 date. I didn't know then that all three victims stopped answering their phones between 7:30 and 8:00 p.m. on Sunday, September 11. The victims had gathered to watch a football game. The Cowboys were playing the Jets; it's unclear if the three men lived to see kickoff. But I did guess that the three men were murdered at night—that's when killers tend to strike. A triple homicide on the tenth anniversary of 9/11. What did it mean? Anything?

In the immediate wake of a homicide, journalists and law enforcement are generally aligned in their sense of urgency. Back then, I did not question Leone's early statements. It was his job to reassure the public. But I didn't totally buy his nothing-to-see-here public statements—at least that's how they came off to me. It wasn't just the coincidence of the date, or the location, which I knew well, or the number of bodies, which was remarkable from the jump; the fact that the assailants took the effort to stab the victims, a difficult feat compared to a gun killing, made it that much more unusual and violent.

Granted, I did not know with certainty that the Waltham victims were stabbed; the neighbors' rumors would not be confirmed until Leone's office sent out an email with the medical examiner's report and the victims' names days later. Nor did I know where or in what manner the stab wounds had been inflicted, or even if all three victims had been killed in the same way. The additional bizarre and macabre details would be revealed to me later.

What I knew was this: around here drug killings are conducted with guns—and silencers—if the murderers are true professionals, and they are done quick. Every extra second spent at the murder scene increases the risk that the killers might get caught. Time is not the only factor at play in a stabbing crime. Stabbings are intimate affairs, physical feats that require a nearly maniacal determination, in addition to strength, to complete. Unless they have the distinctive markings of a gang warning, stabbings are crimes of passion, for the most part, and usually suggest a personal rather than a professional motive. This did not look like a New England drug murder.

Yet, it was reported that there were drugs on the bodies, which, I guess, technically made the Waltham murders a drug killing—drugs were involved—but on what terms? The killers seemed to want police to think it was drug related. So was the marijuana on the bodies a message or misdirection? That the killers stuck around the murder scene to dump weed on the corpses demonstrated a taste for drama and theatrics that I'd only ever seen enacted by serial killers—and yet I knew of no similar crimes.

Nor had I heard of anything like this in an insanity trial. *Insanity* is a legal rather than a psychiatric term. Usually state law requires that the defendant be physically unable to follow the law or be so delusional that they are unaware they are committing a criminal act. Nonetheless, killers suffering from what a psychiatrist would likely deem to be mental illness tend to behave erratically after the fact, drawing attention to themselves via bloody clothes or careless driving. That is, if they have the wherewithal or the desire to flee. But the Waltham killers were methodical, and they had escaped.

I ran through the list of factors in an attempt to determine the crime's tenor and form. I usually came up with predictions fast, wagering with my colleagues as to what had happened and how the news might unfold. The Waltham murders had too many incongruous angles for me to say either way. My only hunch was that the story had to be good. I was desperate to know more.

Coakley launched her career charging a teenage nanny with murder, Leone made his name on the Shoe Bomber's singed sneakers, and now there were three dead bodies in Waltham. It was my turn.

CHAPTER SEVEN

Lynn

Erik Weissman is not my only friend who was murdered. He is the only one with an open case. Lynn Henneman had hair like running water. She was a flight attendant, but I knew her as the girlfriend—and for a short while, the wife—of one of my father's friends, Valta Us, a Slovenian oil painter. They met while she was waiting tables in Bozeman, Montana. Valta was on a ski trip, and Lynn was saving up for flight attendant school.

Valta and Lynn made a home together in Sag Harbor, New York, in a bungalow near the beach and the woods, where Lynn hung locks of her hair in the trees to scare the deer away from eating her vegetable garden. In the summer, they rented out their home and traveled the world, taking advantage of Lynn's airfare discount. They stayed with my family in our old Victorian between trips.

In those summer months, Valta painted the house pale yellow with blue and gray detailing. Then he moved on to the rooms inside—pink, royal blue, sky blue, two shades of moss green, lavender, and purple. In the evenings, Valta would play guitar in the backyard, Lynn would sing "Oh My Darling Clementine" and Fleetwood Mac, and I'd climb onto a big rock and dance. In the afternoons, Lynn would take me swimming in the neighbor's pool and teach me tricks, like backward underwater somersaults and jumping on one foot and shaking water from your ears.

I have two memories of Lynn that are short and sharp, like video clips. In one, she's sitting at the kitchen table with her back to the fireplace, and I'm drawing her portrait with a set of colored pencils she'd brought me as a gift. My parents and Valta are deep in discussion, but Lynn is looking at me like I've just said something smart. The tip of her nose wiggles as she smiles. In my other memory, we are coming home from the pool, and we are talking about bodies. This was a subject about which, I'd learned, grown women like to complain. I wondered which faults Lynn liked to dwell on. Lynn told me she liked her body, her muscles, her curves. She wouldn't change a thing. She made me want to be a woman too. It was exciting.

I took to following Lynn around, confiding in her about my elementary school crushes and grilling her on the details of her personal life. She and Valta were in love, and her favorite thing to do was kiss him. She didn't wear makeup, didn't follow fashion, and liked her worn pair of cargo shorts because they were comfortable and had pockets so she could collect things like sea glass and heart-shaped stones.

When Lynn was a little girl in Montana, she had wanted to become a flight attendant so she could travel the world, and that's exactly what she was doing. She liked to explore new cities and take walks on her own. The solitude allowed her to focus on things like lightning bugs and the smells of different trees. These things she found as compelling as a good conversation. I was curious. *She likes being alone?* I wondered. Since my half siblings are about two decades older than me, I was perpetually in want of a playmate. After Lynn and I talked, I started to enjoy my solitude more. My parents threw a lot of parties. They were friends with artists, poets, journalists, scientists, lawyers, and professors. I'd interrogated them all. Lynn was the first grown-up I spoke to who seemed truly satisfied. Maybe one day I'd become a flight attendant and travel the world. That's what I told my teachers when they asked.

I'm not sure how much of this I told Lynn, but I suspect all of it. That was another thing about Lynn: I could tell her anything. On her last visits she brought me grown-up presents. A magenta scarf, velvet with long tassels, and vanilla-scented soap.

Lynn and Valta married in a courthouse in Sag Harbor in September of 2000 and made arrangements to honeymoon in Bali the next month. She had a few flights to make first, including a three-day haul from LaGuardia to Boise, Idaho, by way of Chicago O'Hare, then back through Denver and Orlando International. It was a trip she'd made many times before. She left the house on September 24 at 3:00 a.m., according to reporting at the *Bozeman Daily*

Chronicle. When she landed in Boise later that afternoon, she checked into her hotel and went for a walk. First to the Boise Art Museum, where she bought glitter pens and window paint for her brother's kids, and then to the TableRock Brewpub & Grill, where they served a mango chutney spinach salad she liked. At around 7:00 p.m., she paid her bill and made her way to the Doubletree Riverside Hotel, through Julia Davis Park. There was a path along the Boise River, three-fourths of a mile long, that should have led her back to the hotel. It didn't.

My parents asked me if Lynn ever talked to me about running away or leaving Valta. She hadn't, but when I found out she was missing, I thought maybe she needed some more time alone. Maybe she didn't want to get married after all. Maybe there was another man. People are complicated; I knew that much, even then.

Days passed, then weeks. Police found Lynn's wallet and ID under the bleachers at the local high school. Then, by the side of the river, they found her cargo shorts. "It doesn't look good," my father said. He didn't elaborate on what *not good* might mean. *Maybe she went crazy and forgot who she was,* I thought. Like, amnesia. It happened in sitcoms, but it had to have happened to someone at least once in real life too.

I was thirteen years old sitting up in bed, my back against my pink bedroom wall, writing a note to a friend to be folded over into an origami envelope and delivered in class the next day, when it hit me. The only possible explanation for Lynn's sudden disappearance in a city where she didn't have any friends, followed by the emergence of her clothes and belongings, was that she was dead. Somebody killed her.

A few days later, my father got the call. A fisherman found her naked, lodged underneath a log in the Boise River, clubbed in the head, and strangled with her own sweater. Though no one told me at the time, I knew. She'd been raped.

I am sure the memorial in Montana was bigger, but at Sag Harbor, from what I can remember, only her parents, my parents, Valta, and I were there. John Denver's "Take Me Home, Country Roads" was playing on the stereo system when I—in a headband and itchy tights—walked into the small assembly hall full of rows of empty chairs. There had to be others who loved Lynn. I don't know why no one else came. Maybe they were cowards. Maybe they loved her so much they couldn't face their own grief. I didn't plan on speaking, but when

Valta said a few words, and no one else got up to talk, I went to the podium and said what I knew to be true. Lynn was good—more good than the evil that took her—and that was what mattered in the end. I knew that whoever had killed Lynn was still out there, and that unless he was caught, he'd strike again. I bet he liked to scare women. This knowing throbbed in the marrow of my bones. That had to stop. I would not let Lynn's killer scare me too. This is how I came to learn that I possess a special power of sorts. When I'm angry enough, I can turn off my fear like a switch. I practiced by taking walks alone, during the day and during the night, like Lynn did.

~

Two days after my sixteenth birthday, a boy walking his dog along the Boise foothills found the body of a woman buried under some brush near a playground. Cheryl Ann Hanlon had been clubbed in the head, strangled with her own belt, and raped. She was forty-two. Strangulation by means other than hands. The belt was the tell, the killer's signature move and the detectives' first clue that they might have a lead on Lynn's case. An eyewitness linked a man named Erick Virgil Hall Jr. to Hanlon. Hall was a sex offender who had been living under a bridge by the Boise River. He had previously been convicted of raping and choking a seventeen-year-old girl. Investigators arrested Hall, got a swab of his DNA, and tested it with the forensics found on Cheryl Ann Hanlon and found a match. It matched DNA collected from Lynn's body too. Hall was found guilty in 2004 of murdering Lynn, and he was convicted in 2007 of murdering Hanlon. He was sentenced to death twice, in both cases. Decades later, he is still alive, appealing his cases. It's not unusual for the appeals process after a death penalty conviction to go on for decades; these measures are put in place to make sure we don't kill the wrong person. The Supreme Court in Idaho shut down Hall's most recent appeal in May 2022.

A year after Hall was convicted of Lynn's murder, I was on a flight back to Boston from Portland, Oregon, where I went to college. I was watching the flight attendants serve coffee and looking out the window as we flew over farmland, fields that from that distance looked like a green patchwork quilt. I imagined that even with the monotonous roar of the engine and the demands of needy passengers, Lynn used to enjoy views like that. In the years after her murder, I thought about Lynn often. But I only allowed myself to think of her life, never her death. I was strict with myself on that point. I would not be scared. But now that Hall had been put away, I did not have to be brave. As far as I was concerned, the story was over. I could cry if I wanted to. It was a relief.

CHAPTER EIGHT

Stabbed?

I was off work on Thursday, September 15, 2011, so I took my laptop to a Cambridge café down the street from my apartment to see if I could learn anything more about the Waltham case on my own. I logged into my work email and hit refresh every five minutes for updates.

Finally a press release from Leone's office came through with information from the autopsy report. The three men were killed by "sharp force injuries of the neck." Their throats were slit. All three of them. This was more terrible and intriguing than anything I'd imagined.

Then I read the victims' names. Brendan Mess was twenty-five years old. Raphael Teken was thirty-seven. The third victim was thirty-one.

When I got to the words *Erik Weissman* I froze. The blood drained from my hands. Those confusing Facebook posts about Heady E started making sense, and I didn't want them to. With my eyes still fixed on the screen, I reached for my phone and I called my senior prom date, neighbor, and friend since kindergarten.

In a few days Michael would tell a story at Erik's funeral about how Erik never wore a pair of socks twice, in emulation of his hero, Kobe Bryant, and we would smile at Erik's eccentricities through our tears. Michael could always make me laugh, but soon our jokes would become overshadowed by a tangle of anxious questions. His sense of unease and distrust started with the murders, and grew exponentially after the bombing. Erik's murder was one of those "cataclysmic events," he'd explain. He felt lost, and though he wanted clarity, he said, "It's hard because I'm not sure if that's ever going to happen."

"Hello?" Michael's voice cracked, and he was breathing heavy. That's how I knew.

"No," I said.

"Yes," he replied.

"No," I said more forcefully this time.

"Yes," he said again, and by then he was crying.

I ran up the street screaming, tears streaming down my face, gasping for breath. But my adrenaline kicked in by the time I started my car. I stopped crying. I felt numb and at the same time energized, like if I needed to I could run fast and far. I drove straight to Michael's. Michael felt the same way; one minute he would be in tears, the next minute he'd feel nothing at all.

I told Michael about Lynn. I explained that I had been through this before and that the grief would be omnipresent yet slightly out of reach—until the killers are found. Until then, part of us would be frozen in time, waiting for the other shoe to drop, for the killers to strike again. We would not be able to fully process this event, grieve, and move on until we knew what happened.

We hugged once more. Then I drove to Logan International Airport. My parents were on a flight to Boston from Ireland—where my mother is from—and I could not call them while they were in the air to change plans. Their flight was delayed for an hour. I paced by the arrivals gate until they landed.

When I told my parents the news, my father held me tight to his chest and cried. "How?" he asked. "Stabbed?" he said, once I'd explained. "Stabbed?" he said again on the car ride home. "Stabbed?" It didn't make any sense.

A few weeks later my father would receive a call from a state trooper, because Erik had been my father's client. My father told me he informed the trooper he had no idea what could have happened.

There's another factor to stabbing murders. One that I had not considered before but one that gives me a rotten feeling in the pit of my stomach every time I contemplate it today. When people are stabbed to death, and they are killed slowly, the terror and pain are elongated. Those last moments and hours matter, I've learned. For the people who endured them, of course, but for those who remember them too. Especially for those who still have questions. As I strained for answers in the following years, mental re-creations of Erik's last moments would play over and over again in my mind. Every new detail I learned would inspire a new reimagining of his last hour.

For the rest of September 2011, I tried to piece together what happened, talking with my father and huddled with my high school friends. My father agreed with me that Erik's murder was unusual, and he was also upset. But he did not want me to dwell on his killing. Homicide trials are one thing; a friend's brutal death is another. He told me to snap out of it. Journalists question police work, sure. But they don't investigate open murder cases, he said, no matter how compelled I felt to do exactly that.

I told the news director at NECN everything I knew, which also meant revealing my close personal relationship to a drug dealer. She held her tongue if she had questions on that point, but she did not seem interested in following up on the story either. Or maybe she, like my father, was uncomfortable in the presence of my obvious distress.

I was three and a half hours late to work the Saturday after Erik was killed, creeping into the dark production room at 6:00 a.m. smelling of whiskey. "I'm sorry," I whispered to my producer and the camera director. It was just the two men in the production room on Saturday mornings. I told them my friend was murdered, and I'd been having a hard time. The camera director asked me, "Where?"

"Waltham," I told him. And then, as if on cue, footage of the outside of 12 Harding Avenue started rolling with photos of Erik, Brendan, and Rafi, and a reporter relaying the gruesome findings of the medical examiner's report once more. My colleagues did not ask any more questions, but I don't think they reported my tardiness to my supervisors either. The station covered the killings for a week, and that was that. There was no more story.

CHAPTER NINE

Good Kids

"My friend was murdered," Omar told me while we sat together at a booth at Cambridge Lunch, a family diner with an open kitchen and window boxes overflowing with herbs. The restaurant was run almost entirely by my neighbors, a married Jordanian couple and their seven kids. I used to help out with the weekend brunch shift. (The name of the restaurant and the family have been changed.) My shifts were a blur of omelets, toast with homemade rosewater jam, and home fries heaped with vegetables. On weekends, the line stretched out the door. The father, Adam, would give me peaches from his garden and have me read the news to him while he cooked, bragging to customers that I would be a famous reporter one day. The mother, Dana, would box me up big healthy meals to go when I did not have a college meal plan. Omar was one of their children.

The table was covered in crayons and the plate of French toast Adam had prepared special for me. I had come to the diner for comfort food and to exchange pleasantries, hoping the visit would take my mind off Erik's murder, if only for a short while. When I asked Omar how he was doing, I expected to hear more about his quest for a puppy or a report he was working on in the fifth grade. I did not know that Brendan Mess was, like me, a part of the extended family of the place, and that the family was grieving as well. Brendan was not just a customer; he had been Omar's *friend*, and he had been so kind.

Adam and Dana called me a "good kid" well before I became serious about school. They were consistent like family, but without the baggage and complications. My first few shifts, I came in exhausted and hungover. But soon, I tempered down my weekend hijinks so I could get to work on Saturday and Sunday morning without feeling ill. Adam and Dana were not the only reason I became studious, but their encouragement felt so warm.

To Adam and Dana, Brendan was a "good kid" too. They didn't dwell on the fancy cars and the cash. They saw a man who was kind to his friends and their children. Brendan doted on their youngest daughter especially, who had to sit in the booth and color while her parents worked. He let her try on his hats, an assortment of new baseball caps and his camouflage Kangol. He would come to the diner with a rotating cast of friends, he would always pay, and he would often spruce up their orders. If his friend tried to order pancakes, he'd tell them to get the chocolate chip pancakes, Adam's specialty. Brendan ordered eggs Benedict with spinach and bacon every time. Later the family would name the Brendan Benedict after him, and hang his photo above his favorite booth like a shrine, so his friends could still eat by his side. Though in the months leading up to his death, the family had noticed Brendan had changed. More often than not, he came alone with his new girlfriend, Hibatalla K. Eltilib. She mostly went by Hiba. Hiba, then twenty-nine, was born in Sudan, moved to London as a toddler, and then moved to Richmond, Virginia, in her teens. She had recently moved to Massachusetts to be with Brendan. The couple did not seem at ease. Adam and Dana chalked it up to lovers' quarrels.

In August Brendan came into the diner alone, and he was dressed up like he was going to a job interview, with a blue button-up, black pants, and dress shoes. "Everything okay, Brendan?" Dana asked. Brendan said it was, and he ordered his usual. Dana heard him make jokes with Adam about parties. Adam likes to joke about parties and drinking since he doesn't drink because he is Muslim. That's the joke. It's a routine Adam does with almost everyone, me included. But this time Brendan didn't play along.

"We're going to have a party downstairs," he told Adam.

"Like he meant hell, like all will go to hell. That's how he meant it. Which is something that at that moment, knowing Brendan, gave me goose bumps. Like sometimes you have [a] gut feeling like something's wrong," Dana told me later.

But when Brendan came to the diner for the last time, in September, he was his normal cheery self. Adam told him that Omar wanted to start boxing. Adam wanted his son to be like Brendan, to work out and be strong. Brendan offered to take Omar to Wai Kru, a local MMA gym. He gave Adam his number and said he and Omar would go the following Monday, after school.

On Monday afternoon, Omar had his gym bag packed and was waiting by the restaurant door after school. Brendan never came.

~

In the weeks after the murders, my feeling that something uniquely terrible had taken place in Waltham had multiplied tenfold. Even though my reasoning was much the same as it had been before I learned Erik was a victim, everyone I spoke to seemed to think my fixation was personal. I did speak to a senior investigative reporter at another outlet. (I was introduced to him by Michael's mother.) But instead of listening to me, the reporter turned a coffee meeting into a dinner date and dangled a work opportunity in front of me while making comments about my appearance. I started to question my instincts. At work, every new murder story that crossed the wire filled me with dread. Would this case involve someone I knew too? I paused before opening emails, checked the names of homicide victims on Facebook to see if we had mutual friends, and researched the cases obsessively to see if the crimes bore any similarities to Erik's murder.

My father's lectures on redemption were well and grand, but no one slits three throats and returns to the life of a law-abiding citizen. Prison may be inhumane, but homicides need to be accounted for somehow. I was perplexed by the unusual staging of the crime—it seemed as if the killers took pleasure in the act. They were bound to strike again. The question was *when and how?* I thought about Erik's killers all the time. *Who are they? Where are they? Could they be behind me in the checkout line? Driving down my street?*

The only cure for this near-crippling fear was rage. I liked Erik. I really fucking liked Erik. Sure, we argued, but isn't that the test of a real friendship? Someone with whom you can speak your mind? Our conversations were honest and real. He was funny and smart, tender and kind, and he got me in ways few others did. He had me recite my freshman-year poetry for goodness' sake, and he listened, like, *really listened*, to what I had to say. He never hit on me or made me feel uncomfortable, not once. He was a great guy. So why did he have to get himself killed? As much as his death didn't look like a typical drug murder, I still thought the fact that he was operating in a criminal world factored into his killing in some way. I told Erik to stop selling drugs and he didn't listen to me. I was mad at him even if I knew it wasn't fair. There is no returning to your old life after events like these—not all the way. I'd lost Lynn, I'd lived in fear for half a year because of my ex, and I'd done everything I could so I would not have to contend with that sort of terror ever again. I went to college, worked hard at my job, stopped dating drug dealers, and traded my club clothes for oxford shirts. And then Erik got himself killed, and now here I was, contending with a fresh new horror coursing through my veins. Worse, I knew that my childhood friends and my neighbors at the diner would never be the same. Erik did not deserve my anger on top of everything else. But anger can be an easier emotion to bear than fear, and I didn't know where else to direct my feelings.

I was also confused and concerned that the Waltham murder case slipped so quickly out of the headlines. At the news station, when cases went unsolved, we would often receive statements from district attorneys and police encouraging the public to come forward with information. I'd write out the tip lines in the chyrons. Neither the police nor the district attorney requested information about the Waltham murders case or provided a number to call. The seeming lack of interest and urgency made me uneasy. Especially since the district attorney said that the victims likely knew the assailants. But thinking about Erik's death was so overwhelming I shelved my thoughts away. I convinced myself that the detectives were doing everything they could to find Erik's killers. Why wouldn't they? They had the time and the resources to work the Waltham case. When, two weeks later, my old history professor offered me a position as a media coordinator at a university research center, I took it. I thought I was leaving crime reporting for good.

PART II

Cambridge and the Caucasus

CHAPTER TEN

Nothing Is Solved

Bellie Hacker has a thick Israeli accent, applies an intimidating red lip, and does not want anyone's pity. When people hear about her son's murder and everything that followed, they often ask, *How do you go on?* She hates that. Yes, some days, weeks, months, or even years, she is consumed by grief. But the tragedy does not define her. On Facebook she continues to post photos of her late son on a Facebook memorial page: Erik with a birthday cake, Erik with his violin, Erik flashing a peace sign, Erik in a suit dancing with his little sister, Erik with a fake mustache, Erik in a silly wig, baby Erik in suspenders, and teenage Erik lighting the menorah. But Bellie also draws every day, a practice of joy. On her own account she posts photos of her floral ink sketches, studies in architecture, and abstract designs.

"He was a perfectionist. That was his best trait and his worst trait," Bellie told me of her son, flipping through a photo album of Erik's elementary school report cards at her tidy Harvard Square apartment. "Whatever came easy he could master, so he was always waiting for something to be perfect before he went ahead and accomplished anything. That's what held him back," she said. Erik was amazing, intelligent, creative, and smart, but she told me his life had still been on hold. "He got involved with this. I don't know why." She paused again, not wanting to mention his weed dealing—his clandestine career pained her when Erik was alive as well. When I began interviewing Erik's family, cannabis was still illegal in Massachusetts. It's not anymore. Dispensaries are everywhere, and the state has set up a social equity program to prioritize licenses for those impacted by the War on Drugs—historically African American people have been four times as likely as white people to be arrested for marijuana possession despite roughly equal use. The program also prioritizes those arrested on nonviolent weed charges, like Erik.

Bellie had not known for sure that Erik was a dealer, but she had an inkling, and it scared her. They often fought about his future and his plans, how he was wasting his potential—the kind of arguments loving mothers often have with their sons. Erik adored his mother, though he would not leave the career into which he had placed his whole identity. Erik was innovative, extremely successful in his trade, and had a plan for when marijuana was legalized. Had he lived, he would have prospered like many of his friends have since. "But he was extremely intuitive and wonderful, sensitive, caring, loyal. Just a really unique human being," Bellie went on.

My first introduction to Erik's family was at his funeral on the edge of a Jewish cemetery in Roxbury. I stood around his grave with my childhood friends, scanning the crowd for suspects. Erik's father, Nikki Weissman, an Israeli Army veteran, paced in circles around the mourners. Bellie held on to her only surviving child, Erik's younger sister, Aria. The women's wails cut through the late summer air and punctuated the rabbi's prayers. I had never heard grief so bare.

In the months after the murders, I tried to forget their pain. I tried to forget Erik. I tried to forget everything. I went to the *Yahrzeit*, the graveside service on the one-year anniversary of Erik's death, but that was it. To say I regret not reaching out to Erik's family in the weeks and months that followed would be an understatement. If I had known then what I know now—how they were treated by law enforcement, the questions that were and were not asked—I would not have let this story go. I would not have turned away. I don't know what I could have done, exactly, but it would have been better than nothing. And maybe, it would have made a difference. I know this thinking is not altogether rational—it's grandiose, even—but no matter how many times I try to forgive myself, I am plagued by regret. I could have done better. I could have tried, at least.

Not that the news coverage after the bombing helped the victims' families exactly. Bellie still feels like the focus of the reporting is always on the Tsarnaev brothers, and Erik's death remains "in the shadow." When a story does mention the Waltham case, Bellie inevitably gets contacted by her friends and acquaintances congratulating her, thinking the case is closed. *Did you read that? Did you see that?* they ask. *Now we know.*

"Nothing is solved," Bellie tells them.

Some days, Bellie is fed up with me too. She wants answers from someone official, not the media, and not me. Nothing I write or say will ever equal a statement from the district attorney or a ruling from the courts. She asks, *Why are you doing this? Writing a book? Producing a docuseries? It will never bring Erik back.* I tell Bellie it's because I have to find the truth. I tell her I'm grateful to her and to Erik, that Erik saw me as a writer before I did. Then, in his death, he gave me a story I had no other choice but to tell and ignited a discipline I could not conjure on my own. She tells me Erik lives in the seeds he planted in me—in my craft and my creativity—and also, *Why are you so thin?*

CHAPTER ELEVEN

The Triple-Decker

In early 2011, while Erik was couch-surfing, life in the Tsarnaev residence was also growing increasingly dire.

Who was Tamerlan Tsarnaev? In the wake of the bombing, this question became the focus of international news, books, and films. The Tsarnaev family history also became central to the bombing trial and subsequent appeals. Naturally, Tamerlan, the man who allegedly slit my friend's throat, became a point of my own personal fixation.

If I've learned anything about Tamerlan, it's that he would have liked the attention. I'm not sure if his parents, Anzor and Zubeidat, knowingly named their eldest son after Tamerlane, the brutal fourteenth-century Turco-Mongol conqueror. But Tamerlan did at times call himself Timur, just like the conqueror did, among other self-aggrandizing nicknames, and the military ruler's mythic legacy just about tracks with the Tsarnaevs' own deluded aspirations for their firstborn.

The first two details about Tamerlan's life blasted across news networks was that he was Chechen and he was a boxer. I learned who the bombers were from a law enforcement source about an hour before the story broke. The first hit I found about Tamerlan online was a 2009 photo essay titled "Will Box for Passport" by a French student photographer named Johannes Hirn. The essay includes fifteen photos of Tamerlan taken at Wai Kru, the MMA gym where he trained with Brendan Mess. I am pretty sure this essay was how other journalists first sourced their reporting too, inadvertently spreading some of the myths that Tamerlan told about himself.

In the essay there are photos of Tamerlan posing before an American flag, stretching on the mats, curling his upper lip, sweaty and shirtless and training with an unidentified woman. In another photo, Tamerlan is seen looking at his phone, posing in front of a silver Mercedes, his gym bag slung over one shoulder. His hair is gelled, and he is wearing purple-tinted sunglasses and black leather pants. "I'm dressed European-style," he is quoted as saying, beneath a close-up of a pointed white leather shoe.

Tamerlan told Hirn he was originally from Chechnya and his family fled the republic in the 1990s. Tamerlan thought of himself as Chechen. He had a group of Chechen friends in Boston, but even they would point out that he wasn't like them—he spoke with a Dagestani accent. It makes sense that Tamerlan identified as Chechen, but he was actually born in the Republic of Kalmykia, near the border of Kyrgyzstan in Central Asia, where his father, Anzor, was born. Tamerlan's grandfather was one of hundreds of thousands of Chechens dragged from their homes and shipped off in trains after World War II. Tamerlan's mother, Zubeidat, was not Chechen at all. She was the youngest child in a family of shepherds from the Avar ethnic group in Dagestan. Zubeidat's mother died when she was still a little girl, and she was passed back and forth between her brothers' families.

Hirn wrote that despite living in America for five years, Tamerlan didn't have a single American friend. "I don't understand them," Tamerlan told him.

After the bombing, those who knew Dzhokhar, a polite student and mild-mannered stoner, voiced a near universal chorus of shock. It was inconceivable that Dzhokhar, or "Jahar" as he was known on the Cambridge Rindge and Latin high school wrestling team, had taken part in violence at all, let alone terrorism. But people who knew Tamerlan distanced themselves from the elder bomber, essentially claiming that they never liked the guy. They said he was aggressive, fixated on his religion.

Tamerlan was indeed aggressive. He was prone to political and religious tirades. But he did make American friends in Cambridge, many of whom confided to me that the Tamerlan they knew was also a self-deprecating jokester who loved *Family Guy* and gave his buddies silly nicknames. He was charismatic and loyal—at least he seemed so. That's what made the allegations that Tamerlan murdered Erik, Rafi, and Brendan all the more disturbing: by all appearances, Tamerlan loved Brendan like a brother.

~

Anzor and Zubeidat's marriage was controversial. Neither family approved. In Dagestan, Zubeidat was known as the flamboyant cousin. She took particular pride in flashy, fashionable, colorful clothes. Her family was Muslim, but not especially devout. The women did not cover their heads, and the family celebrated New Year's with Christmas trees. Anzor's family was not especially religious either. The point of contention was cultural. Though both cultures emphasized the role of the firstborn son, there were differences, in wedding customs, for example. Also Zubeidat was who she was: a distinctly outspoken woman. She quickly learned Chechen, and her family eventually accepted Anzor, but his family never liked Zubeidat. Later they would blame her for all of the family's misfortunes, call her a "witch," and claim Anzor was Zubeidat's "zombie," a "mental cripple" under her spell.

Anzor's psychiatrists had a different diagnosis and believed he was tortured in a Russian filtration camp. The Tsarnaevs likely spent a brief period in Chechnya in 1994, at the beginning of the First Chechen War. Zubeidat told the same shrink that Anzor was not tortured in a camp; he was tortured by the mob because he was a prosecutor. According to journalist Masha Gessen, Anzor did sign up for a correspondence course to become a lawyer and may have had run-ins with organized crime, but according to Gessen and the *Boston Globe*, he was never actually an attorney.

It's unclear what Tamerlan knew about Chechen history or how he placed himself in his family's conflicting lore. But he did understand himself to be Chechen, a history that had been shaped in part by mythmaking and harmful narratives.

My trips to the library to learn about the tiny, mountainous North Caucasus republic, less than a third the size of Vermont, would invariably lead me to titles like these: *To the Heart of a Conflict*, *The Sky Wept Fire*, and *A Small Corner of Hell*. Before David Remnick became editor of the *New Yorker*, he wrote from the war-torn region. The "independent spirit" of the Chechen people is a Russian obsession that has come to represent "an image of Islamic defiance, an embodiment of the primitive, the devious, the elusive," inspiring Kremlin leaders to acts of war, and Russian poets to verse, he wrote in a 1995 *New Yorker* article. Chechens were famous for bowing to no ruler, having no royalty or system of government other than their familial bonds. They are said to have revered *abreks*, legendary Robin Hood–like bandits who stole to support their clans.

Chechnya was late to adopt Islam. The religion didn't really take off there until the early eighteenth century, when the Russian Empire tried to take over the North Caucasus. Because the Chechen people did not have a system of government, Islam became a unifying bond for the otherwise autonomous mountain communities, who against all odds fended off the Russian Empire in a series of resistance efforts lasting more than a century.

After the fall of the USSR, under the leadership of Dzhokhar Dudayev, Chechnya once again declared independence and thoroughly embarrassed Russian leadership for their inability to control the republic. (Dzhokhar Tsarnaev was born shortly after Dudayev became president.) Dudayev was not known to be observant, but in the First Chechen War (1994–1996) he used Islam to distinguish the Chechens from Russian oppressors.

Chechnya won the first war but the region was left poverty stricken, cut out of international trade, and became a hub for organized crime. This left an opening for Wahhabi extremists from abroad to move in to the area and rally support for their beliefs by providing jobs to those who joined their movement. When the Second Chechen War began, in 1999, the nationalist resistance movement had essentially been co-opted by these outsiders and conflated with their agenda to fight a holy war and establish a caliphate.

What I found really interesting about the Second Chechen War is that it was instigated by what is potentially a real deal false flag operation. False flags are a favorite among conspiracy theorists. Some of the most unbelievable and detestable conspiracies, like that the Sandy Hook school shootings were a hoax, are structured around this idea that an attack, shooting, or bombing was carried out by an unseen power as a means to justify some other action, like war. A lot of 9/11 conspiracy theories are centered around the same premise. Before the bombing, Tamerlan was becoming more and more enamored with conspiracy theories, many of which involved false flags as well. The Second Chechen War may explain why he was so susceptible to this kind of thinking.

This war also established Vladimir Putin as a household name. Putin had been recently appointed as acting prime minister in place of Boris Yeltsin and was the former head of the KGB, but most Russians had no idea who he was. Then in September 1999, a series of deadly bombings in apartment buildings across Russia killed at least 243 people and launched Putin into the public eye. Putin posed as a strongman, vowing revenge. He blamed the attacks on the "Chechen terrorist nation," despite the fact that the bombings were unlike attacks orchestrated by Chechen nationalists in the past, and leaders from the Chechen nationalist movements did not claim responsibility for these attacks as they had previously done.

Then local officials thwarted what appeared to be a fourth attempted apartment bombing and seized bags of explosives, which were linked to the FSB, or Federal Security Service (the modern iteration of the KGB). Kremlin officials claimed it was a test and the bags contained sugar. The false flag theory that Putin orchestrated the apartment bombs himself as a pretext to invade Chechnya—though never definitively proved—is accepted by a wide array of Western journalists and academics and is part of Chechen lore. When, years later, Russia closed the apartment bombing case, none of those convicted were Chechen.

After Russia regained control of Chechnya, bands of resistance fighters, who increasingly also identified as jihadi fighters, moved the struggle to neighboring Dagestan. The movement was especially popular among the Avar ethnic group. The fighters also worked to expand their reach online, posting videos of heroic-looking men dressed in black and their exploits. The rebels lived in the steep, thickly wooded mountains. Going to "the Forest" soon became synonymous with joining the resistance movement.

The Tsarnaev family lived a ping-pong existence, moving constantly across Central Asia and the North Caucasus. Zubeidat's aunts and cousins would complain that the Tsarnaevs lived out of suitcases, rarely staying put for more than a year. Then they came to America on a refugee visa and settled into the top floor of a triple-decker in Inman Square.

The family was welcomed by the landlady, Joanna Herlihy, a Peace Corps veteran who spoke Russian and lived downstairs. Located near a cluster of auto shops, the Tsarnaevs' was one of the last Cambridge neighborhoods to gentrify. Tamerlan would spend the entirety of his decade-long stay in America at this singular address on Norfolk Street. Anzor and Zubeidat arrived first with their youngest, Dzhokhar, in 2002. Along with his two sisters, Bella and Alina, Tamerlan joined his parents the following year. By then, he was an awkward sixteen-year-old with a unibrow. The Cambridge apartment would be the family's first and only consistent home. Over the course of the next ten years, behind the walls of the cramped third-floor apartment, Tamerlan's disdain for the United States would grow to a violent boil.

CHAPTER TWELVE

Lizards

In the "Will Box for Passport" photo essay, Tamerlan told the French photographer of his plan to fight in the national Golden Gloves boxing competition. He believed entry to the national championship would pave the way for him to fight for America in the Olympics. Even though he was not a citizen, Tamerlan was under the belief that if he made the nationals, immigration officials would grant him citizenship. How he arrived at this idea is unclear.

This was not Tamerlan's only delusional aspiration. He had big dreams but did not seem to have the know-how or discipline to achieve them. He aspired to become an actor or a musician, or alternatively a lawyer or a dentist, and intended to go to an Ivy League school while working full- time to buy a house, according to *Wall Street Journal* reporter Alan Cullison, who connected with the Tsarnaev family during their first years in Cambridge.

In high school Tamerlan paid little attention in his ESL classes and instead tried to teach himself English by reading Russian translations of Sherlock Holmes books side by side with the originals. He fancied himself an intellectual and gave himself the nickname "the Professor." But ultimately, he was a C student. In the photo essay, Tamerlan said he was only taking a break from college to focus on boxing and would soon go back to school and become an engineer. He had enrolled in community college but dropped out after a few semesters.

When Tamerlan first arrived in America, he walked down the halls of Cambridge Rindge and Latin high school with his boxing gloves over his shoulder. He was a fighter, and he wanted everyone to know it. One of his classmates,

Shane McCarthy, was impressed by Tamerlan's height and encouraged him to join the volleyball team. Shane would eventually invite Tamerlan to pickup basketball games with his other Cambridge friends in Inman Square, including Brendan Mess's younger brother, Dylan. Tamerlan wasn't serious about volleyball as a sport, but he was a good enough player, and he liked to shoot the shit at practice. He would brag to his teammates about his father, Anzor, who he said had been a champion boxer back home.

Anzor Tsarnaev gave firm handshakes. He was like a cowboy, a muscular man of few words, even in his native Russian. He fixed cars for a living, working on the street in front of the apartment, or in a nearby parking lot. He could be found with his back on a car roller, working away with his bare hands on hot summer days and frigid winter mornings, impressing clients with his tenacity and cheap prices. But he also had warm eyes and was quick to extend an invitation for tea. Though neither parent ever attended Dzhokhar's wrestling matches, Anzor was devoted to Tamerlan's boxing career, trailing Tamerlan on a bike as he jogged around Cambridge and interjecting as he trained at the gym—much to the dismay of Tamerlan's coaches.

Anzor began seeing psychiatrists almost immediately after he arrived in America. He complained of flashbacks, and he also suffered from what his doctor said were paranoid delusions. He thought the Russian KGB was following him in Cambridge, and he would look for agents from the window of the apartment.

Anzor's medical reports reveal a deeply afflicted man. He was startled by loud sounds, and he could not tolerate light. He was diagnosed with post-traumatic stress disorder due to the flashbacks, but also agoraphobia, psychosis, and impaired cognition from his own years as a boxer. By 2006, Anzor was complaining to doctors that he felt a "presence" next to him, had visions of "little lizard-like creatures," and thought he heard someone calling his name. As his condition worsened, these calls grew to screams.

Despite Anzor's health, the Tsarnaevs did okay for themselves for a while. In Central Asia, Anzor made money in part by flipping cars. Gessen notes that the legality of his trade was likely murky. The *Washington Post* reports that in Cambridge, at a local parts yard, employees would regularly catch him walking away, his pockets stuffed with merchandise he hadn't paid for. Though he never publicly advertised this service, it appears Anzor carried over some form of his side hustle of flipping cars in the United States. To what extent and with what means and assistance Anzor flipped cars is unclear. But Anzor did sell a Mercedes to Brendan Mess, originally listed in Tamerlan's name.

In his early twenties, Tamerlan at least maintained the appearance of affluence. He drove a Mercedes himself and claimed to work in the auto industry. Then Anzor's health took a dramatic turn. In late 2009 he was hit in the head with a pipe in a fight in the parking lot of a Russian social club—Anzor claimed he was attacked when a patron wrongly believed he had bumped into a woman's chair. The Arbat Banquet Hall was an Allston restaurant with elaborate chandeliers, and it once ran into trouble with the Boston licensing board for selling whole bottles of vodka. It also served as headquarters for the Russian Benevolent Society. Anzor and Tamerlan often frequented its premises. Anzor was hospitalized after the incident. He couldn't walk straight. He saw animal faces. The voice screaming his name had grown to an unruly chorus.

Zubeidat had been determined to make her mark in her new country. She took quickly to English and acquired a cosmetology degree with an emphasis on tattoo cosmetology, inking women with a permanent eyeliner or a crisp brow. There is an inherent financial downside to operating a cosmetic tattooing company: repeat customers are rare. For whatever reason, business never took off. When Zubeidat first arrived in America, neighbors believed her to be an agreeable complement to Anzor. Zubeidat was a kind of spark—lively, talkative, with a high sort of singsongy voice. In 2011, her high-pitched voice began to come off more like neurosis. She spoke constantly of her financial anxieties at such a fast clip it seemed she was always on the verge of tears. Zubeidat had exchanged her colorful outfits and loud jewelry for a black hijab. The color of the hijab worried her family in Dagestan especially, as they viewed black as the uniform of the Wahhabi resistance movement that had recently crossed the border. Zubeidat had been fired from a beauty salon in Belmont, and in 2011 she was working as a home health aide and giving facials in the apartment, whispering to her clients about 9/11 conspiracy theories with increasing fervor.

By February 2011, a year and a half after the parking lot fight, Anzor had lost his muscular physique and was suffering from stomach pains. He was thin and often too sick to fix cars. The landlady, Joanna Herlihy, drove him to medical appointments. "If I am not getting better, my wife would divorce me," he told his doctor. This was no delusion. Their marriage was falling apart. In August 2011, in the weeks leading up to the murders, Anzor and Zubeidat filed for divorce, according to the *Boston Globe*. In September 2011, the same month as the triple homicide, the Tsarnaev family filed for food stamps. By then Anzor had given up on America for good and returned to Dagestan. Zubeidat would abscond to Dagestan within the year, fleeing a shoplifting charge after she was busted at the mall for allegedly stealing $1,624 worth of merchandise from Lord & Taylor.

CHAPTER THIRTEEN

Golden Gloves

When Tamerlan arrived in America, he began training at the Somerville Boxing Club with John Curran, a longtime local coach. The Somerville Boxing Club was a "boxing gym, not necessarily a health club," as Curran described it. But Tamerlan shined in the dingy gym. Back then, Curran also found the athlete to be charming and kind.

Unlike his American peers, Tamerlan fought in the European style. American boxers keep their weak hand up to protect their face when they punch. Tamerlan boxed with his left hand down low. This gave him the freedom to inflict more force with his jab, but it also left him open to a right hand or a power shot to the face. Tamerlan also preferred to spar without headgear. He usually won. But when he didn't, he would be left coughing up blood. Over the years Tamerlan would develop a kind of performance outside of the ring as well, wearing flashy outfits or unnerving his opponents with piano concertos before the match.

Curran tried to steer Tamerlan away from the European style for years, but Tamerlan wouldn't hear of it. Especially not when Anzor was there to interject. Curran cautioned Anzor against interfering. "We're trying to teach him stuff and he's not listening," he said. This did not go over well. The regional New England Golden Gloves tournaments are held every year at Lowell Memorial Auditorium in January and February. Tamerlan won two back-to-back novice championships. But when he graduated high school he left the Somerville Boxing Club, dropped Curran as a coach, and for several years, seemingly gave up on his athletic ambitions.

In the years after high school, Tamerlan was a bit of a drunk. He primarily socialized with the close-knit group of Chechen men his age. *Chechens stick together,* one of his friends told me, in explanation of his relationship to the Tsarnaevs. In all likelihood, I crossed paths with Tamerlan and his friends in their bar-hopping days. We lived only a short walk from one another, and they went to the same clubs I did back then, like the Middlesex Lounge. Several of the men rented an apartment in Cambridge around the corner from the Tsarnaev home. Tamerlan was at his friends' place almost every day, day and night, drinking and smoking weed in the basement. It was a nuisance, Rogerio Franca would later claim. Franca is Brazilian, and though he lived with these men, he was apparently less interested in partying. Once Franca found Tamerlan in his room, dividing up marijuana on his table.

In addition to his Chechen friends in Boston and Cambridge, Tamerlan was close to Elmirza Khozhugov, who was also Chechen. The two had met when the Tsarnaevs lived in Kazakhstan. Elmirza followed the Tsarnaevs and immigrated to America about one year later. He and Tamerlan remained close, and Elmirza eventually married Tamerlan's sister Ailina—the marriage ended when she called the cops on him for strangling her. Tamerlan paid Elmirza's bail.

Elmirza noticed Tamerlan began to change around 2008, when he sought out a copy of *The Protocols of the Elders of Zion*, according to the Associated Press. The infamous book is a fabricated text first published in Russia at the turn of the twentieth century purporting to reveal a secret cabal of powerful Jews set on world domination. Basically, it is a reimagination of the medieval blood libel myth told to justify the persecution of Jews for hundreds of years. Tamerlan did eventually get ahold of a copy, according to the *Wall Street Journal*, and marked up the book with Russian translations of words such as *gentile* and *Mason*.

When he wasn't getting wasted with his friends, Tamerlan was growing increasingly fixated on conspiracy theories. As Elmirza understood it, Tamerlan was trying to make sense of the world and his place in it. Tamerlan's theories did involve religion, but that was not his initial focus, according to Elmirza, who testified in the bombing trial. When Tamerlan visited Elmirza in Washington, in 2008, he had Elmirza watch the film *Zeitgeist*, which claims that 9/11 was a hoax. Elmirza said Tamerlan was also a fan of Alex Jones's InfoWars.

Elmirza claimed he was not interested in what Tamerlan had to say on these matters. Yet inside the Tsarnaev family home, Tamerlan's interests were

0

not only tolerated but encouraged. Tamerlan shared his ideas with his mother and with a man named Misha, an Armenian convert whose real name is Mikhail Allakhverdov. In an interview with the *New York Review of Books*, Misha admitted to visiting the Tsarnaev home, but he claimed that he stopped talking to Tamerlan when he moved to Rhode Island in 2009. According to his testimony, Elmirza said he heard Misha and Tamerlan discussing Islam and politics, but they also spoke at length about hearing and talking to demons. Elmirza left the men alone. He didn't like these conversations in which they intermixed "politics and conspiracy theories and Satanism." But Zubeidat approved of Misha's teachings, believing he was helping her floundering son. She would forbid Anzor from interrupting, even from walking through the room to take a shower, when Misha and Tamerlan spoke.

While doctors' records confirm Anzor's health was deteriorating, Tamerlan may also have suffered from mental health issues of his own. He told his mother he felt there were two people living inside of him, according to the *Boston Globe*.

Tamerlan sometimes accompanied his mother to work, to visit a client, Donald Larking in Newton, whom Zubeidat began caring for in early 2011. Larking suffered from a brain injury after he was shot in the head in a robbery attempt, which a family attorney would emphasize to excuse Larking's relationship to the Tsarnaevs in later interviews with the press.

Larking shared Tamerlan's passion for conspiracy theories and Tamerlan confided in Larking. He told Larking he believed he was the victim of "majestic mind control." Larking explained to the *Boston Globe* that as Tamerlan understood it, an evildoer had inserted an alternate personality inside of him, and this personality was being activated with specific signals, phrases, or gestures. Tamerlan told Larking he felt forced to obey their commands, though he was attempting to coexist with this being peacefully.

Larking apparently followed along with Tamerlan's logic. In fact, it appealed to his interests. Larking subscribed to *The Sovereign* and *American Free Press*— outlets that propound conspiracy theories ranging from flu shot fears to the need for domestic terrorism to fight big business. They also write a lot about the Rothschilds. Tamerlan had his own subscription to *American Free Press*, according to the *Wall Street Journal*. A copy of *The Sovereign* was found in his apartment, according to court documents in Dzhokhar Tsarnaev's trial. In the years leading up to the tenth anniversary of 9/11, these publications were especially fixated on the event and the idea that not only were the attacks a hoax, but that the Israeli government was to blame. After the bombing, *The Sovereign* and others would disseminate new unfounded myths about the bombing.

~

In the fall of 2007, Tamerlan met the woman who would become his wife at a nightclub.

Katherine "Katie" Russell grew up in North Kingston, Rhode Island, the daughter of an emergency room doctor and a nurse. The Russells were a Catholic family with a dash of New England blue blood. Her father and grandfather went to Phillips Exeter Academy and Yale, according to the *New York Times*. The photos that surfaced of Katherine Russell before she met Tamerlan reveal the wholesome beauty of a Vineyard Vines model, a brunette with long earrings, as well as a teary-eyed mug shot from a teenage shoplifting bust.

In a photo taken of Tamerlan and Katie in the early days of their courtship, he is wearing a pin-striped fedora with a snakeskin band and a leather coat with a fur collar. Katie is leaning into his shoulder in a short-sleeve blue top. Her hair is dyed red, and she wears a nose ring, black nail polish, and a smug grin. That year Katie was a freshman at Suffolk University. Her roommate, Amanda Ransom, saw that Tamerlan was outgoing and flashy, but Amanda was not sure what he did for a living. "He said he worked with cars, delivering cars . . . He was driving a Mercedes," Amanda said. Despite his spotty résumé, Tamerlan seemed to be doing well for himself. Since Amanda and Katie were both underage, Tamerlan flashed cash at bouncers at the club doors.

~

In her sophomore year Katie found out Tamerlan was cheating on her, and they broke up. This breakup coincided with the publication of the "Will Box for Passport" photo essay. In the essay Tamerlan said he was dating a half-Portuguese, half-Italian woman who had converted to Islam. "She's beautiful, man!" This woman, Nadine Ascencao, was living with Tamerlan in the triple-decker on Norfolk Street. In July 2009, Ascencao called the police to report Tamerlan had slapped her. According to the complaint, they were arguing about another woman—possibly Katie, maybe someone else. The charges were later dropped, but they would complicate his application for US citizenship.

After Ascencao left, Tamerlan apparently started lurking around Katie's apartment. Katie told Amanda that she had run into Tamerlan again in the street, and they decided to get back together. This time, the relationship was serious and potentially violent. That fall Tamerlan gave Katie a copy of the Qur'an, and she started observing holidays with him. Katie had grown distant from her friends. Her friendship with Amanda reached a breaking point when one night Amanda awoke to hear screaming and banging from Katie's room. She tried to intercede, to protect her friend. But Katie took Tamerlan's side, as Tamerlan turned his ire on Amanda, threatening her from the bottom of the stairs. Amanda took this threat seriously. She barricaded her door with her desk until Tamerlan was asleep, then fled the apartment in her pajamas. She would never live under the same roof with Katie and Tamerlan again.

Soon Katie started calling herself Karima. When Katherine's mother, Judith Russell, paid her daughter a visit, she found she was wearing a hijab. It was the first time Judith saw her daughter covering her head. On that same visit, Katherine told her mother she was pregnant. Tamerlan and Katherine married on June 21, 2010, in a private religious ceremony without family or friends.

In October 2010, Katherine gave birth to a daughter, Zahara. Judith Russell welcomed her daughter and grandchild into her home. Katherine and Zahara stayed for ten months before joining her husband in the Tsarnaevs' Cambridge apartment in August 2011, just as Dzhokhar was leaving for college. Katherine began working as a home health aide like her mother-in-law. Finances were tight. Tamerlan no longer wore flashy outfits, no longer drove a Mercedes, no longer had hopes of boxing in the Olympics. Instead, neighbors would find him outside the apartment taking care of his daughter in tattered sweatpants and a wifebeater tank top. Meanwhile Katherine could be found in the courtyard in a hijab speaking to other women in Russian and Arabic. When she did speak English, she talked very slowly, like it was her second language, according to the *Washington Post*.

CHAPTER FOURTEEN

The Gym

For all his outsized dreams, Tamerlan was truly an extraordinary boxer.

Wai Kru consisted of one windowless basement room with red mats covering the walls and floors and a boxing cage in the corner. The gym was founded in 2006 by Boston College wrestler John Allan and Steven "the Sandman" Dunn, who was arrested and later convicted for trafficking OxyContin.

MMA, or cage fighting as we know it today in America, was officially established in 1993 with the launch of the Ultimate Fighting Championship. When the creators of the UFC pitched the entertainment-turned-sport to networks they explicitly compared their vision to the video games *Mortal Kombat* and *Street Fighter.*

Wai Kru was one of the first gyms in Boston to offer the full roster of MMA practices: muay thai, jujitsu, boxing, kickboxing, karate, wrestling, and sambo. Videos of Wai Kru fighters in clandestine bare-knuckle matches were occasionally leaked online—in one instance sparking a local scandal when a participant, Sean "the Cannon" Gannon, was revealed to be a Boston Police officer. Wai Kru is an MMA gym, not a place frequented by boxers. Which was probably why Tamerlan liked it. There was no one to critique his style. He was the best boxer the gym had, and Tamerlan liked nothing more than being the best.

The way gym owner John Allan saw it, Tamerlan was a "peacock." He was always putting on a kind of show. Even when he was just working out at the gym, he was always aware of attracting attention.

In the winter of 2009, Tamerlan was in fine form at the New England Golden Gloves competition and was sent to nationals in Salt Lake City. Unfortunately for Tamerlan, he and several of his teammates caught the flu on the flight over. He lost. He was certain he would win the following year. His dream of fighting in the Olympics was just in sight.

CHAPTER FIFTEEN

The King Man

Brendan Mess loved weed, women, and MMA. He also liked urban streetwear, flat-brimmed baseball caps with the sticker still on, new sneakers, and bucket-style Kangol hats. He listened to Jay-Z and had a white bearskin rug. His friends called him "the King Man," and he was kind of a legend, even when he was alive. His quick reflexes and his high threshold for pain often factored into stories of his antics. He was not someone you wanted to mess with, but he was a great guy to have on your side. He was a prankster, and when he was in Cambridge he was almost always surrounded by a close circle of friends. He was a leader and he was loyal. The same group of boys who came to his house to eat cereal and watch cartoons before elementary school would join him for pickup basketball games in his early twenties.

He started selling weed in middle school. In those days, he had a different look. He dyed a red streak in his hair and wore JNCO jeans. But at heart he was the same Brendan, extremely social and with a thirst for excitement. He befriended a group of high schoolers who sold him weed by the ounce, which Brendan would divide and sell as dime bags. He used the extra money to spoil his friends, buying them sneakers and CDs—whatever would make them happy. Brendan also sold weed through high school, but he stayed away from Cambridge gang fights and the long-standing dispute between North Cambridge and a neighborhood dubbed the Port. He did not always apply himself at school. He was a bit of a class clown. But he was smart, his teachers loved him, and he harbored real artistic ambitions. Though he did not mention this fact often, he came from an academic family. His father, Derek Mess, is a professor of chemical and biological engineering at Tufts. Brendan himself wanted to be a writer.

After high school he went to Champlain College in Vermont and quit smoking weed for a few years. On campus he stuck out from kids from Connecticut who showed up wearing Abercrombie & Fitch and later evolved into hacky sack "hippies." He had a commanding voice and a thick Boston accent, though he would probably have noted features in his speech that were distinct to Cambridge if someone said that. He lived off campus and adopted two pit bulls, Hazel and Ruckus. On campus his peers found him to be a surprisingly good writer, outshining his classmates with his authentic and empathetic voice in writing groups. He was known to borrow a classmate's computer, stay home, and study when the others went out to parties. In his class assignments Brendan wrote a lot about Cambridge and his childhood, which by his own account was a little rough. He wrote this in one assignment:

> I always loved to go to the courts of parks ever since I could walk down the street. I can remember almost every day there would be royal [rumble] matches on the playground. Fighting was how you solved your problems and got respect. It was . . . until a family of [pacifists] moved above my apartment. There were two kids roughly my age, and I recall going to the park like every other day; something sparked up conflict, and where another day there would have been a fight, these kids just walked away. I never saw anyone talking to those kids again; I did not understand why they did not fight for a long time. As I got older everyone fought less except for the girls, but when there was a fight it was a lot more serious. Respect or maybe intimidation is a big thing where I'm from. The messed up thing is the next man will take everything you have if he does not respect you; and I'm dead serious.

In his writing Brendan identified as bilingual. He went to a public Spanish-speaking school, and he identified with "the Coast," a neighborhood in Cambridge that also appears to have been central to Southern New England Indians—potentially where they cured fish. The African American history dates to shortly after the American Revolution. This was before the Charles River was dammed. Back then, the shellfish banks were likely destroyed, and the land here was made up of muddy and (to the colonists) undesirable riverbanks. It was not central to Cambridge, and there was no easy access to Boston via bridges. The community was founded by people who had been enslaved by the British and had been taken to America from the Caribbean. The people who enslaved them were Royalists during the war. After the revolution, the Royalists abandoned their homes in the Boston area. A number of formerly enslaved people were left behind and gained their independence this way. For centuries the Coast was a vibrant community and was home to prominent figures in African American history, such as W. E. B. Du Bois. The soul-food restaurant The Coast Cafe and Riverside Pizza, both on River Street, pay homage to this history. In Brendan's day there were still a few Coast clubs left, like The Ebony, and the reggae bar Western Front. Brendan wrote that most of his friends were Caribbean and Hispanic and wrote about his appreciation for people from different backgrounds. He was upset about the impact on the community after rent control was lifted in 1995. "There is nothing to fear about another culture," he wrote.

Brendan also wrote that he was a "hustling salesman," though he did not detail what exactly he sold in the college essays I obtained. In college Brendan was meticulous about his clothing. He wore a beige leather jacket and new sneakers. He told his friends he shopped for his little brother, Dylan, as well.

Brendan was protective of Dylan and kept him away from his drug dealing. "He made a huge point of it," Dylan told me. "He was always trying to encourage me to do something else." The brothers were close, only a year apart in school, and they fought a lot, as brothers often do. Brendan, the big brother, was used to winning every scuffle. "When I started playing football I got bigger than him," Dylan explained. This was during Brendan's first year of college, when Dylan made the Cambridge Rindge and Latin varsity football team. Dylan's size advantage didn't last long. "Sure enough, he learned jujitsu, and I couldn't wrestle him anymore," Dylan said. Brendan was passionate about MMA and deeply involved in the fighting community in Burlington, Vermont. He received a purple belt in kickboxing, and in his spare time he would mentor younger athletes. He taught children at Wai Kru as well.

After Brendan graduated college in 2008, he moved back to Cambridge. The Mess brothers shared an apartment in the multifamily property where they were raised. Tamerlan and Brendan were not friends in high school. But they had mutual friends, and the two kindled a tight bond when Brendan returned to Cambridge, what with Brendan's new interest in MMA and Tamerlan's acquired appreciation for marijuana. Tamerlan may have hated America, but he sure liked American weed. By then, Tamerlan had stopped drinking, but he still smoked all the time. Outside of the gym, Brendan's friends saw Tamerlan as Brendan's "new sidekick." They called him "Tim" or "Tam," and he was always hanging around. He was different. He walked around on the balls of his feet, like he was in a boxing ring, ready to fight. He could be intense and prone to political rants. But for the most part he actually mixed in well with Brendan's group of stoner jocks.

∼

Tamerlan introduced Brendan to the owners and trainers at Wai Kru as his "best friend." They trained together three or four times a week, reeking of weed every time they walked in the door. Brendan let Tamerlan borrow his clothing to help him fit in and show off at matches. Tamerlan would often accompany Brendan on weekend trips to Burlington, where Brendan maintained ties to the MMA community. They'd go to Friday night fights, then out to bars, then smoke, eat food, and watch sports all the next day. Tamerlan talked about his religion sometimes. But for the most part he was there to have a good time. He would gulp down Red Bull at the clubs, get hyped up, jump around, and start dancing and cracking jokes.

CHAPTER SIXTEEN

The Final Round

Tamerlan never did make it back to nationals. In 2010 New England Golden Gloves officials enforced an old policy blocking non-Americans from all national competitions. Whether or not this policy was enforced to spite Tamerlan directly is a point of debate. In any case, the rule was reinstated shortly after an incident in which Tamerlan stormed into the locker room, as the *New York Times* reported. He was dressed in his typical flamboyant prefight fashion, wearing a cowboy hat and alligator-skin boots, loaned to him by Brendan Mess. Tamerlan began taunting his opponent. Taunting a rival was unsportsmanlike, but not entirely without precedent. But Tamerlan being Tamerlan, he escalated things and began taunting the other fighter's trainer, Hector Torres, as well. Torres lodged a complaint. New England Golden Gloves officials later claimed that this complaint just so happened to coincide with an ongoing decision to update tournament policy. Previously noncitizens were allowed to compete in nationals in non-Olympic years. This rule would still have disqualified Tamerlan from his Olympic dreams, though it appears that Tamerlan either was not aware of the rule or thought he could be an exception.

Tamerlan won every match in regionals, but he never made it to nationals. A guy Tamerlan squarely beat, an American, went in his place.

In the years after Tamerlan graduated from high school, it had become painfully clear that in regard to education, or a career in medicine or business, his lofty aspirations were not attainable. But if Tamerlan was American, maybe he could have made it as a boxer. When that route was cut off to him, it appears that the self-described "Professor" began working on a thesis to account for the gulf between what he believed was his rightful destiny and his actual predicament based on conspiracy theories, warped interpretations of the Muslim faith, anti-Semitism, and nationalist Wahhabi propaganda from the North Caucasus region. Tamerlan was as smart and strong as he and his mother had always claimed. His failings were the fault of seen and unseen enemies keeping his people, and Tamerlan specifically, down.

In this way, Tamerlan came to believe that the Golden Gloves officials were plotting against him personally. His theories about who was behind this plot and why grew in scope and significance at a frightening clip. There was a hidden hand responsible for this foul deed, a secret group of powerful individuals intent on keeping him, the great Tamerlan Tsarnaev, down. As Christopher Swift, a national security studies professor at Georgetown University, told me, in the realm of conspiratorial thinking, anti-Semitism is like "the glue that holds disparate ideologies together." Anti-Semitism and conspiracy theories about powerful cabals are often similar in form, even when the theories are not about Jews at all—though Tamerlan's theories were explicitly about Jews. Tamerlan was vocal about his thoughts at Wai Kru. "He liked to engage in conspiracy theory discussion with Jewish people, it seemed, whenever possible," gym owner John Allan told me. Another trainer told me Tamerlan was openly disgusted when he learned the trainer was Jewish.

Tamerlan had introduced another Chechen fighter, Ibragim Todashev, to the gym in 2009. Ibragim lived in the apartment where Tamerlan used to go to drink and smoke. From the outside, gym patrons said it was hard to decipher the dynamic between the pair. They spoke to one another in Russian, but it didn't seem that they liked one another much.

Ibragim was significantly smaller than the heavyweight Tamerlan. He was 155 pounds and five feet eight inches—with dark mushroom-cut hair and a faraway look in his eyes. He broke his nose several times over, and his ears were swollen from regular blows to the head. Concerns of vanity in no way deterred Ibragim. He would do anything to compete in the UFC. Ibragim was a cage fighter, not a boxer. He wrestled in the Eastern European–Russian sambo style, which meant he kicked. Tamerlan thought kicking was cheap and dirty. He was really pompous about it, "whereas Ibragim didn't give a fuck," Allan said. According to one patron, Allan had tried to give him a nickname, "Ibragim, the Chechen Killing Machine." But Ibragim didn't like it. After one match he revealed to his carpool he carried a knife in his gym bag for protection.

After Tamerlan was barred from the Golden Gloves tournament, he became more tolerant of Ibragim's eclectic style. They became a kind of odd couple. The spectacle that was Tamerlan evolved as well. He toned down the flashy outfits and distinguished himself by provoking people with his bold worldview. Ibragim had always taken breaks to pray at salat—the five daily prayers observed in Islam. He would kneel on a mat in the corner of the gym. Tamerlan began joining him. Tamerlan and Ibragim also spent time together outside the gym, though Allan was never sure what exactly they did. On one occasion, they got into some sort of brawl. Tamerlan knocked out a couple of people, he told Allan. Meanwhile, Ibragim came back to the gym with a black eye.

When Ibragim first came to Wai Kru, he had no money and his English was terrible. "It was really hard to communicate with him at the beginning," Allan said. "I always assumed the problems and conflicts that happened were because of miscommunications. But, I later learned, Ibragim . . . He's a very hotheaded guy. He could just really flip his switch. If it flipped he would just . . . He would lose control."

Despite the regular flare-ups, Allan let Ibragim train at Wai Kru for free. Ibragim had trouble holding down a job—he was always broke—but he was a good sparring partner.

~

Tamerlan and Brendan remained close and kept up their training at Wai Kru. In August 2010, Brendan bought a black 2004 Mercedes-Benz C320 from Anzor Tsarnaev. Brendan told his friends he got it for a good price. Oddly, there is no record of ownership for the 2004 vehicle prior to April 30, 2010, when the car appears under Tamerlan's name.

Meanwhile, Brendan Mess's friends noticed that Tamerlan had grown increasingly prone to political rants. Any mention of President George W. Bush would set him off. *Americans have no idea what they do to other nations,* he raged. *Millions and millions of American tax dollars are spent on weapons. For what? To drop bombs everywhere.*

Usually when Tamerlan got upset in front of his Cambridge friends, Brendan would take them aside and explain that Tamerlan had lived a hard life. He would do the same with Tamerlan when he got agitated: take him aside and explain where his friends were coming from. Brendan often played peacemaker—at least when he was among friends. Though it was becoming more and more difficult to calm Tamerlan down. In late 2010, Tamerlan stormed out of Brendan's Christmas party, upset because Brendan was drinking.

And sometimes, it seems, Brendan took pleasure in riling Tamerlan up. He allegedly said things that were offensive. Specifically, he taunted Tamerlan about Israel. He would tell Tamerlan that Jews were smart, and that's why the Israeli government was able to steal land from the Palestinian people. "That's why the Jews be fucking you up," Brendan said on one such occasion. One can imagine how this might make Tamerlan, or anyone else, upset. That was the point. Tamerlan would get so enraged that Brendan actually found it amusing. Brendan didn't take anything he said seriously.

By 2011, Brendan and Erik had become closer. They had met around 2003 through their Cambridge weed connections, when Brendan was in high school and Erik drove around Cambridge in a baby blue Mercedes Benz. After Erik's January 2011 bust, he needed help, and Brendan would do anything for his old friends. So Brendan let Erik stay with him in his new place in Waltham.

CHAPTER SEVENTEEN

The Interview

In April 2011, FBI agents interviewed Tamerlan and his parents in their Norfolk Street apartment. It is difficult to categorize these interviews exactly. In the wake of the bombing, the FBI was not immediately forthcoming about what happened, and while intelligence agencies have since released more information, many questions remain. We do know that after this interview, the FBI apparently failed to pursue logical steps and leads, which could have provided law enforcement and intelligence agencies with information about Tamerlan's radicalization before the bombing. FBI agents also failed to follow up on electronic alerts when Tamerlan traveled to Dagestan in early 2012 and returned six months later.

A year after the bombing on April 10, 2014, the inspectors general of the intelligence community—who oversee seventeen different agencies, as well as the inspectors general of the CIA, DOJ, and Department of Homeland Security—issued a classified 168-page review of intelligence information sharing and handling in the lead-up to the bombing. A redacted version of this report was released to the public. Notably, officials from the FBI did not author the report. I do not have access to the classified copy, but apparently the inspectors general ran into conflicts with the Bureau. The review states that "As described in more detail in the classified report, the DOJ's [Office of the Inspector General]'s access to certain information was significantly delayed at the outset of the review by disagreements with FBI officials over whether certain requests fell outside the scope of the review or could cause harm to the criminal investigation. Only after many months of discussions were these issues resolved, and time that otherwise could have been devoted to completing this review was instead spent on resolving these matters."

According to the report from the inspectors general, the inquiry into Tamerlan was sparked by an unusual tip from Russian intelligence officials, who informed the FBI that Tamerlan and Zubeidat were followers of radical Islam and had changed drastically since 2010. Russian intelligence officials sent this tip to the FBI's attaché in Moscow in March 2011 and said that Tamerlan Tsarnaev was preparing to travel to Russia to join unspecified "bandit underground groups" in Dagestan and Chechnya.

Unsealed court documents in Dzhokhar's trial reveal that an unidentified Tsarnaev family member overseas may have shown Russian intelligence officials an inflammatory text message sent by Zubeidat. It's unclear if this text sparked Russia's investigation into the Tsarnaevs or was retrieved as part of an ongoing inquiry. The Associated Press would later report that in early 2011, a Russian intelligence agency secretly recorded phone calls between Tamerlan and his mother in which Tamerlan reportedly expressed his desire to wage jihad in conjunction with a desire to visit Palestine. He then reportedly thought better of it since he couldn't speak Arabic.

The Tsarnaevs' earlier interactions with the FBI raise serious concerns about American intelligence, and at the same time lingering questions about these interviews have created a breeding ground for conspiracy theories. After the bombers were identified, Russian news outlets immediately reported that Tamerlan had been questioned by the FBI. "My sons are innocent!" Zubeidat told *Russia Today* (*RT*). The bombing was a setup, and the FBI "followed them for years," Zubeidat said. She also told *RT* that FBI agents were "controlling" Tamerlan. She did not explain how—did she too subscribe to Tamerlan's majestic mind control theory, or did she think agents were directing him in some other way? *RT* also quoted a veteran Russian military officer who speculated that the bombing was likely premeditated and planned by American intelligence, and the Tsarnaevs were framed.

Anzor and Zubeidat's claims and the false flag theory put forth by *RT* caught on fast. Posters declaring the Tsarnaev brothers had been framed were plastered on lampposts in Dagestan. Dzhokhar's face was stenciled on streets in Chechnya above the word *INNOCENT*. Meanwhile the #FreeJahar movement echoed on internet channels all over the world. Today *RT* is widely recognized as an efficient branch of Russia's disinformation campaign, but this was not as obvious or well understood in 2013.

After the bombing, then–FBI director Robert Mueller told the Senate Appropriations Committee that the agent tasked with looking into Tamerlan's case did a "thorough investigation." The report from the inspectors general released a year later would make evident that this was not exactly so. By then Mueller was long gone. Ten weeks after Mueller addressed lawmakers about the bombing, he stepped down from his role as FBI director and was replaced by James Comey.

The FBI had entered their 2011 assessment of Tamerlan in a database, along with thousands of other entries. While technically this report could have been accessed by the Boston Regional Intelligence Center—a hub where state, local, and federal agencies are supposed to share information—law enforcement there would have had to know where to look. Boston Police Commissioner Ed Davis told the Senate Homeland Security and Governmental Affairs Committees in a July 2013 hearing that the FBI should have done more to alert other law enforcement agencies about Tamerlan's growing extremism. (Controversially, FBI officials did not attend the hearing.) Perhaps they could have done more to circulate this information in their own departments. Even if the FBI was not able to prevent the bombing, why weren't they able to apprehend Tamerlan from photos of the suspects? Instead the brothers remained at large for four days. "There is a gap with information sharing," Davis said.

In the wake of the bombing, politicians on both sides of the aisle raised questions about what the FBI knew about the Tsarnaevs and when. Congressman Bill Keating (D-MA) accused the Bureau of stonewalling. "I got more information from Russia than I did from our own FBI," Keating told *GBH News*. Keating had traveled to Russia in May 2013, with other members of the Congressional Homeland Security Committee. Russian officials purported to share what they knew about Tamerlan with the politicians in a gesture of transparency. Keating feared that the same intelligence failures outlined in the 9/11 Commission had been repeated and the guidelines to amend these failures had been ignored.

Senator Charles E. Grassley of Iowa went so far as to ask the FBI point-blank in an open letter if Tamerlan had been an FBI recruit. The FBI responded flatly that he was not. Though of course, the FBI's denial by no means put an end to this speculation The theory has lingered for more than a decade and directly impacted my ability to report on this case. Several potential sources informed me that they were so consumed with fears about nefarious plots involving the FBI or the CIA that they would not speak to me. Many more people were simply freaked out.

Derek Maltz, the now-retired head of the DEA's Special Operations Unit—which was instated to better synchronize criminal law enforcement efforts around the world in the wake of 9/11—was especially upset about the FBI's failure to share intelligence about Tamerlan in 2011. He was also irate at Mueller's insistence that the FBI had done nothing wrong. Maltz told me that his unit was specifically designed to share information about terrorism and other crimes. The FBI's Joint Terrorism Task Forces (JTTF) were also supposed to cooperate with other agencies. Maltz said sharing information about Tamerlan would also have been useful to investigators in the Waltham case. "Had the police been told that Tamerlan was a radical terrorist, maybe somebody would have put it together," he told me.

It wasn't just the Waltham murders. Maltz said the research his team was able to do after the bombing strongly indicated that the Tsarnaev family was involved in other kinds of crime as well. According to Maltz, a phone number registered to the Tsarnaev home, which the FBI later told Maltz belonged to Bella Tsarnaev, was linked to a federal drug investigation and calls placed to a New York prison. The prison calls would have been recorded, but by the time of the bombing, it was too late to retrieve them. Maltz was also suspicious of a $70,000 bank withdrawal Anzor Tsarnaev made on March 23, 2012, according to analysts at a DOJ fusion center—an office for intelligence sharing. That substantial transfer was made after Anzor had left for Dagestan, the analysts informed Maltz, and during the time Tamerlan was there. This was all information that could have been shared with law enforcement before the bombing, said Maltz.

The ACLU came to a different conclusion about the FBI's closed investigation into Tamerlan. In the wake of the Twin Towers attack, the federal government created the Department of Homeland Security and expanded the powers of federal agencies to surveil Americans. After the bombing, the FBI claimed to have been managing thousands of other tips, as context for why the Russian tip about Tamerlan was not more vigorously pursued. The way the ACLU saw it, federal agencies had cast such a wide net they were unable to notice a real terrorism threat in their midst.

～

Much about the tip from Russia and the FBI's investigation into Tamerlan remains elusive to me. However, over the course of nearly a decade, the report from the inspectors general, records requests, and unsealed documents in Dzhokhar Tsarnaev's trial have allowed me to account for this interaction in more detail.

JTTF agents first interviewed Anzor and Zubeidat at the Norfolk apartment on April 14, 2011—two years and a day before Tamerlan and Dzhokhar Tsarnaev bombed the Boston Marathon. On April 22, 2011, the agents went back and interviewed Tamerlan. Anzor was present for this interview as well.

The FBI has not released a report on their first interview with Anzor and Zubeidat. But in 2017, the Bureau released a redacted copy of the second interview, with Tamerlan. The FBI formulates interview notes on what is colloquially called a 302 report. The 302 report of this encounter is bizarre; reading it, one might conclude that Tamerlan and Anzor called the FBI back to the apartment, and the agents were there at the Tsarnaevs' request.

The 302 report begins with an account from Anzor, in which he claims that he had been approached by four men who also claimed to be FBI agents. It is unclear if he is referring to the first FBI interview a week before, but retired FBI agents inform me that the FBI almost never approaches an individual as a group unless it is an arrest situation, and they are trained to provide evidence of their credentials. If they want to get ahold of someone, they usually leave business cards.

According to the report, the four people Anzor said he saw before were "all young, handsome men in suits." They said they wanted to "talk to Tamerlan." They did not leave business cards or contact numbers. The men said they would be back the next day but evidently did not return. Anzor did not think they had accents, in response to what appears to be the agent's questions, and he did not see their car when they left. Tamerlan told the agents that he did not know anyone who would be looking for him or would be upset with him.

Who were these four mysterious men? Did this encounter really happen? According to Anzor's doctors, by 2011 he had been experiencing paranoid delusions about the KGB and others for years. Or perhaps was there an element of truth to Anzor's paranoia that his doctors overlooked? After all, according to the AP's reporting, Russian intelligence officials did in fact listen to at least one family phone call.

We do know that in this second interview the FBI questioned Tamerlan about his relationship with Russians. Tamerlan told the agents he'd never had any problems with Russians, and he did not take the political tensions between Russia and the rebellious Chechen republic personally. Then the report notes a series of statements that appear to be attributed to Tamerlan, such as "Wars are fought between leaders of countries and not individual citizens." Veteran FBI agents tell me this is unusual: 302 reports usually include a lot of detail, whereas this report reads more like a transcript of one of Tamerlan's grandiose rants. It reads as if the agents were taken in by the boxer.

Tamerlan told the agents he didn't think there were any Islamic radicals in Cambridge, and he did not read extremist material online, which we now know was a lie. It does not appear that FBI agents pressed him on this point. Nor did they monitor his YouTube account after concluding the interview. If they had, they would have later found him spreading said radical material. The report notes that Tamerlan was interested in Spartan warrior culture and had not thought about joining the American military because he wanted to become a professional boxer. "TAMERLAN doesn't like to fight for the sake of violence. TAMERLAN has fought to protect others," the FBI agent wrote, adding that Tamerlan stood up for kids when they were being bullied. According to the FBI's 302 report, Tamerlan seemed like a really great guy.

~

Even though the Russian tip included specific details about Tamerlan's plans to join "bandit underground groups" in Dagestan and Chechnya, the FBI never asked Tamerlan about his interest in traveling to those places. Nor did the FBI agents question his wife, Katherine Russell, who at the time was still living with her mother. Judith Russell was vocally concerned about her daughter and son-in-law's dramatic changes. The FBI didn't question Tamerlan's ex-girlfriend, who had filed an assault charge against him in 2009, and who would later say she also had concerns about Tamerlan's shifting ideology. Neither did the FBI reach out to other American law enforcement and intelligence agencies.

Instead, the JTTF requested more information about Tamerlan from Russian intelligence. When they did not get a response, the JTTF set up an electronic alert to notify the Bureau in the event that Tamerlan left the country and then closed the assessment. In September 2011, the month of the Waltham murders, Russian intelligence officials reached out to the CIA about Tamerlan's growing radicalization. According to the report from the inspectors general, this tip contained substantially the same information as had been provided to the FBI earlier that year. The CIA determined that Tamerlan had already been assessed by the FBI and closed their inquiry.

Four months after the Waltham murders, on January 21, 2012, Tamerlan, who had recently filed for food stamps, packed his bags and took a six-month trip to Dagestan. It was his first time back to the North Caucasus region since immigrating to America as a young teen. He left Katherine and his infant child behind. The same day a complete set of *Inspire* magazines, a jihadist publication purportedly distributed by al-Qaeda, was downloaded onto Dzhokhar Tsarnaev's computer. The *Inspire* collection included an article titled "How to Make a Bomb in the Kitchen of Your Mom."

After the bombing, Tamerlan's 2012 trip to Dagestan was identified as his turning point toward radicalization—the notion being that he picked up this violent ideology abroad. This theory was articulated by Secretary of State John Kerry soon after the attack. "He learned something where he went, and he came back with a willingness to kill people," Kerry told reporters. The Tsarnaevs' violence was foreign, not American, the messaging went, and Tamerlan had not killed before.

Tamerlan's travels and actions in Dagestan were immediately investigated by American intelligence agencies. It is possible Tamerlan became further entrenched in his violent ideology on this trip. But in the decade since, publicly released intelligence material and reporting have not produced evidence to support this assumption. Rather, it seems Tamerlan was already fully committed to his violent ideology by the time he landed in Makhachkala.

∼

If I have learned anything in my lifelong study of crime, it is this: the most dangerous criminals in the world are often the most ridiculous. Tamerlan was one such poser. When he arrived in Dagestan, the other men his age were wearing tracksuits. Tamerlan, meanwhile, was dressed how he thought a jihadi fighter was supposed to dress, based on propaganda he had read online, including a caftan and dark eyeliner, as was first reported by the *Boston Globe*.

Tamerlan apparently tried to join fighters in the Forest, the mountainous region where the insurgents were hiding. He had relatives on his mother's side who were part of a group called Union of the Just. The group, founded with the objective of protecting the rights of Muslims from the police, is also known for organizing mass protests on behalf of suspected jihadi insurgents and advocating to establish a caliphate. After the bombing, the FBI interviewed Tamerlan's second cousin, Magomed Kartashov, who was imprisoned at the time due to his alleged involvement in the group. Kartashov told the agents that Tamerlan did not mince words. "I came here to get involved in jihad," Tamerlan allegedly told his cousin.

If we are to take Kartashov at his word, Kartashov told his cousin to stop talking about jihad and forget the Forest. "You won't make it to the next tree," Kartashov told him.

Kartashov told the FBI that Tamerlan's beliefs didn't come out of nowhere, and that kind of thinking doesn't disappear by itself. He said the two argued a lot, citing passages from the Qur'an. Even when Muhammad was beaten, he talked about patience and not answering aggressively, Kartashov told him. Tamerlan believed he was also paraphrasing the Qur'an and argued that they should hurt unbelievers: "Cut their heads and make them kneel." That's not what the Qur'an says, said Kartashov. But Tamerlan did not know the Qur'an well enough to have a proper argument. "You have convinced my head, but my heart still wants to do something," Tamerlan told Kartashov before he left.

According to Gessen, who interviewed Kartashov as well, Tamerlan also complained about corruption in Watertown and Waltham to such an extent that Kartashov thought Tamerlan lived there and not Cambridge.

Tamerlan apparently made known to his entire family his intentions to meet with insurgents. Zubeidat's cousin, Naida Suleimanova, testified in Dzhokhar's trial that she was also concerned. Word among the family was that Tamerlan was adhering to "some kind of radical Islam." Suleimanova said she hugged Tamerlan, who she called her brother, but she was also afraid and kept her distance.

After his interview in April 2011, Tamerlan was placed on a terrorist watch list. Even though the FBI was explicitly tipped off to Tamerlan's intention to travel and join radical groups, he was never questioned about his travel plans. His flights in and out of Dagestan triggered electronic notifications to the investigating agents. But according to the 2014 inspector general report, Tamerlan was never questioned about this trip.

On April 9, 2014, the day before the report was set to be released and distributed to Congress, the *New York Times* published an article with the headline "Russia Didn't Share All Details on Boston Bombing Suspect, Report Says." The journalists did not read the unreleased report but quoted several unnamed senior American officials to get the scoop. These unnamed officials claimed that the report found that Russia was to blame for the intelligence missteps because Russia did not provide the FBI with more information as the bureau requested.

The unnamed officials also told the *New York Times* that the report matched the FBI's own internal review. It was true that the report revealed that Russia did not respond to requests to provide additional information and did not disclose the intercepted phone call between Tamerlan and Zubeidat until after the bombing attack. But the unnamed officials also brushed over the damning details about FBI missteps. I don't know why the anonymous individuals spoke to the *New York Times* before the release of the report, but in effect these interviews shaped the narrative—so that the news coverage about the report focused on Russia—and deflected criticism about the FBI.

There is a lot we do not know about Tamerlan, the interview, the mysterious men in suits, and his trip to Dagestan. I have not seen information that proves or disproves that Tamerlan was a secret agent, informant, spy, or anything else. Perhaps these theories are correct. Maybe the FBI's April 2011 interview and the CIA's handling of this same tip several months later are not alarming examples of ineptitude. Perhaps these events do not highlight failures in our national security protocols and intelligence handling, but rather are all part of a calculated plan. Maybe the truth lies somewhere in between or somewhere entirely else. From my own read, the FBI looks sloppy. But at the end of the day, I'm just trying to figure out who slit my friend's throat.

∼

In 2011, Tamerlan told Brendan Mess about his interview with the FBI. The encounter became a running joke among their friends. "They think I'm crazy, they think I'm going to blow something up," Tamerlan said, laughing. *Tamerlan, the crazy Chechen terrorist*, they joked, and shook their heads and passed the blunt around.

CHAPTER EIGHTEEN

Rafi

Raphael Teken lived life on his own terms. He was handsome and strong. He had a mole on his cheek, which actually made him more approachable. Rafi always knew how to put people at ease.

More than anything, Rafi wanted to make people happy and follow his own convictions. He had the gift of gab. He spoke on the phone several times a day with those he was closest to. He could run his mouth about more or less anything: sports, marijuana, politics, cell phones. He was humble and loving, like a puppy, as several of his friends described him. He grew up in Brookline, the city next to Newton, and, like Erik, his family was Israeli. His father, Avi Teken, is a prominent spiritual leader in the Jewish community and just so happened to officiate at least a half dozen of my friend's Bat and Bar Mitzvahs in middle school and one childhood friend's wedding. Rafi studied history at Brandeis, a college with a large Jewish population in Waltham. He read constantly; he was like a sponge for information. A true intellectual, his mother, Tina, would tell me. He applied the same intellectual rigor to his love of marijuana. He collected dozens of strains, which he stored in glass jars in a special freezer. He would analyze and experiment with their various properties. To Rafi, smoking weed was almost spiritual. He was a medicine man, a healer.

Rafi loved Waltham. Living there kept him close to the Jewish community at Brandeis, like-minded friends he could speak Hebrew with. He took special joy in rollerblading up and down the banks of the Charles River.

Rafi was the big brother of Brendan Mess's friend group. He was twelve years older than Brendan. They met when Brendan was still in high school, through the older brother of a classmate at a pickup football game. Rafi's Waltham apartment became a sanctuary for Brendan, a safe place to smoke away from the watchful eye of his parents. They had stayed close ever since, practically like family. They talked almost every day.

Like Brendan, Rafi was also into personal fitness. Rafi had a fully equipped gym that took up the entirety of his living room with squat racks, dumbbells, treadmills, and rowers. He was a licensed personal trainer and once had aspirations to become a bodybuilder. For the most part, he wasn't interested in material wealth or acclaim. He prioritized his relationships and his community. He wanted his friends to feel at ease, body and soul. He experimented with ways to vaporize marijuana to avoid harming the lungs, more than a decade before the era of vape pens. He took special pride in always selecting the right strain for the right occasion, set friends up with workouts, and consulted with them on their diets as well. "He'd always give you a protein shake or tell you some workout to do," Dylan Mess told me.

He was also a little bit of a risk-taker, as marijuana sellers back then often were. He gambled on sports. In fact, he'd bet on just about anything. It was almost comical—when he was watching TV with friends, he'd try to bet on what the next commercial would be.

Among Brendan's friends Rafi's reputation was that of a more low-key dealer than Erik and Brendan—the third wheel in their enterprises—whereas Erik and Brendan "wanted to take over the world." This may speak more to the kind of reputation Rafi sought to maintain. Rafi would keep inconspicuous jobs at the Vitamin Shoppe, at a phone kiosk in the Arsenal Mall, and as a valet at an Italian restaurant. But this might have been more to suggest a legitimate source of his earnings than anything else. He spoke to another friend about how, throughout the course of his career in the trade, he had accumulated close to a million dollars, which he had hidden in the woods. He had plans, literal blueprints, for a business once marijuana was legalized, and it would be. That was one bet he was sure of. He shared his aspirations with his parents, who were deeply concerned. But he said he had a plan. "I know it's going to get legalized," Rafi told his mother. Rafi spoke to his parents regularly. His marijuana use deeply upset his mother. Though now that marijuana is legal in Massachusetts, Tina looks back on these arguments as evidence of Rafi's foresight. One thing was certain, Tina told me: her son had a "wonderful heart." He was generous to a fault.

Rafi regularly took in friends to live with him at his Waltham apartment on Brown Street, often for months at a time, without asking for rent. Daniel Mastey was one such friend, who had initially come to the area to be close to his girlfriend, a Brandeis student. Like Rafi, Mastey came from an Israeli family and spoke Hebrew. "Rafi was very proud of being Jewish," Mastey told me. "That was like a big part of who he was." Rafi didn't go to temple or preach. But it was part of who he was. He was a Zionist, Mastey told me, "for lack of a better term." Rafi was especially proud of his father's service in the Israeli army, and he was comfortable jumping into debates about religion. Most of Brendan's friends just rolled with it. They didn't have strong opinions about what Rafi was saying, unless he was talking about sports or weed.

Rafi was like "the dispensary before the dispensary," Mastey told me. Better than that, it seems, according to Mastey's description. Rafi collected a quarter ounce of between sixty and seventy different strains. If customers weren't satisfied with the product, Rafi accepted returns. Mastey soon became incorporated into Brendan's social circle as well and often found himself in Brendan's apartment at 12 Harding Avenue. There, before heading off to Indonesia for a six-week surf trip, Mastey met Tamerlan Tsarnaev. Mastey noticed Rafi would hug most people he came into contact with, but not Tamerlan.

~

Mastey would be surprised to learn that that summer, while he was away on his surf trip, the dynamic between Rafi and Tamerlan seemed to change. Contrary to Mastey's impression, Rafi's friend George Becker thought Rafi "really liked Tamerlan." In Rafi's mind it was a positive thing: he was Jewish and Israeli, but he was able to have a friendship with a Muslim man, Becker explained. On at least one occasion, Tamerlan was seen at Rafi's apartment when Brendan was not there. The two had grown closer, but it was not clear if the relationship was entirely amicable. In the weeks before his death, Rafi asked his father about Chechnya on two occasions. Avi told his son there were many jihadi fighters in Chechnya. Rafi told his father he had a Chechen friend, who would sometimes leave the group to pray. The next time he brought it up, Rafi said he and the Chechen friend had had some sort of argument. As Rafi said, he told this friend that his father had special training in the Israeli Defense Forces, and "could kick your ass." It would be one of Rafi's last conversations with his father.

PART III

3XMX

CHAPTER NINETEEN

The Breather

If it wasn't for his borderline homelessness and the $50,000 he owed to a California drug cartel, Erik might have enjoyed his last afternoon. Sunday, September 11, 2011, was blue and cloudless. The college students had returned, and the streets and shops were busy again. The humidity of summer had passed but the warmth remained. It was one of those perfect September days in New England where it feels like the whole world is back in focus. That afternoon Erik went to visit his sister at Zoe's, a Cambridge diner with fifties-style Formica booths, around the corner from the apartment where he and Aria had grown up. Zoe's was a second home for Aria; she'd waitressed the weekend brunch shifts since she was fourteen, her best friend working by her side. Later her partner and children's father would bus tables there too. In 2011, Aria also had a full-time paid internship as a social worker. She worked seven days a week. If anyone wanted to see Aria, they had to go to Zoe's. Aria wore her sleek dark hair in a loose ponytail, painted dark rings of eyeliner around her large brown eyes, and tied a black apron around her waist when she waited tables. After the bombing, I'd meet Aria at Zoe's, sitting at the bar in the same seat where Erik sat the afternoon before he was killed.

She wasn't expecting Erik that Sunday, and she jumped on him when he walked through the door, gave him a full-body hug, and teased him about the nerdy wire-rimmed glasses he always wore. The siblings looked little alike, but they had the same dimples. Aria was starting her master's degree in social work at Salem State the next day, and Erik had come to wish her luck.

After high school Erik enrolled in City Year, a nonprofit that sends young adults on their gap year before college to volunteer at high-risk schools. Erik never completed the program. He could have—he had only a few weeks to go before receiving a certificate—but instead he flew to Amsterdam for the Cannabis Cup. There were some new strains of weed he just had to try.

Even though Erik couldn't lead by example, he pushed his sister Aria to excel in her classes. In high school, Erik told Aria that he had signed her up for a scholarship program. It wasn't until years later that Aria realized Erik was the one slipping her cash for her As and Bs, money she carefully stashed away for college. When she graduated, Erik set her up with the social work internship she had in 2011, through one of his friends.

Aria relished her time with her brother. As much as the two teased each other, Erik was the first person she confided her problems to. He wouldn't live to see her rekindle her love with her high school sweetheart, launch a career, buy a house, and start a family of her own. He'd never meet his nieces: Mia, with whom he shared the same mischievous smile, and baby Shai. But in those uncertain years in her early twenties, Erik always knew how to cheer his sister up. Aria kept her brother informed about the ups and downs of her dating life. He consistently reminded her that she was special, that whatever guy she was stressing over wasn't worth it. Then he'd send her silly text messages to make her laugh.

Erik was sparse with the details about his own affairs. Aria knew that he worked in the music industry, briefly invested in a glass shop in Boston, and had plans to open a weed café in California. Though Aria knew about his legal woes and had her suspicions about how he made his money, she did not pry. So Aria was surprised when, on that visit, Erik mentioned a girlfriend, Victoria Jackson. Erik showed Aria a photo of a beautiful woman in a red swimsuit from a trip they had taken to Florida. Erik said she lived in Virginia and was friends with Brendan's girlfriend, Hiba. Aria noted that the two women looked a lot alike. She told Erik she was happy for him before sending him off with a bowl of home fries and avgolemono soup.

~

The house at 12 Harding Avenue was built in 1920 with some of the practical features found in local triple-deckers and others more commonly seen in

Victorian-style homes. In 2011 pale yellow paint covered the subtle shingle detailing. Three arched Palladian windows peered down on the dead-end street from the top floor.

I made my first pilgrimage to 12 Harding Avenue in the summer of 2013, months after the bombing. It was my first door-knock as a journalist, the first time I'd ever shown up at someone's door with my notepad and pen, unannounced.

It was late afternoon. The landlord, Charlie Paquette, who lives in the first-floor unit, was sitting on the front porch, talking on the phone. I sat in the car and waited for him to finish talking while a neighbor practiced piano by an open window. The delicate chords mingled with the chirps of house sparrows taking dirt baths in the crumbling road.

Charlie was sucking on a cigar, squinting in the afternoon light, and staring me down with one eye. I wore a purple floral dress, to try to soften the intrusive nature of my visit. Charlie didn't buy it for an instant. Though he would later confirm basic facts about the case, on that day I hadn't so much as closed my car door when Charlie told me he would not be giving interviews. I can't blame him. If I saw what he saw on September 12, 2011, I'd yell and scream if a stranger pulled up to my front yard uninvited and tried to hit replay.

~

For Erik, Brendan, Rafi, and other East Coast distributers of high-grade black market cannabis, 2011 was a year of upheaval and growing tensions. Brendan Mess's concerns also included his tumultuous love life.

Rumors about Hiba spread fast. They reached me in the days immediately after the murder. *Brendan had a girlfriend. They had a fight. She left town. She wasn't supposed to return. She did not have a house key. She asked the landlord to open the door.* The rumors Erik's family heard were more explicit. The theory going around was that "Hiba hired someone to kill Brendan" and that Rafi and Erik just happened to be there, Erik's mother, Bellie, told me. After the bombing, theories about Hiba persisted among some of the victims' associates, at times merging with wholly discredited conspiracy theories about the terrorist attack, reimagined to feature Hiba as some sort of highly connected criminal mastermind or agent.

Brendan was not Hiba's first, nor her last, romantic partner to meet a violent end. Accounts of Hiba's other dead lovers compounded the speculation that Hiba may have played a role in the Waltham killings. Hiba's ex-boyfriend, Jahmare H. Smith, 33, was shot and killed on September 1, 2011, in Henrico County, Virginia, ten days before the Waltham murders. A man named Jeffrey Runion was later convicted for the crime. Hiba had separated from her husband, Johnson Aimie "Jay" Edosomwan Jr., but they remained legally married. Jay died in his Richmond, Virginia, apartment on October 7, 2011. Investigators at the Richmond Police Department found that Jay died by suicide.

Five dead bodies in a five-week timespan.

Hiba also spoke of another boyfriend who was murdered prior to her relationship with Jay, according to four separate accounts. Hiba allegedly told two individuals that the boyfriend had been killed in a home invasion.

According to Brendan's high school friend Ray Filmore, Brendan found Hiba's complicated past alluring. He respected her alleged know-how and experience. Brendan was fixed on having a certain lifestyle, Filmore explained. "He was drawn to things that were dangerous," he said. Later the qualities that once endeared Hiba to Brendan would exacerbate his friends' suspicions.

These suspicions appear to have been shared by law enforcement. Records I obtained from the Richmond PD show a Massachusetts state trooper traveled to Richmond to question Hiba and Jay in separate interviews shortly before Jay's death. Joe Vizard, a former Waltham city councilor, spoke to Waltham police chief Thomas LaCroix about the murder case in February 2012. LaCroix told Vizard that the focus of the investigation was on a "friend or a girlfriend" of one of the victims who was "out of state." In September 2012, city councilor Gary Marchese also told a *Wicked Local Cambridge* reporter that the investigation had led detectives out of state. It appears investigators continued to point fingers at Hiba long after the bombing. According to a 2018 *GBH News* report quoting anonymous law enforcement sources, "Investigators believe that she knows more than she's let on." The Middlesex office claims that the murder case is still open and investigators are still looking into the "potential involvement of additional undisclosed person or persons in connection with these homicides," according to their most recent statement. The office did not respond to inquiries pertaining to Hiba and Jay.

But I too have had my share of dark luck and there are reasons to be skeptical about law enforcement's veiled claims and their stated reasons for keeping this case open. Investigators apparently harbored other suspicions about the case that, in retrospect, do not appear to be founded. We all have our types. Hiba apparently preferred men who allegedly sold drugs and also allegedly partook in robberies. She dated risk-takers who lived dangerous lives, so it's not as surprising that a handful of these men met a violent end as it would be if she liked to date, say, dentists.

Hiba told me several times over that speculation about her role in the murders is unfounded and has compounded her trauma and pain. "I'm still trying to deal with all of those deaths at the same time," she said in a 2014 Skype interview. She said she was not a James Bond villain, as others have described her to me. "I feel like I'm being punished because people around me died," she said. "I just don't really know what people want from me. What could I have done to make people not be so suspicious of me? I did a lot of soul-searching. And I'll admit, maybe I wasn't the best person. And I'll admit, maybe I had my issues and my flaws. I'm working on those things. Maybe I was selfish, and maybe I was aggressive, and maybe I didn't really treat people well. But at the same time, I don't know what they want from me. What would make people happy? What could I do to make people less suspicious of me?" She later said, "It was an awful thing to go through, and I'm still going through it."

Hiba told me that she had "no involvement" in the Waltham crime. She doesn't understand how anyone could think that she might. *What could possibly be the motive for doing something like that?* she asked me. "Like, I have no reason whatsoever," she said. Practically speaking, she wouldn't even know how. "There is no way that I could ever imagine that happening, let alone orchestrate it."

"First of all, I would never want anyone to die. I don't have that much anger toward anyone. I don't think I could ever have that much anger toward anyone. And second of all, I don't have the means or the ability to pull something like that off—or the connections. I don't know anyone who would do something like that," she said.

Hiba and I spoke on a video call in 2014 after she emailed me from her home in Khartoum, Sudan. I had been trying to reach her for months, calling phone numbers—hers and her associates'—and searching for her on social media. By then, I had already spoken to more than a dozen individuals who had shared concerning accounts of Hiba's behavior, how she came to discover the bodies, and her fights with the victims. After months of deliberation, my editors and I decided to detail some of the substantiated reporting about Hiba in *Boston* magazine. Hiba emailed me immediately after the story posted online and asked why I had not contacted her first. She said that she was reachable on social media. Neither I nor my editors or producers had apparently been able to find her. She did not confirm whether any of the numbers I had previously tried were hers.

Hiba wrote that after the deaths, she spent a year sedated on her parents' couch, and then she tried to move on with her life. She began to travel, and at the time of our conversation, she said she was volunteering her time on charity boards and working with disabled people and orphans. She thanked me for my conscientious, objective reporting and said that Brendan, Rafi, and Erik were lucky to have me. But she wanted to clear some things up. She is a victim. She loved Brendan, and he loved her. He was her angel and she knew that he was with her at all times. She was devastated by his murder, and after he was killed, she lived in fear—*she could have been there*. Brendan knew she was coming back and was supposed to pick her up from the airport. She wrote that she was "actually supposed to be there the night they were murdered but couldn't get a flight for that [S]unday night and ended up flying out that [M]onday morning."

What mattered to her most was "finding out the truth." She felt she was forced to speak to reporters to "squash the lies." But she would have preferred to stay out of the picture to "grieve my silent grief" and pray for the strength to forgive those who, she said, only accused her out of "hopelessness and hurt." She said that she appreciated my diligence. "Without knowing you, I admire you," she wrote. But she wanted me to leave her out of my reporting. The other journalists didn't care about the truth like I did, and accounts about her were based on "NO FACTS and NO EVIDENCE." My reporting was "more dignified than that," and she cautioned me not to stoop so low as to include her in the story, considering her trauma and pain.

Going off record, or not naming Hiba, was not something I could agree to—she and I would return to this point on several occasions throughout the Skype interview—although I very much wanted to hear her account and appreciated her perspective. She asked me to look at the situation on the flip side:

What if she was innocent? Before the string of deaths in 2011, she had "never even experienced the death of anybody" in her life, other than her grandmother, and she asked me to imagine how painful it would be to experience such profound loss while also being ostracized. At the time, I had yet to hear accounts of Hiba's other boyfriend, who she allegedly claimed was killed prior to 2011. She did not respond directly to accounts of this reporting in a 2023 email.

I thought the 2014 interview went well. I thanked Hiba for her time and told her I respected what she had been through. I truly did. She seemed to be on the edge of tears at several points during the conversation. "I really respect you too, Susan," she said. While speaking to Hiba, I found her account believable. We continued to email back and forth and she thanked me again for "pursuing the truth." Later she would move to England, and then, according to Facebook, she married a man in Saudi Arabia and began teaching English classes online. (Earlier she told me she was interested in pursuing work in education or as an au pair.) Meanwhile, I set aside my reporting on Hiba, until, years later, it no longer became feasible to do so.

In addition to Hiba's concerns, I was hesitant to report on Jay's death, or on any death by suicide. Her series of dead lovers seemed like a bizarre sidenote, not central to the Waltham murders story. I was concerned her seemingly tragic luck may have unfairly exacerbated speculations about Hiba even if the events were in no way connected. Journalists are generally advised against reporting on suicide except in unusual situations. Unfortunately, this situation is indeed unusual, and Hiba's accounts, Jay's accounts, and Jay's death are fundamental to the story of the Waltham murders, what happened, the initial investigation, the aftermath of the bombing, and where the case stands now. There is a direct and significant connection. In the years to come, I found myself coming back to the questions about the tenor and significance of this connection but was unable to reach a definitive conclusion. I cannot answer those with any degree of certainty. The scenario Hiba initially asked me to entertain—that she is the victim of circumstance, many times over—may still hold true. Perhaps many of these questions could be cleared up in an additional interview. Yet, she and Jay are still squarely a part of the Waltham murder story.

Over Skype, Hiba said she understood why I had questions about her movements the weekend of the murders and her dead lovers—the ones I knew about at the time. It was truly a remarkable series of events. "These are questions that

I've had for months and months and months and months, which I'm sure you understand, which is why I'm asking you about them," I said.

"I totally understand," she told me.

Hiba was not so understanding in February 2022, when I invited her to appear in *The Murders Before the Marathon* docuseries. She wrote that while she was grateful someone was still chasing down the truth, she did not want to be a part of this narrative. She had lost someone close to her, suffered alone, and said she had been "demonized for no rational or logical reason other than the fact I was a [B]lack foreigner with [M]uslim heritage." She said the focus should be on the victims and the perpetrators, "NOT ME because I found them and definitely NOT ME because I'm different."

In our final exchanges, it seemed increasingly possible that Hiba was making these allegations at least in part to deflect my questions. Yet, it is also crucial to contextualize speculations about Hiba and the actions of law enforcement before and after the bombing through this lens. The fact that the bombing was labeled an act of "jihadi" terrorism presents a heightened risk that people may have drawn unfair connections simply because Hiba's family is Muslim. This is another reason why I was concerned that suspicions of Hiba were overblown, especially after our 2014 conversation when she first introduced racism as the reason for her disagreements with Brendan's friends. Hiba told me that she does not harbor any anti-American sentiment, and this assertion is consistent with my reporting. Although previously, in May 2013, the *Boston Globe* quoted an individual who suggested otherwise. This person claimed to have been friends with Brendan, Tamerlan, and Hiba, but asked to remain anonymous for fear of retribution from a potential killer at large. The anonymous associate said that Hiba and Tamerlan grew close shortly before the Waltham murders and that the two swapped "stories of their distaste for American culture." The associate also told the *Globe* that Hiba was aggressive and violent and "had this radical way of thinking." I did not speak to anyone who could substantiate this account on or off record.

In 2023, I wrote to Hiba regarding reporting in this book and suggested that discrepancies I found in the account she provided to me could potentially be resolved in an additional telephone interview, although I would understand if she did not wish to speak to me again or respond to my emails. I would try to be fair regardless and would not hold her silence against her. I also told her

I took her claims that she had been discriminated against seriously and would articulate them in the book. When I didn't hear back, I emailed her a detailed list of my reporting. "You may wish to provide comment," I wrote.

Hiba wrote back ten hours later: "Susan, what is wrong with you?! I am a victim!" She instructed me to "take a long hard look" at myself and called me a "prejudiced," "racist," "sens[at]ionalist tabloid journalist."

In regard to Hiba's allegation that I am sensationalist: my reporting is sound. This isn't tabloid journalism; it's a ten-year investigation. I have included reporting to contextualize Hiba's patterns of behavior, motives, and credibility, as I have with other actors and institutions. In Hiba's case, this additional information was especially necessary due to the difficulties I encountered sorting through some discrepancies in her account. Prejudice and racism are ingrained into almost every aspect of our society, from land ownership, to city management, politics, health care, the rules of law, and those who enforce them. Not to mention the spike in Islamophobia in the wake of 9/11, and other terrorist attacks in which the perpetrators were found to be Muslim. It's important to question one's own potential for bias and the bias of others when reporting a story. Islamophobia is especially pervasive. Pigeonholing the Tsarnaevs and others in this story into a simplistic "jihadi" terrorist narrative also misses the point.

I have thought about how prejudice and racism could impact reporting on Hiba before we spoke, after we spoke, and throughout my reporting on this book. I can think of few things more shameful than acting on racist or prejudiced inclinations. I have actively worked to uncover and identify racism and prejudice as it pertains to the Waltham murders. But I don't think actions in one instance can absolve you from criticism in another. In response to Hiba's allegations, all I can say is that I stand by my reporting, and that includes articulating Hiba's account as fairly and as accurately as I am able to. Her concerns deserve to be heard before fully diving into my reporting on her and the inconsistencies I'm left to question.

"Your little bullet point list is unfounded and rooted in prejudice and has no bearing on finding the truth," she wrote, referring to the detailed list of reporting. "I haven't plotted or engaged in any robberies or criminal activities, haven[']t hurt anyone, bad mouthed anyone and I don't have any knowledge of any criminal activity by anyone else. Asking me is in itself inflammatory. I haven't been arrested nor have I been anything but a victim in all of this." As a point of note, I asked Hiba if she had prior knowledge of a plan to commit crimes in Waltham the night of September 11, 2011, in response to additional information and allegations made by others. I also asked her the same question, in less specific framing, in 2014. I wanted to give her an opportunity to respond. When Hiba wrote that she had never been arrested, engaged in criminal activity or "hurt anyone" I believe she was referring to matters directly pertaining to the Waltham murders and the deaths of her other former romantic partners in 2011. In her email, Hiba told me in very clear terms that she did not wish for me to contact her again, so I did not reach out for clarification. Yet, as another point of note, according to records I obtained in Henrico County, Virginia, Hiba was convicted on a misdemeanor assault and battery charge in 2002. She received a thirty-day sentence.

~

Hiba's friends told me they were initially struck by her beauty, her charm, and her international accent. She seemed to know everything and everyone. Brendan and Hiba met in 2006 after Brendan traveled to Richmond to visit a friend, Ian McCleod, a fellow boxer he met in Vermont. According to Ian, the pair had a drunken hookup after a social gathering. Brendan went back to New England, and for many years, it appeared that this single encounter would be where their relationship would begin and end. Brendan remained with a longtime girlfriend.

Hiba dated Jay, who came from a wealthy Christian family. His parents were Nigerian and were leaders of a church. Jay grew up in a large home in Fairfax and was described as warm and well liked at his private high school, Hargrave Military Academy. He was tall at six feet six inches and played on his high school basketball team.

They married in Richmond on November 24, 2009. Hiba was twenty-seven, Jay was twenty-three. Hiba told me that Jay's mother was aware of the marriage, but his father was not. In an interview, Jay's mother said the fact that Hiba was older—she was his first girlfriend—and was not Christian was upsetting to the family. They did not want Jay to date or marry outside of his faith. Jay would later claim that Hiba's family did not approve either.

At the time of his death, Jay was trying to start a business—apparently some kind of restaurant or health food store—and was enrolled in seminary school. For many years, the couple also sold weed together, according to three people who were intimately involved in their dealings. A police officer at Virginia Commonwealth University claimed that Jay was a "major marijuana distributor" and in 2007 and 2008 Jay was moving fifty to sixty pounds of marijuana from Northern Virginia into Richmond. But Jay was never arrested or charged with selling narcotics. Sources also informed me that at times Hiba was the primary supplier in these dealings. On at least one occasion Hiba allegedly introduced a buyer to Jay, helping him find a new client. (Again, Hiba denied engaging in criminal activities.)

By early 2011, Jay was in financial distress, and their marriage had apparently fallen apart. Jay was served an eviction notice to get out of his apartment, and the paperwork was filed on January 10, 2011. This was just the start of his troubles. One week later, on January 17, 2011, the landlord of the commercial property Jay had been leasing filed paperwork to evict him and collect past due rent and damages, totaling $153,094. Then, on January 28, 2011, nine days after paperwork on his commercial rental was served, Hiba hit Jay with another round of legal documents in an attempt to annul their marriage. Her request was denied two months later, on March 21, 2011. Hiba would never formally divorce Jay.

Meanwhile, Brendan broke up with his longtime girlfriend on March 4, 2011, according to a source familiar with their relationship. Upon learning they were both single, Ian, the friend who introduced Brendan and Hiba in 2006, put the couple back in touch.

The spark was still there. According to Hiba's friend in Richmond, Barbie Kerr, Hiba was enamored with Brendan. "She gloated about him all the time. You know, *He's handsome. He treats me so well. He's so much fun. He pays for things.* You know, he just, he took pretty good care of her. She didn't have anything negative to say about him, ever. It sounded like she was extremely happy, and I was happy for her," Kerr told me.

Hiba left her job at Saks Fifth Avenue in Virginia and was living with Brendan, his brother, and his two pit bulls in their Cambridge apartment by April. By May 2011, Hiba and Brendan had moved in together in the second-floor apartment of 12 Harding Avenue in Waltham. Brendan left his dogs with his brother.

Because Brendan could not state his real occupation as a distributor of high-grade marijuana on a lease application, Hiba applied for the apartment.

According to the landlord, Charlie Paquette, Hiba initially listed a Cambridge halfway house as her employer and source of income. Charlie happened to have a family member who worked at that very institution. The relative told Charlie that Hiba was lying. She didn't work there and never had. (Hiba did not respond directly to the account that she'd lied to her landlord.) When Charlie confronted Hiba, she admitted she had lied, apologized, and explained that she had been embarrassed to tell him the truth, that actually she received alimony, according to Charlie. Hiba then put Charlie in touch with Jay. Though they were not legally divorced, Jay allegedly told Charlie that he gave Hiba $1,200 a week in alimony payments. And that's how Brendan and Hiba moved into an apartment in a two-family home on a quiet leafy dead-end street in Waltham.

Save for his stint in Burlington, Vermont, Brendan had always lived in Cambridge. Waltham was only a few miles away, but it was a departure. He wouldn't be a local anymore. *You're living in someone else's town,* one friend warned him.

∽

From the best I can tell, the way Brendan's business usually worked was that he would get five to ten pounds at a time shipped in from Oakland as his regular source of income, from grow houses he helped establish. He would also purchase shipments from a Vietnamese organization based in Malden, and Brendan would meet with a female courier to receive these shipments. It wasn't high grade, but it was decent. Then he would get designer strains like Grand Daddy, Blue Dream, and OG Kush, in two- to three-pound shipments mailed to his associates in flat-rate boxes.

Waltham operated under a different code than Cambridge, I would learn after familiarizing myself with the federal agents, felons, real and wannabe mafiosi operating in Waltham and neighboring Watertown and Newton at the time. In 2011, the peaceful suburbia I knew as home was a cesspool of drug rivalries, arrests, rip-offs, and hired hits. Whether Brendan knew it or not, he had moved into someone else's territory. *Whose* territory was actually an active point of dispute.

∽

On April 20, 2011, less than two weeks before Brendan moved to Waltham, Homeland Securities Investigations (HSI) made a big bust. HSI is the principal investigative arm of the US Department of Homeland Security along with Immigrations and Customs Enforcement (ICE). Most people aren't as familiar with HSI as they are with, say, the FBI or the DEA. The agency's relative lack of notoriety is known to irk HSI agents on occasion. Especially when they go home for Thanksgiving. HSI collaborates with other law enforcement agencies in task forces, but it is its own separate investigative agency, with more than six thousand agents, according to the government website. The agency is tasked with investigating transnational crime and threats. The transnational crime in question on this day involved the large-scale trafficking of hydroponic marijuana over the Canadian border into Waltham and Watertown. The investigation also turned up prescription pill, money laundering, and extortion charges. The agents dubbed this investigation Operation Blackstone, and the central target, and the first name on the twenty-person indictment was the alleged plumber turned local kingpin of the semiorganized Waltham- and Watertown-based cartel, a steroid-pumping Syrian national named Safwan Madarati. The agents spent more than a year looking into Madarati and his associates, following trucks of marijuana over the border and wiretapping his phones. A local Watertown police officer who had a personal relationship with Madarati was also charged and convicted in the sting, for impeding the investigation and lying to federal agents.

Despite the fact that Madarati was locked up at the time of the triple murder, after the bombing others put forth theories—by word of mouth, social media, blogs, and in books—about potential connections between Madarati's case and the Waltham murders. This included a theory that Madarati could have orchestrated the Waltham killings himself. I spent a good part of the last decade trying to figure out if any of this was true. I knocked on doors, visited auto shops, pizza spots, and federal prison, and I interviewed the clean-shaven HSI agents in a windowless conference room in their Boston office. The theories did not match up with the facts I found on the ground, but Operation Blackstone did come to shape my understanding of Erik's death and the events that followed. Madarati's clandestine relationships with local law enforcement raises serious questions about the Waltham murder investigation, which I will address later.

Madarati's arrest also impacted the last months of Erik's, Brendan's, and Rafi's lives in other ways. There was a direct link between Madarati and the Waltham murder victims, according to federal agents. Apparently Madarati was one of Rafi's suppliers.

According to these federal agents involved in Madarati's case, Rafi showed up on the Operation Blackstone wiretaps. "He was a large customer of Madarati's," agent P. J. Lavoie said. Madarati appeared to supply Rafi with marijuana outside of Rafi's Waltham apartment on Brown Street on several occasions, interactions the agents watched and listened to via various means of surveillance. Another time, Lavoie said they met at the parking lot outside of the Arsenal Mall, where Madarati handed Rafi a giant trash bag full of what Lavoie estimated was about fifty pounds of cannabis. Of course, to make a charge Lavoie would need to do more than cast an eyeball guess at what was being exchanged between the two men, likely in the form of a seizure. But this proved difficult, seeing as Rafi did not contact Madarati on a regular basis, much to Madarati's chagrin. In one intercepted phone call Madarati complained that Rafi did not call him like he used to, according to Lavoie. "You're off and on," Madarati said. According to Lavoie, Rafi did not seem to be a regular part of the crew, which is why "He didn't make our list," Lavoie said. Meaning Rafi was never indicted. Derek Maltz, who had been the director of the Special Operations Division at the DEA and assisted the HSI agents in the case, also confirmed that Rafi was found to associate with Madarati over the course of the investigation.

Operation Blackstone put Erik, Rafi, and Brendan on their heels, an individual familiar with their endeavors told me. It was a warning of the inherent challenges of working in an illicit economy. But it also meant that there was one less supplier and a market to fill, if they could find the product. Back in 2007, Brendan got great weed from Canada, but he didn't want to cross the Canadian border after Madarati was arrested. Meanwhile, Erik had lost his Sour Diesel connection. To the frustration of nearly everyone involved, in 2011 weed prices on the East Coast were down across the board. This was due in part to an influx of mass-produced chemically grown low-grade cannabis—known as "beasters" or "schwag"—one grower explained to me. Brendan had been talking about a deal with folks in Colorado, and a "mother" was going to receive the Colorado package in Newton. But the Colorado people wanted the cash in advance, and Brendan and Erik did not want to pay until after the weed had been delivered.

That deal fell through in July 2011. In the last months of their lives Erik and Brendan had concocted a plan to cut out the middleman and build a grow house of their own. They did just that, setting up a nearby operation that would have produced about ten pounds a month, had their plants made it to harvest.

~

In the weeks leading up to the murders, Hiba was in conflict with Erik and Rafi. In at least one instance these arguments escalated to violence.

At first, Erik and Hiba got along. Hiba introduced Erik to Victoria Jackson, her old friend from Richmond, when Victoria came to visit her in Waltham. When I called Victoria in the months after the bombing, she would not speak to me. She told me she did not feel the murder case had been "resolved." Victoria knew about Hiba's fights with Erik leading up to his death and initially feared Hiba might have been involved in the Waltham killings. "I thought it was coincidental that she wasn't in town when it happened. And I also thought if I walked into a house and I saw one dead body—and I said this to her—I would run out and scream. I mean, it would be my initial reaction if I saw just broken vases or dishes, or if it looked like the house was in disarray, I would run because I would be scared, like, that maybe someone's in there. When she described that she'd gone to every single room and saw a dead body in different places, it just didn't make sense to me, because I know I would run." But when Victoria and I spoke again in 2021, her thinking on the matter had changed. Hiba was made aware of my recent reporting and contacted Victoria before I did. Hiba apparently told Victoria that she had already provided numerous on-the-record interviews with reporters. "That was another thing that made me feel like she didn't have anything to do with it is because she was steadfast with trying to figure out what happened. She was very vocal and she was well—this is what she told me—she was very vocal," Victoria said. After reconnecting with Hiba, Victoria told me she had second thoughts about her suspicions. "Maybe I treated my friend poorly at a time where we were mourning, you know? I never wanted to believe that she had anything to do with it. It's just some of her actions didn't make sense, but everyone acts differently," Victoria said.

~

When Hiba introduced Victoria to Erik, Hiba only had good things to say. Hiba said he was amazing and sweet and Victoria agreed. In Victoria's eyes, Erik was "pure light." In the last months of his life, Erik made trips to visit Victoria in Virginia. They FaceTimed regularly when they were apart.

Victoria and Hiba had been friends for a long time, although their friendship was not without its ups and downs. They met when they were twenty or twenty-one, through Victoria's cousin, Crystal. "I remember thinking that that was a beautiful girl that she just brought by," Victoria said of their first meeting. Back then Hiba went by the name Nubian, which is what Victoria called her throughout the duration of their friendship. Hiba and Crystal lost touch, but Victoria ran into Hiba again a few years later. Together they did "everything you're not supposed to do together when you're in your twenties," Victoria told me. "We were the ones who jumped on the speakers, dancing at the club," she said. They had a lot of fun together. That is, until, according to Victoria, Victoria found out Hiba was sleeping with her boyfriend. That put an end to their friendship for what Victoria thought was for good.

Years went by. Victoria and the boyfriend broke up, and Victoria's life hit a bit of a lull. When she wasn't working at a bar called the Matrix Room, she was watching *Sex and the City* episodes on repeat, bored out of her mind. One of the other waitresses at the bar, Cindy, was having rent trouble, and Victoria invited Cindy to live with her so she would have a little company. One day Cindy asked if she could bring a friend over. Victoria told her of course; she didn't need to ask for permission.

The friend walked up to the door. "And lo and behold, if it wasn't her," Victoria said. It was Hiba. The two women locked eyes, and Hiba ran right back out the other way. "She cannot come in here," Victoria told Cindy. But Cindy said Hiba just wanted to come in and apologize. "I, for some reason, forgave her. And we became friends again," Victoria said. Hiba made life more interesting. "I didn't trust her. I wouldn't trust her around my boyfriend or anything like that, but she was fun, and she always knew the bouncers at the door, so you never had to wait in line when you went to the club," she said.

At this point, Hiba was married to Jay. "I met him through her," Victoria told me, "and he was just a pretty cool dude. I mean, he was extremely laid back. Inappropriate at times, as far as hitting on her friends, including myself, which is why she went off the handle that night."

According to Victoria, what happened "that night" was this: They were at Hiba and Jay's apartment. They were about to go out to a club and Victoria had borrowed Hiba's dress. Victoria went to look for a lighter in the basement, where the couple had a pool table. Jay followed her down. "He wasn't aggressive or anything, but he was hitting on me and putting it on pretty thick, and time just flew by. I never did find a lighter, but I believe we still had drinks. And he was, you know, propositioning me. And I was like, *You do understand that I am going to have to tell,*" Victoria said. But Victoria never got to tell Hiba anything, because when they got back upstairs, Hiba broke a glass table. "I remember her screaming," Victoria said. "She was in a rage, breaking everything and breaking the table, throwing stuff, and I remember her screaming and taking off my fucking dress, and I'm like, *Oh my gosh,* like, you know?" Jay, meanwhile, kept his cool. "She's throwing stuff at his head and she, you know . . . He was calm. He was just laid back. He was a laid-back guy." (Hiba did not respond directly to this allegation.) Later, Hiba apologized for the outburst, Victoria said. Hiba thought Victoria was trying to get back at her for Hiba's sleeping with her boyfriend years earlier, according to Victoria. "Why would I do that?" Victoria asked. "What would be the point of being your friend?"

I heard other accounts of Jay and Hiba's arguments, regarding Jay's alleged infidelity. A college friend of Hiba's claimed that even though she did not believe Jay actually had hit on her, and she certainly did not hit on Jay, Hiba accused the friend of trying to seduce Jay, and in this way ended their friendship. Meanwhile, Hiba and Victoria stayed friends for many years.

Being with Hiba was always exciting. At first Victoria enjoyed visiting Erik and Hiba in Waltham.

And then something changed. In the weeks leading up to the murders, Hiba fought with Erik and stopped speaking to Victoria. "I could never understand why," Victoria said. After the murders, Hiba told Victoria it was because Erik wouldn't lock the doors. She also felt that Erik was intruding on her space and overstaying his welcome.

Hiba told me a similar story in 2014. "You know, I liked Erik as a person, but I just thought the whole thing . . . It made me uncomfortable that he was going through such legal situations," she said, regarding Erik's arrest earlier that year. Hiba also told me that she was trying to get Brendan to stop selling drugs and that Erik was a bad influence. "I was trying to get Brendan to stop being in that lifestyle that he was in. I was hoping that we could start our own business," she told me. "It was just so frustrating, you know? Because I'm, like, over here trying to get him to stop, and Erik is over here trying to get him to expand."

In any case, these arguments are why, even though Erik had a room in the attic, in the weeks leading up to his death, he was back to couch-surfing again. "That chick is craaazy," he told a friend he had been staying with.

~

Hiba insists that she did not throw a knife directly at Rafi's head, as others have claimed. That story was "overexaggerated," she said. She threw the knife across the room. "It wasn't anywhere near him," she said. She told me that Rafi was "racist," and that was why they got into heated arguments. "He made a lot of remarks toward me, and I tried not to get frustrated, I tried to be understanding about it. I didn't really appreciate it. But in general. I was all for their friendship." When Hiba made this allegation, I did not press for additional details. In retrospect, it would be useful to have more information. Multiple people close to the couple told me that Hiba was upset at least in part because Rafi was interfering in her relationship with Brendan. At first, Hiba would apparently call Rafi to work through her disputes with Brendan, and to inquire about Brendan's activities. But later, Rafi seemingly tried to step in on Brendan's behalf, like a protective older brother. Hiba and Rafi's arguments were apparently due in part to the fact that Brendan was dating other women. Rafi allegedly supported Brendan in this pursuit and let Brendan meet these women in his apartment.

Though Rafi had once been a frequent visitor at Brendan's place, after Hiba threw a knife, Rafi made it a point to steer clear. According to three sources, in the weeks leading up to the murders, Rafi refused to go to Brendan's place on Harding Avenue when Hiba was home.

On the Skype call, Hiba told me that she was not aware that Brendan had been seeing other women. "I didn't know about that," she told me when I asked in 2014. I immediately felt terrible for bringing it up and continued to feel terrible for years afterward. "I didn't know about that. I didn't feel like that, you know?" she said again. "I don't even want to question his character right now. I'm just going to go from my memory and from what I know. I felt very secure and happy," she said. I can also understand why Hiba would not want to share such personal information with me. But later I did hear from multiple sources that Hiba was very much aware of Brendan's infidelities and viewed his relationships with other women as the root cause of their disputes, including their fight days before the murders.

Hiba did admit she slashed Brendan's tires. "I was really mad at him that day," she told me. Again, she said she was upset because she wanted Brendan to stop selling drugs. It was only that one incident, Hiba said of the fight. Other than that, her relationship with Brendan was "golden." I spoke with nine sources who dispute Hiba's characterization of the cause and frequency of her disagreements with Brendan. I also spoke to three sources who claimed Hiba threw a knife or an axe at Brendan on one or more occasions. The *Boston Globe* also quoted two additional sources who I did not speak to, Christopher Medeiros and Elizabeth Jason, who said Hiba threw knives and beer bottles at Brendan because he would not allow her to have guests in the home. Hiba told me Brendan was paranoid about having guests over because of his lifestyle, and that was part of the reason why she wanted him to stop dealing.

Ian, the friend who introduced the couple, told me that he still has "a lot of love for Hiba," and he would regularly field calls from both her and Brendan about their arguments. In one instance he received a call from Hiba freaking out because she said Brendan had put her in the trunk of a car. When he called Brendan, Brendan apparently admitted that he had done just that but said it was only for a second. "Yeah, she kind of freaked out a bit and threw a knife at me," Brendan said, according to Ian. Ian believed that these clashes were not as bad as they might sound, that the two of them were playing games, although the games could escalate and get malicious. Also Hiba was using cocaine, according to four separate accounts including a police report, and that made everything more intense. The landlord also stated that he found a packet of cocaine in the apartment after Brendan was killed, which investigators had apparently neglected to collect. Charlie said investigators released the apartment back to him less than twenty-four hours after Hiba found the bodies. "They were both completely insane," Ian told me. But he added, "I think she really loved him." (Hiba declined to comment directly on the discrepancies in her characterization of her arguments with Brendan, on allegations she threw knives and bottles at Brendan on more than one occasion, and on her use of cocaine.)

Hiba told me in 2014 that it was because of this one argument, about Brendan dealing and Erik living in the apartment, that she slashed all four tires of Brendan's Mercedes-Benz and flew to Florida that day in September. "I was just frustrated with the whole thing, and I was just really upset, and I felt like I was being ganged up on by everyone. So I just kind of got really mad and I was really drunk, and we had that huge fight. I knew that that wasn't the right way to approach the situation," she said. "That's why I decided to go take time out."

~

Hiba's account of her trip to Florida is as follows. She told me she flew to Miami on or slightly before Friday, September 9, 2011. She said she went to see a girl-friend from college. She said her friend gave her a coupon for a cheap flight. It was a one-way ticket. Though Hiba did not provide me with the name of the individual she was with at the time of the murders, I did track down at least one person she saw on that trip. In a brief interview LaTasha Banks spoke to me from behind the closed door of her Miami home and confirmed that Hiba had visited her that weekend. Banks also stated that she had only interacted with Hiba on two occasions. She did not elaborate further on the nature of Hiba's visit or her relationship with Hiba.

Charlie Paquette was aware that Hiba had slashed Brendan's tires. It had been a loud fight. Brendan assured Charlie that Hiba had gone to Virginia to see her mother, that she was "on the chill-out," and that she would return. Hiba was the only name on the lease. Brendan could run into problems with the landlord if she did not come back. But Brendan told his friends a different story. He told five people, including friends and family members, that Hiba had gone to Miami, and he did not expect her to return.

~

Brendan spent his last Sunday afternoon with a dozen friends at a barbe-cue, smoking weed, drinking beer, listening to music, and taking in the good weather. "Cum thru," Brendan texted his brother, Dylan. Dylan declined the invitation.

After the barbecue, Brendan went back to 12 Harding Avenue and texted several of his friends to swing by to watch the football game. Rafi took him up on the invite. Hiba was gone so the coast was clear. Rafi texted his friend Daniel Mastey to meet him there.

That evening Erik was supposed to be dog-sitting in Newton for one of my high school friends, Caleb Howcroft. The plan was for Caleb and Erik to meet in the afternoon. But in typical fashion, Erik was hours late. Erik arrived in Newton at 7:30 p.m. "Yo, I'm here," he told Caleb on the phone. By then, Caleb had given up on Erik and told him he had gone to Martha's Vineyard with the puppy. Erik replied with his signature "Woooord," and made his way over to Waltham. Friends would later claim the three men stopped answering their phones around 8:00 p.m.

Hiba told me that her trip to Miami had been a "breather." Even though she left for Florida without a return ticket, she'd always planned to come home. She gave me several accounts about the intended length of her stay, which I have not had the opportunity to clarify with her. Again, in her initial email to me she stated that she was "actually supposed to be there the night they were murdered" but couldn't get a flight out that Sunday. Over Skype, she first told me that she was only supposed to be gone for the weekend. Then that it was supposed to be a long weekend. Then that she was supposed to have come back on Sunday, the night of the murders. Then that she was supposed to come back on Wednesday. (Hiba declined the opportunity to clear up these discrepancies in writing or over the phone.)

Then again, it would make sense that her plans might be in flux if she had left after an argument. Her story sounded convincing on first listen. Hiba said that she and Brendan had talked on the phone every day she was gone and once they made up, she wanted to be with him as soon as possible.

Another reason for the confusion, she said, was that she only had cash to pay for the flight back to Boston, and she needed to deposit it at her bank, Wachovia, to buy the ticket. She said that the Wachovia machines in Miami were not working, which accounted for the delay and her not being there the night of the murders. That's why she said she ended up booking a flight back to Boston on Monday morning. "The issue was that I had a Wachovia account but there's no Wachovias in Boston, so I had taken cash with me. I was going to put [the cash] in my account, and that Sunday I was going to buy a ticket, you know, a one-way ticket back to Boston, and I couldn't find any ATM machines to put my cash in. All of them were, like, not working in Miami. So, it was all just really crazy," she said.

Hiba told me she and Brendan spoke for the last time around 7:30 p.m. on September 11, 2011. She also told the *Boston Globe* that on that call Brendan said, "I love you." "I told him I was going to call him back because I was watching a movie with my girlfriend, and after the movie I tried to call him back, but he didn't answer," she told me. Nor did he answer her calls the next morning when she was about to board the plane. Brendan did not answer when she landed at Logan either. By afternoon, Hiba had given up on Brendan's ride. Hiba did not have a key to the apartment. "I have a habit of losing things," she explained. She called Charlie two or three times that day to open the door. Charlie told her that Brendan's car was outside and his friends' cars were there too. "Will you let me in if he doesn't open the door?" she asked on the phone, according to Charlie. At first Hiba told Charlie that she was taking a taxi to the apartment. Then she said she got a ride from a woman at the airport, not a taxi, according to Charlie. By the time she got to the apartment it was 2:00 p.m. Charlie unlocked the door, and Hiba stepped inside alone.

CHAPTER TWENTY

They're All Dead

The smell was Hiba's first indication that something was wrong. The apartment always smelled like weed, but this was different. It smelled like incense and it was strong, like the incense had just been put out.

She saw Erik first. His body was by the door. "My eyes, like, I can't get that image out of my head, and I don't think it will ever go away. But I recognized Erik from his flip-flops." Hiba's mind could not process the whole scene at once. Her vision grew laser focused, starting at Erik's feet and traveling up his leg to where he lay in a pool of blood, her mind skipping over the deep lacerations in his throat. Hiba was in disbelief.

She ran through the living room. The couch was flipped over. When she got to the kitchen she found Rafi, his blood seeped into the cracks of the tiles. She dashed to the bedroom, splashing through the puddles of blood as she moved through the apartment. Brendan was encircled by a massive red stain on the carpet. The mattress the couple once shared was upturned. Hiba saw "brown stuff" on the bodies. But she did not stay to look closer. She half ran, half fell down the stairs backward with blood on her feet, wanting desperately to leave but unable to turn away. She was sick in Charlie's bathroom and ran outside and screamed, "They're all dead! They're all dead!"

Some neighbors noted Hiba's wails as she ran from the apartment as their first memory of that terrible incident. But in another account, Hiba was quiet at first. She walked across the street barefoot, leaving a trail of bloody footprints in the road. "My boyfriend is dead," she told a neighbor. She asked for a phone—she needed to call the police—and for a cigarette. There were a few moments of "calm." When the police came Hiba began to wail.

~

That Monday was Aria's first day of graduate school. Erik's sister was twenty-five years old and eager to begin the next chapter of her career. Erik always told her that she had a gift for helping people, that she was a good listener and had a talent for accepting people as they were. He told her she should take those talents and fine-tune them. What Erik said was true. Aria eventually learned to counsel people working through mental health concerns in affiliation with a local psychiatric hospital. The work is challenging at times. Aria is not immune to the strain. But she genuinely likes her clients. She learned what it was to go through a difficult period and appreciates the opportunity to help others in their time of need. Aria went to school in the evenings and worked during the day. Even after her brother's murder, she didn't miss a class or turn in an assignment late. Her education had been Erik's final wish for her, and she was determined to fulfill his dreams.

Aria was on the Salem State campus, taking notes on Monday evening, when she received a strange Facebook message. The professor was still introducing herself. "If you can't complete an assignment on time, let me know. Life happens," the professor said. *Life happens, life happens.* The words would ring in Aria's mind because at that very moment, her phone lit up. "I'm so sorry for your loss," the Facebook message read. It was from someone Aria didn't know well. *What are you talking about?* Aria thought. Then a stream of messages and alerts rolled in, and she got a call from her father. That's when a light bulb went off in her mind, and she knew something had happened to Erik. She ran out of class and called her dad. Nikki Weissman was already with detectives by then. He handed over the phone, and the detectives told Aria that her brother was dead. *This can't be happening,* she thought. She made it to the parking lot of the school before she started screaming and collapsed on the pavement.

~

Erik's mother, Bellie Hacker, works part-time as a set designer, and she was putting finishing touches on costumes for a production of Tom Stoppard's

Rosencrantz and Guildenstern Are Dead. Her partner, Wade, was the stage man-ager. On the evening of September 12, 2011, the cast was in dress rehearsals, and Bellie was trying to pin on Rosencrantz's cloak when her phone started ringing. *Oh my god, what do you want, what do you want?* she thought. Aria kept calling so she finally picked up. At first, her daughter's yells were unintelligible, then they became clear.

"Someone shot Erik! Someone shot Erik!" Aria yelled. Aria did not yet know how Erik was killed. She assumed he had been shot.

"No, it's not true," Bellie insisted. "No one shot Erik." But Aria's panic was too much to ignore, and Bellie started to yell too. She ran through the set and out of the theater screaming.

Staff at Aria's school had come outside, then, everyone—classmates, janitors, and the dean—to see what was wrong. One of Aria's friends who was on campus drove her home to her mother's apartment. On the car ride, Aria started making calls to family in Israel. Bellie and Wade arrived home as she did. More than a dozen of their friends were already there. Together they waited for the police.

When police arrived they informed Bellie that it was true: Erik was no longer alive. There was no mistake. They had identified the victims. Bellie said they reassured her of that over and over again. "I kept asking, and they said they wouldn't be here unless it was him."

That night Bellie said the police told her, "He was probably in the wrong place at the wrong time." Bellie was vomiting and crying hysterically, but she grasped on to that line, *wrong place, wrong time. They were watching a sports game, Erik might not have been there that night.* She would ruminate on that possibility for the rest of her life. Then police promised Erik's mother that they would be back when they caught the killers. They would knock on her door, they assured her. "Even if it is midnight. We will come and tell you what happened," Bellie remembers they said. A decade later Bellie is still waiting for that knock.

CHAPTER
TWENTY-ONE

Middlesex Mafia

In 2011, District Attorney Gerry Leone and his team of state troopers had a nickname in law enforcement circles: the "Middlesex Mafia." The title was tossed around in jest and used among the team with pride. Well resourced and led by the thick-haired Leone, Middlesex was popular among area cops and agents; it was the cool kids' table. That its members were tight knit and insular only added to the prestige.

In most Massachusetts towns and cities, homicides are assigned to the county's district attorney's office, rather than to the local police, and the cases are investigated by state troopers assigned to a county office. The Middlesex County District Attorney's Office had jurisdiction. But the state cops and lawyers were assisted by task forces and other departments, including detectives from the Waltham Police Department.

Leone said he got on the phone with Waltham police chief Thomas LaCroix right away. LaCroix was born and raised in Waltham. He started his career at Bentley University, a business school on the outskirts of Waltham, before working his way up the ladder at his hometown police department. In 2011, LaCroix was pushing fifty, kept what little remained of his blond hair in a tight buzz, and was quick to smile.

After confirming with LaCroix that they were likely dealing with a homicide, Leone assigned the triple murder case to Assistant District Attorney John

Verner, a tall well-built man like Leone, with glasses and wisps of dark hair. Verner wore a suit and green tie to the crime scene. The "brown stuff" Hiba had seen on the bodies appeared to be marijuana, the buds having turned soggy and dark in the blood. The killers also left $5,000 cash at the scene.

LaCroix and Verner also consulted regularly with the Suburban Middlesex County Drug Task Force about the triple homicide. This task force would become increasingly interesting to me. It was started by the Waltham Police Department in 1996 to target narcotics trafficking in the county. Under its umbrella, officers from local departments—including Waltham, Watertown, and Newton—work together and regularly call in assistance from state police and federal agencies. In 2023, I asked the current Waltham police chief, Kevin O'Connell, who oversees the taskforce. He said, "I guess all the chiefs do." Then he added that because Waltham Police Department started the task force, "It would have to be me." He said that the Waltham Police Department assigns a sergeant to the task force, who also participates in oversight.

$\sim$

Five weeks after the killings, on October 18, 2011, Gerry Leone, Assistant District Attorney John Verner, and Waltham police chief Thomas LaCroix appeared before a community meeting at a nearby school gymnasium. All of ten residents, the majority of whom appeared to be senior citizens, were in attendance. The Waltham community television network, *Waltham Newswatch*, was the only news outlet to report on the event. I would obtain the recording of the meeting in its entirety years later.

The meeting was led by Gary Marchese, a local city councilor and real estate attorney with a salt-and-pepper goatee. Marchese previously told the *Waltham Patch* that he hoped the murders could serve as a lesson for Waltham's youth— that drugs can lead to problems not only with addiction but also violence. Later he would tell the *Patch* that he actually knew Rafi, who parked his car when Rafi was working as a valet on Moody Street. "He was fascinated with the law . . . We kind of forged a friendship over that common ground," Marchese told the *Patch*. "I know him to be a very decent, intense young man."

At the meeting Marchese gestured to Leone, Verner, and LaCroix, who were seated before a beige fold-up table, and introduced them as guests who in the wake of the murders could talk about what was being done to keep drugs and drug dealers out of the community, and what neighbors could do to help.

All three emphasized the date the bodies were found, September 12. The words *September eleventh* were not uttered, not even when Leone was questioned about the time of death. Nor would the word *terrorism* be mentioned.

Stephen Gilpatric, the assistant district attorney tasked to Middlesex's anti-terrorism unit, was not present at this meeting. Incidentally, Gilpatric was in the throes of a crippling opioid addiction. In 2011 he was spending the entirety of his paycheck on oxycodone, according to court documents. He was later busted for trading information from inside the Middlesex DA's Office to his drug dealer for pills.

~

In the year and a half leading up to the bombing, Leone, Verner, and LaCroix would all step away from the case. In June 2012, LaCroix was arrested for assaulting his wife. The chief's mug shot, with dark rings under his defeated eyes, ran beside news reports of his arrest. LaCroix was convicted and sentenced to eighteen months' probation. He died on August 5, 2014, at age fifty-one, in his home. His cause of death was not listed in reports. LaCroix was replaced by Chief Keith MacPherson. In 2021, MacPherson retired and was replaced by Chief Kevin O'Connell. Neither O'Connell nor the Waltham Police Department responded to questions or clarified or refuted a detailed list of the reporting featured in this book.

ADA John Verner left the Middlesex DA's Office in August 2012 to work at the Attorney General's Office as chief of the Criminal Bureau under Martha Coakley, where he would later face scrutiny in connection to a drug lab scandal. In 2017 a judge recommended Verner for a public reprimand. The Supreme Court of Virginia upheld the decision to reprimand Verner but declined to suspend his license. Verner has since been transferred to an ADA position in Suffolk County. Verner declined to comment for this book and referred my queries to the Middlesex office. Assistant District Attorney David Solet is assigned to the Waltham murder case at the time of writing, according to the Middlesex DA's Office, who released this information in response to a records request. The Middlesex office did not respond to questions or clarify or refute a detailed list of the reporting featured in this book.

Gerry Leone announced he was quitting his role as Middlesex DA in March 2013. Governor Deval Patrick appointed Marian Ryan, a thirty-four-year veteran of the Middlesex DA's Office, to the position on April 23, 2013, shortly after the shoot-out in Watertown.

In an email, Leone, who is currently general counsel of the University of Massachusetts public university system, stated that because the Waltham murders remains an open and unsolved case at the Middlesex office, he "cannot and choose[s] not" to comment on the matter and issues related to it. I had written to Leone with a list of reporting and questions about the homicides and his role in the investigation. But I also asked him if he had heard the term "Middlesex Mafia" during his tenure, what years he refereed the Golden Gloves championships, and if he refereed any of Tamerlan Tsarnaev's matches—officials at the boxing organization said they were unable to provide that information to me. I asked if Leone had watched any of Tamerlan's fights and if he knew of Tamerlan prior to the bombing, and in what capacity. In a follow-up email, I asked if Leone could answer these questions alone. He wrote back that "any and all of this is off-limits" as it relates directly or indirectly to the open case. I thanked Leone for his response and advised him that if and when he is ready and able to answer these questions to please be in touch. Leone wrote that he would "welcome that if and when the right time and situation arises."

~

LaCroix began the October 2011 meeting by assuring Ward 5 residents that the triple homicide was "Nothing that the good people of Waltham need to be afraid of." The victims were specifically targeted and the violence was isolated, the Waltham police chief explained. The implication being that the Waltham murders victims were not "good people" themselves. "I know the Hastings Ave. issue was very disturbing," said LaCroix, mixing up the street name. But while he could not discuss the specifics of the case, he wanted to assure residents that Waltham did not have a murder problem; they had a drug problem, no different from any other town. "I hope that calms your nerves a bit," he said. What the good people of Waltham could do to help was to report suspicious activity. "You guys are our eyes and ears," LaCroix said. He told the gray-haired audience to call the police on their neighbors if they saw strange cars pulling up at short intervals. They had made an arrest like that recently, LaCroix added, with help from the Suburban Middlesex County Drug Task Force. "We threw them at the problem, and we shut down a drug house," he said.

ADA John Verner also stressed that he was working in coordination with the task force. "I speak to members of that unit at least two or three times a week about ongoing issues in the community," said Verner. "Drugs aren't particular to Waltham. They're in Newton, they're in Watertown, they're in all the towns around you, so the task force and we, we attack it as a global problem," he said.

The problem with Waltham was the same problem as everywhere, the three men agreed: drugs. "They get the drugs from somebody," Leone told the audience, with his hand in his fist and his head cocked to the side. If you know someone who is using drugs, get them to stop, he said. "It's a cash-and-carry business. If there aren't drug users who are going to pay for drugs, drug dealers go away." He added that residents should ask drug users where they get their drugs and tell the police. He said it was all about getting information into the right hands. "It's frankly as simple as that."

"Do you rate police departments with one, two, or three?" a gentleman in the audience asked.

"Well, I start with Waltham as number one," Leone said with a chuckle.

As far as the triple homicide went, Leone said they were working on it. "We like crimes to be solved in the first seventy-two hours. That doesn't always happen. It's not a TV show," Leone said. "Sometimes it takes longer than that. But we don't give up on running down the cases, following the leads, running down the evidence. And John and our team of prosecutors and investigators are doing that. Okay?" He concluded with another punch to his palm.

CHAPTER
TWENTY-TWO

The Robbery

On September 11, 2011, Daniel Mastey had plans to go to Brendan's to watch the game. It was supposed to be a reunion of sorts, after his six weeks away, surfing in Indonesia. Daniel would joke with Brendan and exchange quips in Hebrew with Rafi. Daniel expected he might see Erik as well. A typical Sunday evening. But Daniel did not account for his jet lag. He fell asleep around two or three in the afternoon and did not wake up until early the next morning.

"Brendan and Rafi were like brothers to me. I should have been there," Daniel told me later. He is grateful he wasn't, of course. But he hates himself too, he says. He feels guilty. He wonders if there is something he could have done.

When Daniel woke up that morning he didn't have any missed calls or texts. That was unusual; Rafi was very communicative and would almost certainly check in if plans had been set. More unusual still was that Rafi wasn't answering his phone. Neither was Brendan. The calls went straight to voice mail. Daniel was worried. He still had a key to Rafi's apartment, so he made his way over to check in.

Rafi socialized in the attic. He had a leather couch, a collection of leather easy chairs, and a freezer, where he kept his collection of cannabis strains. Guests entered the apartment from the back door. Daniel arrived at the apartment sometime between eleven and noon. The back door was ajar. Now he was nervous. No one was home, but it looked like someone had ripped through the apartment. Drawers were open, and furniture had been moved around. Daniel went upstairs and opened the freezer door. The jars were gone. So too were Rafi's concentrates, his dabs, his whole collection, everything was missing, and Rafi's couches and chairs had been pulled apart. Daniel knew where Rafi stored pounds of weed and knew Rafi usually had at least $10,000 cash on hand. It was all gone. Now Daniel was panicking. He ran out of the house, locked the door, and started calling around to his friends to see if anyone knew what had happened.

Cory, one of Brendan's high school friends in Cambridge, was supposed to watch the game with Brendan on Sunday evening, but his girlfriend, who was also close to Hiba, wanted him to have dinner with her family—a meal that may well have saved his life. (Cory is not his real name—he asked to protect his identity due to safety concerns.) The afternoon of Monday, September 12, 2011, Cory was in his Cambridge basement apartment when he received a call from his girlfriend. Then he spoke to Hiba.

"They're all dead," Hiba said.

"Who's dead?" Cory asked.

"Everybody," she said.

Cory ran through the streets of Cambridge to the Mess family home barefoot to tell them the news. Brendan's father, Derek, was outside doing yard work. Dylan was inside eating a sandwich. It was the hardest thing Cory had ever had to say.

The news got to Daniel shortly thereafter, and he drove directly to Harding Avenue. Rafi's parents arrived on the scene as he did. He saw Rafi's father, Avi Teken, dressed in a suit, marching toward the officers as they sealed off the street with yellow tape. Hiba was speaking to investigators, visibly distraught. Daniel collapsed on the street corner.

When he got his bearings, Daniel walked up to the nearest officer. "Drug dealers were murdered," Daniel remembered he was told. The way the officer described what had happened seemed entirely oriented around the narrative that the victims were criminals.

This same messaging was reflected in early news reports and my interviews with neighbors. "They told us that it was drug related and that things like that don't usually happen twice," said Krystina Miller, who lived across the street.

Daniel told the officer that he knew the men, and he believes he told them about the robbery at Rafi's apartment right then and there. Daniel isn't sure if they took down his name. But he said investigators never called. Daniel went to the Waltham police station of his own accord, several days later, to see if he could be of any help. Rafi's parents had asked him to. So he went.

CHAPTER
TWENTY-THREE

Questioning

Daniel insists he told investigators about the robbery at Rafi's again at the police station. He thought there might be a connection to the murders. "I wasn't about to hide anything. I wasn't trying to protect anybody, you know. I just wanted to give them as much information as possible," he told me.

Rafi was murdered in Waltham. Rafi's apartment was in Waltham. Rafi's apartment was apparently robbed within twenty-four hours of the time he was killed. Daniel had gone to the apartment and observed signs of a robbery hours before the bodies were found, when no one except the murderers would have known Rafi was dead. I do not have investigators' case files or notes. But according to my own interviews, investigators appeared disinterested in looking into this crime at all, let alone in connection to the triple homicide.

Rafi's roommate, Dwayne, who went back to the apartment shortly after the bodies were found, also said he noticed the marijuana in Rafi's freezer was missing. Dwayne was in a state of shock. George Becker, Dwayne's cousin, helped him gather his things and leave. The apartment no longer felt safe. I asked both Dwayne and George if perhaps they took Rafi's cash and weed. This would not be an unreasonable or nefarious thing to do, for a multitude of reasons, including concerns of police scrutiny. Other than a small pollen box of Rafi's, a personal token from his friend that George says he treasures to this day, they both insist they did not take Rafi's belongings.

Dwayne said that investigators did go to Rafi's apartment and took Rafi's computer and other cell phones. But to his knowledge, they did not dust the apartment for prints. Nor did investigators ask Dwayne or George about the robbery in interviews. Neither George, Dwayne, nor Daniel was questioned after the bombing.

Paul Juliano, a friend and neighbor of Rafi's, said he called Rafi several times in the hours before the murders and that he briefly visited Rafi's home. Juliano told me that he was never contacted by investigators. Ten years after the murders, Juliano said he did not believe he had any useful information. He and Rafi met for a short while. Juliano declined Rafi's invitation to go to Brendan's to watch the football game, because he didn't like sports, and then he went home. But police didn't know that; they never contacted Juliano. After Rafi was killed, Juliano was scared and momentarily immobilized by grief. He figured investigators would reach out eventually, and he wasn't sure how to go about getting in touch with them. Weeks, months, and then years passed, and still Juliano was not contacted.

On the other hand, investigators asked a lot of questions about narcotics. "A lot of the questions to me were very oriented towards them being dealers," Daniel said. He felt like the investigators were going after the victims' marijuana connections, hoping to make a drug arrest, regardless of the connection to the homicide. Of course, the killers could have been connected to the victims' sources. But the killers could also have known the victims in some other way, Daniel thought. He said he provided investigators with a list of names, people who were in Brendan's inner circle. Daniel said he included Tamerlan Tsarnaev in that list.

An investigator called Daniel about a week later. Daniel brought up Tamerlan again. "Tamerlan Tsarnaev didn't show up to the memorial service, you know. He didn't show up to the funerals. You know, it was understandable at the time he didn't show up to Rafi's or Erik's, but he didn't show up to Brendan's. And that, like, that raised flags to myself and other people in our inner circle," he said. "I mentioned Tamerlan's name in that interview. I know a handful of other people did as well," he told me. But again, Daniel said, the investigators' questions seemed focused on the victims' distributors and suppliers. "I think they were looking for, you know, somebody, like, in the drug realm, and Tamerlan was not that profile. It didn't fit what they were necessarily searching for." Of course, there is also a chance investigators were trying to throw Daniel off.

Brendan's friend Sam—who asked me not to use their real name due to concerns about safety—had driven past Harding Avenue the night of the killings and seen an unfamiliar car parked outside. Sam told me they went to the police station on Tuesday. For some reason, the investigators did not appear interested in the car. "I don't think that's what you saw," one detective said, according to Sam. Instead, detectives were interested in the victims' weed connections. They asked Sam a lot of questions about drugs. "Whose toes were they stepping on in Waltham?" investigators allegedly asked. Sam did not have insight into Brendan's business operations. But Sam did know who Brendan's close friends were. They said they also wrote down Tamerlan's name in a list of about a dozen other people.

In the days after the murder, Brendan's friends all camped out at Cory's place in Cambridge. They used the buddy system every time they left the house. They were scared. The only one who was missing was Tamerlan. Nobody could get ahold of him or figure out where he was. When Hiba and Tamerlan did not show up at Brendan's memorial—held at a jazz venue in Inman Square—Sam called up Waltham detectives to tell them Hiba and Tamerlan were absent. Sam wasn't overly concerned about Tamerlan at the time. Sam thought that maybe, because Tamerlan was Muslim, he mourned differently. Still, it was odd, and Sam wanted detectives to know.

Cory spoke to police three or four days after the murders and went in to the police station a few days later. He spoke to Patrick Hart, a detective at the Waltham Police Department, and Erik P. Gagnon, a state trooper assigned to the Middlesex County District Attorney's Office. Investigators wanted to know who Brendan was dealing with, what he was up to, what cell phones he was using, and if he had any guns. "We don't care that you sold a pound of pot or pounds of pot. We just want to know who the players are," they told Cory at first. But he wasn't sure how much he could trust them. Someone had apparently told investigators that Brendan had orchestrated the robbery of several antique firearms from a law enforcement officer's home in Vermont. When investigators started questioning Cory about the stolen guns, he got nervous. Cory came in to the station to try to help them solve his friend's murder case. Now, because he had lived in Vermont, he felt like they were trying to link him to a weapons charge and the home invasion and robbery of a cop. They had Cory in there for hours, playing good cop and bad cop, he said. "I only knew what I knew, which wasn't much," Cory told me.

Meanwhile, thoughts about the homicide were spinning around Cory's head. *Was it a bad deal? Where's the money? Last phone numbers? Traffic cameras? Car rentals? Plane flights? Was Hiba involved?*

Police were in contact with Cory over the next week, asking him to help get others in to talk. Then that was it. He didn't have any communication with them after the first month, ever again. Until the Boston Marathon was bombed.

Andrew Jeune, Brendan's childhood friend, went into the police station a week after the murders on his own volition. He had texted Brendan the night before he died. He thought investigators would have gone through Brendan's phone and called. But they didn't, so Andrew went into the station to see if anything he knew might help. Andrew said he had stopped selling marijuana after being convicted on federal charges a few years before the murders. He said he straightened his life out after that, but investigators couldn't have known he had changed, he told me over drinks at a Somerville bar. "I'm sure they were doing their job by being accusatory," he said.

Ray Filmore, who, again, was a friend of Brendan's from high school, also went to the Waltham police station of his own accord, a few days after the murders. He wanted to make sure they knew about Brendan and Hiba's relationship. "Yeah, yeah, yeah. We've already been told that by other people," Ray remembers they said. He said investigators kept him in the station for all of five minutes.

Caleb was the last person Erik called on his phone, detectives told him. They called Caleb on Friday morning, four days after the bodies were found, while Caleb was getting dressed for the funeral. Later I would learn that Erik's family had asked for police presence at the burial for security reasons, a request that law enforcement denied. Detectives told Caleb that he had to come to the station right away. "These types of things move fast," they said. Caleb was one of the half dozen or so men who helped Nikki Weissman carry his son's casket that warm September day. He rushed to the police station as soon as Erik's body was in the ground.

The detectives sat him down. Caleb was still visibly upset from the funeral. They asked him if he knew who killed Erik or who might have been involved in Erik's murder. Caleb said he was ignorant on both points. As the questioning progressed, Caleb began to feel like he was being interrogated as a party to a drug crime. "You didn't know your friend as well as you thought you did," Caleb remembered one of the investigators repeating over and over again. Like they were implying Erik was to blame for his own murder. Caleb wanted to help in any way he could, so he provided investigators with Daniel Adler-Golden's contact information. According to Caleb, the questioning lasted all of twenty minutes.

Caleb's account was concerning. Twenty minutes did not seem like a long interview for one of the victim's last points of contact. I did not learn about this encounter until after the bombing, when I started to call around and ask questions. When I called DAG, to my shock I learned that even though Caleb claimed he provided investigators with his information, investigators never contacted DAG at all.

∿

Admittedly, the victims and many of their associates had an antagonistic relationship with law enforcement. For example, at the time of his death, Brendan had a pending charge for allegedly assaulting a cop. The case actually stemmed from an incident involving the documentarian John Wilson. Coincidentally, this is the same John Wilson who would go on to direct one of my favorite TV shows, the HBO series *How To with John Wilson*.

The documentarian briefly met Brendan the summer of 2010, in a 7-Eleven parking lot in Inman Square. John lived in the Boston area at the time. He told me he was walking through the parking lot with his friend Chris Maggio when Brendan drove by in his black Mercedes-Benz, the one Tamerlan sold to him. John said the car almost hit them, so Chris slapped the car with his hand as they drove by. Brendan did not appreciate this gesture. John told me Brendan jumped out of the car and started "windmilling" on the pair, leaving John bloody, with broken glasses.

The next thing John knew, a man working at the 7-Eleven, who witnessed the scuffle, called the police. "I can knock you out if I wanted to," Brendan told the Cambridge cop who pursued him, according to the police report. Three more officers were called to the scene, pepper-sprayed Brendan in the eyes, wrestled him to the ground, and slapped on a pair of handcuffs.

Even though the dynamic between law enforcement and the victims' associates was strained, it's quite common for murder victims and witnesses to be immersed in the criminal world. I interviewed former Boston police commissioner Ed Davis, who became a kind of figurehead after the bombing. John Goodman played Davis in the Hollywood film *Patriots Day*, a fictionalized account of the bombing emphasizing the tireless work of first responders. Davis would not discuss the Waltham case directly but did talk to me about his experience as a homicide investigator. He's worked hundreds of homicide cases in Boston and in Lowell, and he says that most of the witnesses he encountered had some kind of record. When they don't, he says that presents unique challenges too. Almost everyone he questions in murder investigations is emotionally distraught. The families especially are angry at everybody, he says. They're angry at the police. They're angry at the murderer. They're angry at the government for allowing it to happen. "But you have to cut through that and make sure that people realize as police that we're there to solve the case no matter what. Even if you don't like us, we're going to work really hard to hold the person who did this accountable," Davis said.

Regardless of the inherent difficulties of this work, "All the leads should be run to ground," Davis said. No exceptions. And the stakes are in no way lowered if the victims have a record. "The type of behavior that we're trying to prevent here is actually more likely to occur among criminals who want to handle things themselves. And if there are no ramifications to that, then that killing will continue. That bad activity will continue. So it's really necessary to protect the rest of society so that we're living in a civil environment," he told me.

Ian McCleod flew in from California after Brendan died. When Ian heard that Brendan's friends were suspicious of Hiba after the murders, he told Hiba to get out of town. Everyone was so emotional, and Ian didn't think their suspicions had any credence. "Yo, get the fuck out of there," he told her. That's why she wasn't at the memorial, he explained. There wasn't anything suspicious about her being gone, he told me.

～

Hiba went to the Waltham police station the day she found the bodies. She said she didn't remember how long she talked to detectives. Only that when she went into the station it was light outside, and when she stepped out it was dark. They put her up in a hotel that night, and she spoke to them again before leaving for Richmond three days later. She told me the investigators were respectful. She said they didn't give her a hard time. "I wondered what was going on, but I didn't have any worries because I knew that I wasn't involved in anything. But they repeatedly told me that I wasn't a suspect. That I didn't have to worry about anything," she said. Later, when I asked again, Hiba added that investigators were hot and cold in their last interview but that she didn't really have an opinion about them either way. When I asked if investigators were ever confrontational with her, and noted other accounts where individuals stated investigators had been confrontational, Hiba said that yes, that night, she essentially broke down. Investigators said she neglected to tell them about Brendan's other phone. Hiba said that initially she didn't think about the other phone "because it was literally a couple of hours after I had walked in and found the bodies." She wasn't thinking straight. Otherwise, she said that investigators asked her about any gangs the men could have been affiliated with and about the victims' friends. She said she gave the investigators a list of the people who came regularly to their home. She said she included Tamerlan's name on that list.

She said she and Tamerlan weren't close and never spent any time together alone. "I didn't have any qualms with him, you know. Like, I thought he was a little bit strange and strict," she said. She thought it was odd that he came over so often when he had a family and a daughter at home. On one occasion that spring, Hiba and Brendan had gone out for the day and Brendan didn't answer Tamerlan's calls. "We got back to the apartment, and he was sitting, like, outside the house in his car," Hiba said. She thought that was strange too. But Brendan just laughed it off. "That was usually his response about anything," Hiba said.

"He had some religious views, but he wasn't aggressive or rude with it. You know, like, that was just his opinion, I think. Like, he talked about his sister and how she wouldn't have been allowed to do any of the things I did," she said. "That was that one-time conversation. Other than that I don't remember having conversations with him, like, unless there were people around," she said. She also told the *Boston Globe* she cooked Tamerlan halal meals when he came over. Ian was with the couple and Tamerlan in one of Hiba's first interactions with

Tamerlan. Tamerlan was upset about Israel, and Ian distinctly remembered Hiba disagreeing with what he said.

After the bombing, Hiba said a specific memory about Tamerlan did come to mind. She said Tamerlan came over to the house shortly before she left for Miami. "So we going to do that thing later?" Tamerlan asked Brendan.

"Yeah," Brendan said.

"What thing?" Hiba asked.

"Nothing, don't worry about it," Brendan said and brushed it off. Hiba said she didn't want to pry.

Hiba said she did not think Tamerlan had anything to do with the murders. She said she only mentioned him to investigators because he was around. "Brendan was a very good friend to him so I thought they were friends, you know," she said. "I didn't even think about any of Brendan's friends as possible suspects. I thought that it would have been mostly something to do with Erik," she said.

Erik's girlfriend, Victoria Jackson, said investigators came to speak to her in Virginia twice before the bombing. She had voiced her suspicions about Hiba to law enforcement and had refused Hiba's offer to reconnect after the killings. Victoria was scared. "Everything was running through my mind. I was a wreck. I couldn't even play *Pac-Man*," she told me. Even the simple video game triggered her anxiety. Victoria said law enforcement accused her of being a sex worker, which made her even more upset. "The police asked me if I was a madam of an escort service," Victoria said. "They said that Hiba told them that, and they asked me that question so much that I started to wonder if I *was* the madam of an escort service," she told me. "The only thing that brought me back to reality was my Camry. And I remember saying if I was the madam of an escort service, why would I be driving a Camry?" she said. "I'm, like, *Am I being set up? What is happening here?* Like, I am not a madam of an escort service. I work at Wachovia." After the bombing, investigators also asked Cory and Dylan if Hiba and Victoria were sex workers.

Hiba said investigators flew her back to Boston in December 2011 to testify in a grand jury hearing. She said she was asked to testify as a material witness. According to Hiba, her testimony lasted all of ten minutes. She was asked about a man who came to visit Erik from Vermont—potentially an individual who helped him set up the grow house. She was also asked about the courier from

Malden. But for reasons I have never been able to pin down, Hiba said that the primary focus of questioning in her grand jury hearing was Brendan's dear childhood friend, a Black man with dreadlocks. He would later release a tribute video in which he articulated the anguish of losing "my friend and my brother" in moving detail to the tune of "I Knew You Were Trouble," by Taylor Swift.

At the time of our interview in early 2014, Hiba told me she regularly called investigators for information about the murders and made herself available as much as possible. "Is [there] anything new? Is there anything happening?" she asked. "They were just, like, we'll get back to you, they didn't have anything for me," she said. Hiba said she called investigators again after the bombing, but she said, "They weren't, like, interested in talking to me."

Dylan and several of his friends picked Hiba up when she left the police station after her first interview. Shane McCarthy was there. "I'm protected," Hiba said. She repeated this phrase. Shane wasn't sure what she meant. Protected by who? God? Hiba told them her story about what had happened, about waiting for Brendan to pick her up at the airport, about getting a ride to Waltham when he didn't show, and asking the landlord to open the door. She repeated the same story over and over again, like a script. She would not answer specific questions. She would just start from the top all over again. Shane was suspicious, although her behavior sounds totally understandable to me, considering what she had witnessed. The only time Hiba strayed from this account was to talk about Erik. She didn't like him. Never had. She spoke at length on this point. The men thought it was strange, speaking of the dead like that. But if Hiba believed the murderers had been targeting Erik, it would also make sense that she was angry.

Barbie Kerr received a call from Hiba on Tuesday, September 13, around three in the morning. Hiba was calling from a hotel room. Law enforcement had put her up in a Waltham hotel after the murders. She had nowhere else to go. "I found the bodies. They're all covered in blood. Everybody's dead," Hiba said. Hiba sounded afraid. Barbie said Hiba could stay with her in Richmond.

Hiba arrived at Barbie's Richmond home a short time later with several large boxes. They were items taken from the Waltham apartment, including Brendan's clothes and his collection of jerseys. Hiba told Barbie she planned to sell them but never did. Barbie eventually donated the items. Brendan's associates would later complain about the missing items, since they had sentimental as well as monetary value, and there was little inside the apartment to remember them by.

But Hiba told me that her friends helped her pack. She wasn't paying attention to what they took; she was incapacitated by fear, shock, and pain.

In the days and weeks after the killings, Hiba slept with Barbie in her bed. Barbie said Hiba would wake up in the middle of the night, crying that she could smell the blood. Around that time Barbie noticed that a lot of Hiba's friends were distancing themselves from her. But Barbie wanted to help her friend as much as she could. "I'd rather be there for someone who did do something than not be there for someone who didn't," she said. Hiba told Barbie about her argument with Brendan and how it had escalated to the level where "she threw knives and maybe cut his tires," Barbie recalled. "It sparked concern for me because I didn't know that she got angry like that. I honestly couldn't believe that she told me that she did those things," she said. But Barbie made a note to address these issues with her friend later, after she had calmed down.

Hiba told Barbie she thought the killers were either other drug dealers or the cops. Contrary to Hiba's account, Barbie said Hiba did not feel comfortable talking to the police. It became a point of contention for Barbie and Hiba. Barbie felt like Hiba should speak to law enforcement if investigators still wanted to speak to her, but Barbie also understood her concern. Which is why Barbie suggested that she call a psychic. "Take it with a grain of salt," Barbie told me. But she was hoping the call might encourage Hiba to talk to the police. So Barbie called a psychic and put the call on speaker so they could both hear. The psychic said it was okay to call the cops, according to Barbie, and that they would find out what happened a year and a half later. "He also said that ultimately, he thought a female was responsible. And he described this female as wearing dresses and a lot of jewelry," Barbie said. While the psychic was talking, Hiba appeared to panic. Barbie watched as Hiba tried to take the call off speaker. "It definitely made me feel a certain way. But again, a grain of salt," Barbie said.

~

Ian wanted to speak to investigators and flew from California to Boston after the murders. He was somewhat cautious. He had to be. He was busted on marijuana trafficking charges about a year later and was still behind bars when Tamerlan bombed the marathon and I began reporting on this story. But more than anything, he loved Brendan, and he wanted to help in any way that he could. He said he gave investigators the numbers to all of Brendan's burner phones. The two of them used to buy temporary phones and toss them every few days. Ian said that the investigators' questions led him to believe they were primarily interested in whether or not Brendan was affiliated with gangs or had enemies in organized crime. Ian didn't think Brendan had any affiliations of any kind. Investigators pushed him on this point. They told Ian that the fight at the 7-Eleven—the fight involving John Wilson—was a gang brawl involving the Crips. Ian had not heard of the autobiographical documentarian John Wilson and did not know he'd been nominated for an Emmy for an episode he wrote about singing a cappella in college. The investigators were so insistent that this was a gang fight that Ian wondered if maybe there was something Brendan hadn't told him. I am not sure why investigators brought up the 7-Eleven fight to Ian or presented the dispute in this way. For what it's worth, John Wilson claims that he is not and has never been associated with the Crips.

According to Ian, the theory investigators really seemed to home in on was "Mexicans," as in an organized Mexican cartel. Retired DEA agent Mark Tully, who was in communication with members of law enforcement tasked to the case, also told me that investigators ultimately concluded that Mexicans were behind the triple slaying.

Ian knew Brendan had worked with individuals in California who happened to be Mexican, but Ian said these men were not part of a cartel. They just happened to be Mexican, and according to Ian, "They fucking loved B." (Brendan's friends often called him B. for short.) Plus they wouldn't have been able to find Brendan. None of the people who Brendan worked with who happened to be Mexican knew where he lived or had his real phone number, Ian said.

Investigators seemed to think that because Brendan was selling drugs, he could have pissed off rival drug dealers, according to Ian. They did not seem to be interested in robbery as a motive—based on the questions they asked Ian. Perhaps because there was $5,000 cash left behind. Ian did not know Rafi's apartment had also been robbed. He did know that Brendan typically had about $100,000 cash on hand in his apartment, and multiple sources confirmed that estimate to me. Although, Hiba told me that to the best of her knowledge, it was unlikely that Brendan had guns or a large amount of cash and marijuana in his home at the time of his death. "Brendan said he moved everything out of the house. Because, you know, I guess it was a pretty loud fight, so he didn't want the police to come. So, he moved the, he said he moved everything out of the house. So, the next day when I left, when I left house, apparently there was nothing in the house," she told me. But I can confirm that Brendan had at least $7,000 cash in his home, so it appears at least some money was taken. To Ian, the murder looked like it could have been a coordinated robbery. But he said investigators weren't interested in that idea.

$\sim$

Aria started talking to police over her mother's wails that first terrible evening after investigators knocked on the door. Aria told me she wanted to help in whatever way she could. She also thought that the date of the murders, September 11, 2011, was important. Their family is Israeli. She wanted to make sure investigators knew this. Rafi's parents were Israeli too, she would later learn.

Rafi's father, Avi, also pointed out the date of the killings to police and told them about his experience in the Special Forces in Israel. He thought his son's murder was terrorism right away. Terrorists "like to play with numbers," he explained. He told investigators what Rafi had told him, about his argument with a Chechen. *Chechens. This is remarkable,* thought Avi. And he told police the same. *Have you found any Chechens?* Avi wanted to know.

"I told the state police. One thing my son and I have in common, we're both outgoing and we talk. Maybe too much," Avi told me. "He would ask me random questions as many sons ask their parents," he said. "And that's why I shared it with the state police." Investigators never got back to him about this lead. "They didn't even have the respect to follow up," he said.

Aria arrived at the apartment after Hiba with her father, two of her brother's childhood friends, and two friends of her own. They rented a moving truck and brought trash bags. They didn't know what to expect. When Aria stepped into the second-floor apartment, her eyes fell on a mop and a bucket of water. She wondered if that's what they used to clean up the blood. She headed straight to the third floor, where Erik slept. The place was a mess. It seemed like every single thing he owned had been thrown across the room. Everything that was left, at least. She found a Rolex watch box but no Rolex. There were a few glass pipes, but his laptop was gone. There wasn't enough to fill a bag let alone a truck.

Aria knew Erik had other belongings in storage so she called the storage company to see if she could have access to her brother's things. "Being his sister, like, I just want whatever he had." In the weeks that followed, Bellie would become preoccupied with making scrapbooks with Erik's photos, letters that he wrote, anything he left behind. That's how she got through those first terrible weeks. The storage company said they would get back to Aria. But Aria got a call back from Erik Gagnon, the state trooper assigned to the Middlesex DA's Office instead.

Gagnon accused Aria of tampering with the investigation. He said he could prosecute her for trying to get her brother's things. Aria tried to explain herself. She wasn't trying to interfere by calling the storage facility. She was looking for photos, or a sweatshirt, something that smelled like him. That's what she wanted most of all. Something with his scent. She didn't think these items would make a difference to investigators, but they meant a lot to her. Gagnon did not appreciate Aria telling him how to do his job. "How many murders have you solved?" Aria remembered he said.

"None of the family members or friends ever got charged," Gagnon told me when I asked about his interactions with the victims' families. "If somebody said I was being accusatory, maybe ask them why," he said. "I have nothing to hide on this thing," he assured me. "I did my job. There were plenty of people above me that supervised."

Investigators told Erik's family that they did not need to identify his body. But Aria and her aunt, who had flown in from Israel, demanded to see Erik, just to make sure. "We need closure. We need to make sure we know it's him," Aria told the police. This was on or around September 15, 2011, Aria remembered. Together Aria and her aunt went to the coroner's office and demanded to see Erik's corpse. They said they could only show them a photo. "So my aunt and I were sitting, clenched hands on top of each other, like really scared, and ready to see this picture. And she opens it up and it is Rafi. It's not Erik." Aria did not know who Rafi was at this point. She just knew it wasn't her brother. The woman who showed her the photo left the room. *Maybe this is all a mix-up,* Aria thought while she waited. The passing thought became a burning hope: *Maybe Erik is alive.* Then the woman returned. She showed Aria a new photo. It was Erik.

It would be terrible to see a photograph of her dead brother in any circumstance, but the mortician's mix-up made it worse. If Aria hadn't come, might her family have buried Rafi instead? Rafi's face had no markings that Aria noticed. Erik was pale and had a bloody lip. "It didn't look like him. It did, but it didn't. It was really scary."

To Aria, the visit to the morgue added to an escalating pattern of disrespect. The Weissmans were finally able to bury Erik on Friday, September 16. It was a long time to wait. Aria's aunt made sure to identify Erik's body at the funeral home, just in case. In Massachusetts, families of homicide victims can receive aid—up to $25,000—which can cover burial costs. But a victims' advocate allegedly told the Weissmans that because the murder was drug related, they didn't qualify for any financial support. The Tekens told me they were also denied this service.

After Erik was buried, Bellie regained some of her strength. Bellie had heard about Gagnon threatening to press charges. She realized she had to protect her daughter. Ten days after the murders, Gagnon told Aria he wanted to speak to her again. This time Bellie picked up the phone and called Gagnon herself. If Gagnon wanted to talk, Bellie was going to be there.

The mother and daughter went to the Middlesex DA's Office in Woburn. There, Gagnon and another trooper allegedly accused Aria of knowing who the murderers were. They said she was holding back information and protecting her brother's killer. They presented her with parking tickets she had received in Waltham as proof she knew more than she was letting on. Aria broke down in tears. The detectives gave Aria a few minutes, then admitted they were bluffing.

Bellie told the detectives about Hiba at this meeting. Bellie wondered why they were harassing her daughter when they should be arresting Hiba. "Why is she not in custody?" Bellie asked. The police told her they believed the murders were the result of "a deal that went wrong." That didn't make sense to her. But the investigators did speak to the family with what Bellie believed was a rare moment of candor. They discussed what might happen next.

"Down the line someone might need some plea bargain," they told Bellie. "Probably someone knows the truth, and they'll come forward when they need the plea bargain," they said. They added that usually a family member or friend knows what happened. "It's always like that." Bellie couldn't believe what she was hearing. *That's really how it goes?* she thought. To Bellie, it felt like they were basically waiting for someone to come forward and give them the answer on a silver platter. But they were the experts, and at the time she trusted their judgment. Bellie is not so trusting anymore. "I think they're still sitting there waiting."

~

Three days after the bodies were found, Dylan and Cory were sitting on the front steps of Dylan's Cambridge apartment shaking their heads, when Tamerlan Tsarnaev came strolling by like nothing was wrong. "I heard the news. I'm sorry," Tamerlan said. Dylan asked Tamerlan the same questions he asked of all Brendan's friends: *Was Brendan hanging out with somebody who could have done this? Was there a deal about to go down?* "No," Tamerlan said. And then he asked, "Who else was there?"

"Everybody was there," Dylan said. "Erik and Raf were there."

"No, really? Them too?" Tamerlan said. He seemed surprised.

"Yeah, everybody is gone," Cory said.

Then Tamerlan shook his head and walked away.

The news of the killings reached Wai Kru and the gym's owner, John Allan. Allan tried to offer Tamerlan his condolences the next time Tamerlan came into the gym.

"I'm really sorry," Allan said as he approached Tamerlan. "That's really messed up that that happened to your friend."

But Tamerlan was already laughing off Allan's kind words. "I guess that's what happens when you live that type of a lifestyle," he told Allan with a grin and a shrug. Then he walked away shadowboxing.

Allan was taken aback. Erik and Rafi had also come to the gym with Brendan and Tamerlan on a couple of occasions. Allan figured that Tamerlan's strange reaction was like a psychological defense mechanism, that maybe Tamerlan was laughing so he wouldn't have to deal with the pain. A lot of fighters are like that. Besides, Allan thought, Tamerlan was a showman, and displays of tender emotion had no place in his act.

Investigators apparently never went to Wai Kru to investigate the Waltham murder case. Which is surprising. Brendan went to the gym several days a week. He had a purple belt in jujitsu. There were indications the killers knew the victims. Not only was the murder particularly gruesome, the killers would have to possess a certain degree of physicality and skill to take Brendan down, let alone three men, all with some degree of training. District Attorney Gerry Leone was a boxer himself. Wouldn't he of all people think to consider the victims' and the assailants' fighting skills? Why didn't law enforcement interview more people? Why didn't they reach out to everyone the victims called on the phone that day? Why were they so accusatory with the people who did come forward? Perhaps adversarial investigative tactics work to procure information in some instances. But they can also backfire and shut down the dialogue. Did it make sense to scare so many people away? Why did investigators apparently fail to look into The robbery at Rafi's home?

CHAPTER TWENTY-FOUR

Praying for Answers

In the weeks leading up to the one-year anniversary of Erik's death, Aria contacted a victims' advocate at the Middlesex DA's Office. Aria thought maybe the district attorney could help drum up media attention. She had seen news stories about unsolved cases before, asking for people with information to come forward. She was hoping the Middlesex office would work to put the story back in the news.

Aria did her part to attract attention. She painted *PRAYING FOR ANSWERS* in big black letters on a white wooden sign, along with the date: 9/11/11. On Tuesday, September 11, 2012, Aria, Nikki Weissman, and friends of all three murder victims planted themselves on Lexington Street across from the Waltham Police Department. They lit candles and shared memories while cars whizzed past.

There were no stories about the one-year anniversary in the *Boston Globe* or the *Boston Herald*, or any of the local radio or TV news stations, that I could find. But two local Waltham and Cambridge outlets ran articles. Middlesex County District Attorney spokeswoman Jessica Pastore told *Wicked Local Cambridge*, "Solving this case remains a priority for the office." She said that the office had a designated trial team assigned to the case and that the office was following up on every lead. "We have not forgotten about Brendan, Erik, or Raphael, and our hope really is that we eventually will be able to provide justice for the victims' families," she said. She encouraged anyone with information to call the main office.

Ward 5 Councilor Gary Marchese also spoke to *Wicked Local Cambridge* reporter Ignacio Laguarda. Marchese appeared to have some inside information about the investigation. He said that the investigation had led detectives out of state but that they were struggling due to the lack of eyewitnesses and forensic evidence. He also lavished praise on the investigators. "The police have done a great job," he said. "The DA's office has put some of their best people on the investigation."

Yet Marchese also appeared to blame the victims for the killings. "It's almost like they chose the quietest, safest little cul-de-sac in all of Waltham so that they could fly under the radar," he said. "Maybe it worked for a while, but somebody didn't do something right. They upset somebody in high places, and they paid for it dearly with their lives," he said. "I don't know what the answer is, but I wish that we didn't have to deal with that part of life, the abuse of drugs and alcohol. It leads to so much heartache and crime."

City Councilor Kenneth Doucette, who worked at the Middlesex Sheriff's Department, appeared to share Marchese's sentiment in the *Wicked Local Cambridge* story. "One thing you hope that comes out of something like this is that people learn to make good decisions so that they're not involved in this type of activity," said Doucette. "There's no question that everybody involved in this was not making good decisions."

No one from the Waltham Police Department came out in an official capacity to speak to the mourners gathered outside the station. Instead, a man in an unmarked black SUV drove out of the police department parking lot, stopped by the crowd, and rolled down his window. Nikki Weissman and one other person claim the man said he was a retired cop. "No need to pray," the man told them. "The fucking Mexicans killed him," he said, according to Nikki, who was not aware investigators were tossing around a theory about "Mexicans" before that day and was unaware of my other reporting when he spoke to me. "I was a detective at the time, I'm telling you: it was the Mexicans. Stop praying," the man allegedly said. And then he drove away.

CHAPTER
TWENTY-FIVE

The Bombs

In early 2011, Tamerlan was out of work and had a toddler to support. But on September 22, he bought a new computer. Shortly thereafter, he bought a round-trip ticket to Dagestan. While Tamerlan and his father, Anzor, were in Dagestan, Anzor, who had been unable to work for years due to his injury, was moving $70,000 between bank accounts.

But by the end of 2012, Tamerlan was stressed about money again. Dzhokhar was in the Cambridge apartment for winter break that year, with Tamerlan, Katherine, and their daughter, when the Tsarnaevs learned that they would soon be evicted. After ten years, the landlady wanted them out. She was tired of arguing about the under-market rent and tired of Tamerlan's attitude. They had six months to find a new place. Tamerlan was unlikely to find such a good deal.

A few weeks later, Tamerlan went to the regional New England Golden Gloves competition. He was no longer boxing, and he no longer wore flashy outfits. He sat in the bleachers alone. He was getting older, and it was not clear if he would ever be able to box in nationals again. According to the report from the inspectors general, Tamerlan applied for citizenship on August 28, 2012. Agents at the United States Citizenship and Immigration Services conducted what appears to be a routine background check, searching for Tamerlan's name on various databases, which alerted them to Tamerlan's 2011 FBI interview. The inspectors general report notes that the FBI does not have a standard operating procedure for processing naturalization requests when the subject has a closed case on their file.

A month later, an agent at the Boston JTTF informed Immigration Services that there was "no derogatory information related to national security" that should adversely affect Tsarnaev's eligibility for citizenship. But on December 3, 2012, the FBI provided Immigration Services with information about Tamerlan's 2009 arrest for allegedly assaulting his girlfriend, and agents requested more information from the FBI to confirm that the case did not result in a conviction. Tamerlan was interviewed by Immigration Services on January 23, 2013. Agents later stated that the only reason they did not adjudicate Tamerlan's naturalization was because they were still waiting on those records about the assault from the FBI.

$\sim$

Federal prosecutors in the bombing trial would later suggest there is a lingering mystery about who made the bombs and where. This sensational suggestion was introduced in pretrial hearings, in a retort to the defense, which was trying to bar the government from introducing the statements Dzhokhar made from his hospital bed, before he was read his Miranda rights. The government justified the interview citing national safety concerns. "These relatively sophisticated devices would have been difficult for the Tsarnaevs to fabricate successfully without training or assistance from others," said the Massachusetts US Attorney's Office in the court filing. The office also countered earlier reports that the bombs had been made at the Tsarnaev home. To make the bomb, the Tsarnaevs would have had to crush fireworks filled with fine black gunpowder. According to this government statement, investigators did not find traces of black powder in the Tsarnaev apartment—"strongly suggesting that others had built, or at least helped the Tsarnaevs build, the bombs, and thus might have built more." The federal prosecutors' argument naturally led many, myself included, to question whether the Tsarnaevs were assisted in the attack and to wonder whether a third party might still be at large, adding fuel to the fire of a growing bevy of conspiracy theories.

But when the case went to trial it became apparent that the government had in all likelihood introduced this theory to win an argument—not because they believed it was true. FBI Agent Christopher Derks testified on the stand that the Tsarnaev apartment "almost looked like a construction site." He added, "There were tools everywhere." Agents had in fact seized a soup can lid with black powder on it, as well as a drawer of nails, a pressure cooker lid, a pressure cooker gasket, tape, a hobby fuse, an igniter, wire cutters, wire strippers, Teflon tape, Gorilla Glue, and a soldering gun.

Another agent testified that the first Fagor Elite pressure cooker used in the bombing was purchased on January 31, 2013. On February 8, Tamerlan ordered a series of parts for remote-controlled toy cars, including a transmitter-receiver and a channel receiver. Then Dzhokhar borrowed a Ruger P95 pistol from a friend in Cambridge. He said he was going to use it to rob drug dealers in Rhode Island. He never returned the weapon. In March the Tsarnaevs bought another pressure cooker, paid for in cash, and drove to New Hampshire to buy gun ammunition. Around this time Dzhokhar returned again to the Cambridge apartment for spring break. Dzhokhar's prospects were no better than his brother's. He was flunking out of school and amassing a great deal of debt. When he met with his old high school friends by the banks of the Charles River, he said nothing of his worries when he opened up his backpack and put on an impromptu fireworks display. Everyone was laughing, like old times.

One of Tamerlan's Chechen friends, Magomed Dolakov, ran into the brothers at the Cambridge mosque, two days before the bombing, on April 12, 2013, according to a redacted copy of an FBI 302 report. Dolakov told FBI agents that he tried to make small talk with Tamerlan and asked to go with him to the gym sometime. Tamerlan insisted they go that very instant. Dolakov could borrow his clothes. The three of them drove to Wai Kru in the Tsarnaevs' green Honda. Dolakov noticed a medium-sized cardboard box in the rear seat.

Surveillance footage taken at Wai Kru on April 12, 2013, would later reveal Dzhokhar lackadaisically leaning on the ropes of the ring and a freshly shaved Tamerlan with his arms curled up to his chest, rotating his back in a hypnotic, snakelike motion, shadowboxing, and jumping rope.

One of the stoner guys I used to hang out with in high school also ran into Tamerlan at Wai Kru that day. In high school, Frank—he asked me not to use his real name to protect his privacy—got into predicaments at parties. He had a habit of approaching the wrong people and saying the wrong thing. He doesn't always read the room. Part of the reason Frank started going to Wai Kru in the first place was because he was tired of running away from fights—fights he had a tendency, however unwittingly, to start. So I was not altogether surprised to learn that Frank, of all people, had walked up to the Boston bomber, days before the attack, to chitchat.

Frank talks like the guys I grew up with in Newton; he swears a lot, a habit Tamerlan was allegedly not fond of. When we spoke in Frank's attic apartment on an especially warm day in June, he was twirling a spatula around his finger and swallowing raw eggs, to "bulk up."

Tamerlan first approached Frank in late 2010 when Frank was boxing another beginner. He and his sparring partner looked ridiculous, Frank told me. "Even though we didn't know what we were doing, we were entertaining. Because he was trying to kill me, and I, I was trying to hurt him too," Frank said. Tamerlan came up to him afterward. "Hey, man, your footwork is horrible, and your punches look like shit, man. You never done this before, but I like your heart," Tamerlan told him. "You don't run away." It was a compliment. Tamerlan told him to keep it up, and Frank was really flattered. Over the years Frank would approach Tamerlan for tips anytime he saw him at the gym.

That day Tamerlan went to the gym three days before the bombing with Dzhokhar and Magomed Dolakov, Frank was hitting the bag when he looked over and saw Tamerlan sitting down, lost in thought.

"Yo, what's up, man? Does this look good?" Frank asked Tamerlan and showed him a punching combination. Tamerlan told him to turn his shoulder and went back to his thoughts. But Frank prodded Tamerlan for more. Frank had been doing Brazilian jujitsu and his ground technique was pretty good, but in the ring . . . "That's when I shit my pants," Frank said. Tamerlan was not pleased to hear Frank had taken up MMA.

"All you need is boxing," Tamerlan told him. "You don't need any of that shit."

"What do you mean?" Frank asked. "What shit?"

Brazilian jujitsu, the crazy kicking, Tamerlan explained. Fighting with your elbows and knees. "You just need crisp boxing. And you need to move forward. As long as you're moving forward and your hands are better than their hands, you're gonna beat the shit out of them."

Frank was skeptical. He started asking more questions, posing more scenarios. "I kind of got the impression that I should stop. That he wasn't really down to have a conversation. He was kind of, he was kinda just telling me things. He was, like, talking at me. We weren't really conversing." But curiosity got the best of Frank, and he persisted in his questioning. "Have you ever knocked anyone out with your jab?" Frank asked.

"Of course, man," Tamerlan said. Then he started talking about street fights he'd been in.

"Dude, you punch people without gloves on?" Frank asked.

"Yeah, of course." Frank was amazed. Tamerlan also told him he'd beaten up more than one person at the same time.

"But wouldn't that hurt your wrist? Break your hand?" Frank asked. Tamerlan said that as long as you don't punch the forehead, it's fine.

"Most people, when they say something like that, I usually don't believe them. But I believed him, totally. Not only because he seemed like he was telling the truth. I knew the caliber of fighter he was," Frank told me as he swallowed another egg. "Here's the thing, man: as crazy and fucked up as Tamerlan obviously was, I remember I came away from my last talk with him with a lot of respect for him. He was helping me. He was telling me shit. He was telling me shit so I wouldn't get knocked out." Tamerlan told Frank to train by himself in the backyard with a tree.

"Just get some gloves and just practice your one-two a zillion times, man, and no one can fuck with you," Tamerlan said.

Frank said he started training in his backyard. "I was doing it the day we found out."

"You were outside punching a tree the day you found out he bombed the Boston Marathon?" I asked.

"I wasn't out by the tree, no. I woke up when my girlfriend told me that it was Tamerlan. But I went, and I fuckin' . . . It's my routine. I work out outside, you know what I mean?"

"So after you found out, you went outside and punched the tree?"

"Yeah, the tree outside, I punch the tree." He pointed out the window, at a tall oak.

"Because he told you to?"

"Because he told me to. And I still do it. That's the truth."

PART IV
A Capital Case

CHAPTER
TWENTY-SIX

He Did It

Capital cases are, by their very nature, feverous affairs. The two opposing sides in Dzhokhar Tsarnaev's death penalty trial fought viciously on one point: Should the young terrorist be condemned to execution or locked up for the rest of his life?

Dzhokhar was represented by Boston federal public defenders Timothy Watkins, William Fick, and Miriam Conrad as lead counsel. They also called in outside help from lawyers who specialized in federal death penalty cases: the soft-spoken David Bruck, who has a penchant for seersucker suits; and his frequent co-counsel Judy Clarke. Clarke and Bruck met as students at the University of South Carolina School of Law. Clarke is the antithesis of a stereotypical flashy defense attorney—but is a hero among them. She does not give interviews. She dresses like a kind schoolmarm. In Southern courts she was known to wear thin ribbons tied in a loose bow around her neck. In Boston she opted for fringed scarfs. Clarke made her career saving the lives of infamous criminals like Eric Rudolph, the Olympic Park bomber; Ted Kaczynski, the Unabomber; mass murderer Jared Lee Loughner; and Susan Smith, who sank her Mazda in a lake with her two young children inside. Clarke saved all of them from the death penalty. But not Dzhokhar.

Representing the Massachusetts US Attorney's Office were Assistant US Attorneys Aloke Chakravarty and Nadine Pellegrini. The government's lead counsel was Assistant US Attorney William Weinreb. Weinreb was quick on the draw, like a cowboy in a spaghetti Western film, ready to leap at any moment to an exacting *Objection, Your Honor*. His protests were paired with memorized legal codes and off-the-cuff full-paragraph orations. For these reasons and because of the unnervingly even-keeled manner with which Weinreb delivered arguments and retorts in favor of Dzhokhar's death, and his preference for dark suits, I began referring to him as "the Reaper" in my trial notes. The Massachusetts prosecutors also called in outside help from Steven D. Mellin, a bottle-blond attorney from Texas.

Judge George O'Toole Jr. ruled from his perch in an unrelenting monotone. This would be his last big trial before semiretirement.

Attorneys argued bitterly over whether Dzhokhar was the worst of the worst or had been led astray—at least in part—by the late Tamerlan Tsarnaev. For the most part, attorneys agreed on the basic facts of the bombing. Dzhokhar's guilt was never up for debate. Clarke began her opening statement conceding, "He did it."

~

On April 15, 2013, the two brothers with their chiseled features, dark brows, and high cheekbones strolled down Boylston Street with heavy backpacks hanging from their broad shoulders.

Marathon Monday was a cool forty-eight degrees. Perfect running weather for the more than twenty thousand athletes making their way along the arduous route through the hilly suburbs. A mass of spectators shook off the last shell of New England winter and lined the roads to cheer the runners on, as part of the tradition, more than a hundred years old.

By 2:30 p.m., the winners had already crossed the finish line, and thousands of runners were streaming into the heart of the city. The Tsarnaev brothers neared the growing swell and split up.

Tamerlan, dressed like a spy movie villain with a black baseball cap and a pair of small circular sunglasses, headed closer to the finish line, where spectators sat on folding chairs and leaned over the temporary metal fences. Dzhokhar, in a backward white baseball cap, hung around The Forum restaurant and placed his bag by a tree. Where—as the prosecution would later point out—a group of small children were gathered. At 2:49 p.m., Dzhokhar stepped away from his backpack and called his brother. The explosions went off in quick succession. Tamerlan's first. Then Dzhokhar's. Surveillance video showed fiery red explosions rise from where the backpacks had been and streams of blood flow down the street.

The bombs had been packed with BBs and nails, the purpose of which, the prosecutors would emphasize, was to shred flesh, shatter bone, set people on fire, and cause painful, bloody deaths. The bombs did just that. News reporters were on scene to cover the race with cameras rolling and shared the terrifying images with the world.

But *why?* The bombing was unique in that, although it was ideologically motivated, the messaging was not immediately clear. For four days, the Tsarnaev brothers eluded scores of police officers and federal agents. Tamerlan returned to his Cambridge apartment, while Dzhokhar went back to his college dorm at UMass Dartmouth, joked with friends, and worked out at the gym. Meanwhile, Boston waited in terrible suspense. Then, on Thursday evening, the FBI released photos of the suspects. Tamerlan and Dzhokhar shot MIT campus police officer Sean Collier in the head, hijacked an SUV, kidnapped the driver, and, for their final showdown, drove to a residential street in Watertown, where they shot at local police and set off a new round of bombs.

It was Dzhokhar, of all people, who delivered the last, and perhaps the fatal, blow to his brother. Tamerlan had run out of bullets, and a pair of Watertown officers had him in handcuffs, facedown in the street, when Dzhokhar made his getaway in the stolen Mercedes. Dzhokhar may have been trying to scare off the police officers, but he drove over his brother's body, dragging him about thirty feet before crashing into a police cruiser. Tamerlan tumbled out from beneath the vehicle as Dzhokhar screeched off into the night.

Medics got Tamerlan into an ambulance, where he let out a roar and died soon after at Beth Israel Hospital. After a massive manhunt and regional shutdown, Dzhokhar was detained in a beached boat the next day, bullet ridden yet breathing. Inside the cabin of the Watertown yacht where he'd hidden, Dzhokhar had carved a message claiming that the bombs were retribution for the wars in Afghanistan and Iraq. "We Muslims are one body, you hurt one you hurt us all," he wrote, adding that he was jealous of his brother's martyrdom.

In the hours after the marathon attack, President Barack Obama reassured the public that those individuals and groups responsible would "feel the full weight of justice." But after a throng of officers and agents surrounded the boat, and the lone teenager walked out in a bloody sweatshirt with his hands raised, it was not clear what kind of justice Dzhokhar would receive exactly, or where. The bombing was the worst terrorist attack on American soil since September 11, 2001. Would Dzhokhar be tried as an enemy combatant in a military tribunal? Obama ultimately decided not to go the way of military courts, and Attorney General Eric Holder announced that the government would seek the nation's most severe punishment: death.

CHAPTER
TWENTY-SEVEN

The Terrorists Next Door

Newton's Heartbreak Hill, the notorious climb twenty miles into the Boston Marathon, is the point in the race where people break down or make one last heroic push forward to the finish line. My mother used to bring me to the sidelines with a Tupperware container full of sliced oranges. I'd place the fruit in my sticky palms, arms stretched, fingers flat, like I was feeding a horse, and compete with my friends to see how many runners we could convince to grab slices. The sight of thousands of people with numbers pinned to their chests, whizzing, plodding, and sweating through 26.2 miles, is awe inspiring, anyone from Boston will tell you that. But I'm not especially fond of crowds or day-drinking. So, on Monday, April 15, 2013, I was sitting in an almost-empty Cambridge café, enjoying a mint tea and paying my electricity bill.

At 2:59 p.m. I received a strange message. It was from a police source I made in my NECN days. He was checking to see if I was okay. *Okay?* I checked the news. Nothing yet. I looked at Twitter. There were reports of some sort of explosion at the marathon finish line. Then I did what almost everyone in Massachusetts did that day: I checked in with everyone I knew who could have been there.

I ran home and watched the developing news coverage with my neighbors and close friends Ahlberg and Smith. We'd have another two years before

Cambridge rent hikes would disperse my community of artists and activists, but back then my friends and I lived close.

Who could have done such a thing? I assumed we would have answers in hours. Instead that question dragged on for days. On Thursday evening, I was walking home after an anxious drink at a local bar. Police had released photos of the bombing suspects to the public, but no one knew who they were or where they could be. Just as I was approaching my door, a Cambridge police cruiser drove past so fast I could smell the tires burn. I ran inside and turned on the news to see reports of a shot MIT police officer not far from my home.

The next day, after Tamerlan was killed, but while Dzhokhar remained at large, Governor Deval Patrick took the unprecedented step of issuing a regional lockdown. Everyone in Watertown, Waltham, and Cambridge was strongly encouraged to stay indoors. Smith and I nervously watched the chaotic footage of the manhunt on the news and sipped champagne. It was Smith's birthday. The bottle was initially meant for later that evening, when Smith's friends had planned a party in their apartment on Norfolk Street—the same street the Tsarnaevs lived on, as we learned that morning. Meanwhile, thousands of police officers and agents in military tanks made their way through Watertown's winding streets, looking for Dzhokhar.

Later that evening, we did eventually make our way to Norfolk Street. I watched the glow of police lights a few blocks down before stepping inside to process it all over birthday cake and beer. That's when I heard from Ahlberg. Tamerlan had been in Ahlberg's homeroom at Cambridge Rindge and Latin. Ahlberg was running late.

There were about a dozen of us intermittently trading anecdotes of our hours in lockdown, stories of family members who had run the marathon days before—all of whom were thankfully safe—while we tried to make sense of what had happened. *Who were the terrorists next door?* Smith's friends had moved to Cambridge for school or to work at start-ups. They did not know their neighbors.

When Ahlberg arrived at the party, Ahlberg's head was in another place. How could Ahlberg possibly reconcile the violence of the last few days with the Tamerlan Ahlberg knew from school? Tamerlan asked Ahlberg's friend to prom—a woman I also knew and liked. The friend turned him down, and Tamerlan showed up alone. The image of Tamerlan in a tuxedo, all by himself, throbbed in Ahlberg's brain. Ahlberg sat in the corner, nibbled on a brownie, and left.

CHAPTER
TWENTY-EIGHT

A Shooting in Orlando

On Saturday, the day after Dzhokhar was detained, I was sitting at my kitchen table reading a profile of the Tsarnaev brothers in the *Boston Globe*. Buried in the 3,500-word story was a note about how Tamerlan and Brendan Mess had been "best friends" and trained together at Wai Kru. This was the first I'd learned about Tamerlan and Brendan's relationship.

I read the article and looked at my refrigerator. On the freezer door, I had stuck photos of Erik, part of the pamphlet his family handed out at his Yahrzeit, the one-year anniversary of his death. The date of his death was printed on the card in large, white numbers: *9-11-11*. Was Erik a victim of a terrorist attack? I felt a wave of emotion rush over my body, the kind of wave that chokes you with salt water and bashes your head in the sand. The pain was worse than it was in September 2011. Which may not make sense, but others who knew Erik, Rafi, and Brendan would tell me they felt the same way. It wasn't just the sorrow, which felt just as raw somehow. I regretted those angry thoughts I'd had about Erik, every one. I was mad at myself this time, and I was also ashamed. All those doubts and misgivings I had about the strange nature of the murders and law enforcement's almost dismissive statements—unease that I had tried to quell for too long—came rushing back as well. I thought not only of Erik but also the four dead I did not know: Lingzi Lu, 23, Krystle Campbell, 29, and Sean Collier, 27. Most of all I thought of eight-year-old bombing victim Martin

Richard and the photo of him with his buckteeth, at an elementary school class event holding a homemade sign that read **"No More Hurting People. Peace."** Were Erik's murder and the bombing all part of the same terrible story? I had known in my gut that there was something terribly wrong with the murders in Waltham, and I did nothing.

Two days later, the *Boston Globe* reported that police were looking into a potential connection between Tamerlan Tsarnaev and the Waltham murder case. "Police and prosecutors are stepping up their investigation into the unsolved 2011 triple homicide at the request of victims' relatives who believe that suspected marathon bomber Tamerlan Tsarnaev may have played a role."

While I was open to the idea that there might be a connection between Tamerlan and the Waltham murders, I was in no way convinced. I had not seen any evidence of his involvement. With the same facts, it was possible to speculate and reach an entirely different conclusion. What if Tamerlan Tsarnaev didn't kill those men in Waltham? What if he grieved? What if the loss of his American friend was what pushed him over the edge? But this was a matter of national security now. I tried to trust that law enforcement and intelligence agencies on every level would do everything they could to get to the bottom of what happened.

~

The night of the manhunt, Aria had been glued to the news. In the morning, when the Tsarnaevs' identities were revealed, she learned the bombers went to her high school in Cambridge. That connection alone was surreal. Then a couple hours later, she got a text from an acquaintance: "Do you think they have anything to do with your brother's murder?" A flood of messages asking her about a possible connection followed, but it still didn't make sense in Aria's head. "I barely had time to process the bombing," Aria told me. That the bombing might be related to her brother's murder was too much to comprehend.

Aria called state trooper Erik P. Gagnon on Saturday, the day after Dzhokhar was detained. Was there a connection between Tamerlan and her brother's murder? Was he investigating the connection? Aria had not heard from Gagnon in over a year. He told Aria he would look into it on Monday.

Meanwhile, Erik's family was inundated with media inquiries. Journalists called their phones, sneaked into their apartment buildings, and left notes under their doors. In some ways it was refreshing. For eighteen months, Aria had longed for more media attention on Erik's case, hoping that it might lead to a break in the investigation. Now journalists all over the world were asking questions. But they were only asking questions about Tamerlan, not her brother or the murders, for the most part, she said.

Aria called Gagnon back on Monday. He asked Aria for Erik's cell phone number and the name of the gym where Brendan worked out. *Shouldn't he have that information already?* she thought. The police seized Erik's phones with the rest of his belongings. *Shouldn't they have his phone number as well?* Aria did not bring this up on the phone. She gave Gagnon Erik's number. She said she would ask around about Brendan's gym. Neither Gagnon nor any of the investigators reached out to her with questions again.

~

Cory had plans to watch the marathon but never did. He and his girlfriend grabbed food at Cambridge Lunch and took a nap. He woke up to disturbing calls that a friend's cousin had been hurt. Cory knew Krystle Campbell, a beloved waitress from Medford. Brendan had known her as well, though not intimately.

After the bombing and then the manhunt, Sam was glued to the news. Around 7:00 a.m., Tamerlan Tsarnaev's photo flashed on the screen. Sam knew that face. It was Tam. Brendan's friend. Sam picked up the phone and called the Waltham Police Department. "That's the kid we told you about back then," Sam told them. "Who never showed up to the service."

For Cory, the Friday that the Tsarnaevs were identified as the bombers was especially surreal. After Dzhokhar was detained he drove to Dylan's. The FBI was on their way, Dylan said. Cory had never suspected Tamerlan of murder. Then again, he couldn't imagine Tamerlan would bomb the marathon either.

FBI Agent Aaron McFarlane arrived with a partner. They asked Cory and Dylan if they had anything that belonged to Tamerlan, and Dylan went inside and brought out Tamerlan's boxing gloves and a poster of the word *LOVE* spelled out in knives that Tamerlan had given him the year before. The agents asked where Tamerlan prayed and how religious he was. They asked if he had ever tried to preach to them. They said he had. Then the agents asked what Tamerlan watched and read, and if he ever brought anyone else with him. "He didn't. He kind of traveled solo everywhere. So it was really weird," Cory said. The agents asked them questions about organized crime, if Tamerlan had guns, and who his friends were, where he worked, and about his family. They didn't have many answers, because Tam was not around much after Brendan's death, Cory said. A few weeks later, McFarlane asked to meet the two men again at Dwelltime, a café in Inman Square. McFarlane was accompanied by Detective Patrick Hart of the Waltham PD. They took Cory and Dylan to the back of an unmarked minivan. It was armored inside, and bulletproof vests hung on the walls. The investigators showed Cory and Dylan an array of mug shots. The men looked like fighters. Cory noted their scars. The last one, a bony-looking man with dark hair and a broken nose, looked vaguely familiar. Five days later, the same photo would flash on news screens across the country. The man was Ibragim Todashev, and an FBI agent had shot him dead.

~

On May 23, 2013, I walked across the Charles River to the Boston University campus and my job at the Frederick S. Pardee Center for the Study of the Longer-Range Future. I arrived early to prepare for a conference on emerging economies. My old history professor was no longer the director, and I was now working under a highly acclaimed climatologist, who, though sympathetic, was not entirely pleased that my drug dealer's murder consumed my every waking thought.

There were no new stories about the murders, and in lieu of answers, I read everything about Tamerlan Tsarnaev I could find, including blog posts authored by armchair investigators—people who were making connections about the case via news articles and court documents but were not doing the work of actual journalists, namely, making phone calls and knocking on doors. There was nowhere else to turn for information, so I read through this material carefully, trying to make sense of the speculation.

That morning a story about Erik's murder did break across the news. At first, the connection was not clear. There had been a shooting in Orlando, Florida, involving a Boston FBI agent, two Massachusetts state troopers, and an associate of Tamerlan Tsarnaev's. News helicopters hovered over a beige condo just outside Universal Studios. According to the early reports, the investigators were questioning this individual when, moments after midnight, something went wrong, and the FBI agent shot the man dead.

Later that morning, reporters identified the deceased as Ibragim Todashev and publicized his mug shot, taken after a road rage incident in a parking lot two weeks before. Ibragim was not wearing a shirt, and his clavicles were exposed. He looked at the camera with dark, blank eyes.

For the most part, journalists were crediting anonymous law enforcement officials as sources. According to these unnamed sources, investigators had been questioning Ibragim Todashev about a triple murder in Waltham. I looked at Ibragim's photo, then back at the reporting attributed to anonymous sources. Were the answers to Erik's murder hiding outside Disney World? Who was Ibragim, and what did he know? Emerging economies would have to wait. I clicked link after link, trying to make sense of what I was learning.

Florida TV stations played interviews with Ibragim's friend Khusen Taramov, another young Chechen man with muscular arms and a handsome face, who spoke to reporters outside of the condo complex. He was in distress. Khusen said that Ibragim used to live in Boston and he used to train with Tamerlan at the gym. Allegedly, Tamerlan had a brief Skype call with Ibragim a month before the bombing. Khusen had not heard of a murder in Waltham and believed that it was because of that phone call and that phone call alone that the FBI wanted to talk to Ibragim. Ibragim was a good guy, Khusen said, not a terrorist. "He wasn't radical at all. He wasn't radical. He just was Muslim. You know what I mean? I'm a Muslim. The Chechens are Muslim. He was Muslim. That was his mistake, I guess."

This was not Ibragim's first interview, said Khusen. Agents spoke to Ibragim regularly in the month after Tamerlan was killed. Khusen said agents were surveilling Ibragim and his friends. He thought the interviews were done. Then a couple of days later, a fleet of agents in unmarked vehicles with tinted windows started circling Khusen's home. Ibragim was with Khusen at the time. While the cars were driving around the apartment, an Orlando officer called Ibragim's phone and told him that men had come down from Boston. They wanted to talk to him, just one last meeting.

Ibragim told Khusen he had misgivings. He said they were making up "crazy stuff." Ibragim was afraid of a "bad setup," Khusen told reporters.

But Khusen encouraged Ibragim to go. "If you don't do it, they're not going to leave you alone," Khusen said.

By late afternoon, NBC was reporting that, according to anonymous sources, Ibragim had implicated himself and Tamerlan in the Waltham murders, allegedly claiming that they killed the men after a drug rip-off because they did not want to leave any witnesses. The *Washington Post*, the *New York Times*, and the *Boston Globe* quickly followed with similar stories, all reporting that, according to anonymous sources, Ibragim had confessed. It didn't make sense. How could the murder be an afterthought? Of course the men would be able to identify Tamerlan; Tamerlan had been friends with Brendan.

Each report said that Ibragim tried to harm the officers in some way, and that's why the agent shot him. This was, again, all attributed to anonymous sources. But the news outlets appeared to be citing different anonymous sources, and the sources all had slightly different accounts.

First, NBC and the Associated Press reported that Ibragim was armed with a knife. Then, the *Washington Post* reported that he had tried to grab the agent's gun. The *New York Times* later said he was armed with a pipe. Then there was reporting that he had pushed a table and thrown a chair. Finally the *Washington Post* issued another story, this time citing sources who said Ibragim was unarmed.

I was waiting for a press briefing, an official announcement from the FBI—from anyone—to explain what happened and to address the Waltham murder case. But the only official account was a brief statement from the FBI press office, released the day of Ibragim Todashev's death, explaining that the Bureau was reviewing a fatal shooting incident involving an FBI special agent at 6022 Peregrine Avenue. They also confirmed that two Massachusetts State Police troopers had been present as well—one was assigned to the Middlesex County District Attorney's Office, and the other was assigned to a fugitive task force—and that they had been questioning an individual in connection to the Boston Marathon bombing investigation. No one said anything about the Waltham murders on the record. One week later, the Bureau issued a second statement giving assurances that their internal review was effective and "time-tested" and would be "thorough and objective and conducted as expeditiously as possible under the circumstances."

~

The story about Ibragim Todashev was everywhere, on the front page of the newspapers that lined the boxes I passed on my way to work and on the TV screen at the sushi restaurant when I went out to eat with coworkers. As if I needed a reminder. I'd begin a new search for the story every five minutes or so, clicking refresh again and again, hoping for updates.

I tried to trust the FBI's statement that they would conduct a thorough investigation into the shooting. But weeks passed, then months. I learned about other FBI shooting investigations, and the procedure did not seem as objective or time-tested as the Bureau claimed. Charlie Savage and Michael S. Schmidt at the *New York Times* reported that the FBI had cleared their own agents of wrongdoing in every single internal shooting review in at least two decades—150 incidents in which seventy people were killed and eighty were injured. Then Maria Sacchetti of the *Boston Globe* reported that in other fatal FBI shootings the Bureau had immediately released details, assuring the public that the agents had shot in self-defense. That's not what happened in Orlando.

I first learned of Ibragim's wife, Reni—a young woman with a serious disposition, bright eyes and a svelte jaw—when I watched a video of a press conference in my office at the research center. The Tampa chapter of the Council on American-Islamic Relations (CAIR) organized the event and the director was expressing concern that Ibragim had been held in his apartment against his will. Khusen sat by her side. He said that the FBI's account of the shooting was essentially, "Oh, yes we killed him, but he was a murderer." If Ibragim confessed to murder, why wasn't he arrested? The only person who could refute the FBI's account is dead, and "dead men don't tell tales."

Reniya Manukyan rides a motorcycle and goes by Reni, for short. Her family is Russian, though she was born in Armenia. In America, she became a naturalized citizen, converted to Islam, and found housekeeping jobs working at hotels outside of Atlanta. Reni and Ibragim did not live together at the time of his death. We would speak for hours, over the course of years. Which made it all the more unnerving when, later, I started to question the accuracy of her accounts. She was loyal to Ibragim long after his death. It's unclear if he held her in such high regard.

As I listened to her speak at that initial press conference, she insisted that the allegations about her husband murdering three men in Massachusetts were "absolutely not true."

"Was Mr. Todashev in Boston September 11 of 2011?" an unidentified reporter asked at the May 16, 2013, press conference.

"No, he wasn't," Reni said.

"Where was he at the time?" asked the reporter.

"He was in Atlanta, Georgia," Reni said.

"Was he with you?" the reporter asked.

"Yes," Reni said.

Reni claimed she had bank statements to prove he was not in Massachusetts. She never showed them to me.

In the spring of 2013, Ian McCleod was locked up in state prison in Virginia. But when he learned Tamerlan was the bomber and there might be a connection between the bombing and Brendan's murder, he wanted to help if he could. He said he reached out to law enforcement through his attorney and was interviewed by two FBI agents, shortly after Ibragim was killed. He did not recall the agents' names, but he did recall that one of them had a gash on his head and blood in his eye. The agents showed Ian a series of photos of men who he said "looked like they were in the Taliban." Ian didn't recognize any of them. The agents also asked about Hiba, but from what Ian could tell they were trying to see if Hiba was radical. Ian said they asked a lot of questions about her Muslim faith. They also seemed to be exploring the idea that there was more to Tamerlan and Hiba's relationship. To Ian, it seemed like they were trying to figure out if Tamerlan had been radicalized through Hiba, which Ian thought was absolutely preposterous. Hiba happened to be Muslim, but he never at any point in their yearslong friendship got the impression that she was radical, or even that devout. No one in the decade-plus I have been reporting on this story has ever told me that they believed Hiba to be sympathetic to violent ideology or anti-Semitism. The agents' questions about Hiba's religion and ethnic background made Ian uncomfortable. He worried agents could be targeting her unfairly. Ian said investigators were also curious about other people he knew who happened to be Muslim. He was worried on their behalf as well. It was a frustrating interview. He wanted to talk about the Waltham murders. But investigators did not ask many questions about Brendan. They *did* ask a lot about Jay, Hiba's late husband.

Ian was wary of how Brendan's friends spoke of Hiba. Sure, Brendan and Hiba fought, but around him Hiba was always "Miss Positive." She was a party girl, and she knew how to turn up any scenario and make it "an enjoyable situation at all times."

On the other hand, Ian was a little suspicious of Jay. He wondered if Jay had been jealous or upset by how Brendan had treated Hiba. Jay was a chill dude, but he could be vengeful at times, Ian said. He said he knew Jay had plotted on at least one occasion to get back at someone who had slighted Hiba. But Ian had all sorts of theories rolling around his head. "In my mind I thought anybody—anybody—could have been involved. So I was literally exploring all angles," he said.

In the weeks after the murders, Ian told Hiba to get out of Massachusetts. He wanted to make sure she was safe. But he also had questions. Ian took it upon himself to look into the matter. He kept in contact with Hiba and Jay, kept tabs on what they were up to, and collected information on both of them to see if he could make sense of their stories. Ian was under the impression that Jay and Hiba still spoke regularly throughout Hiba's relationship with Brendan and after the murders. Jay told Ian that Hiba was "devastated" after Brendan died. In their last conversations, Jay also talked to Ian about suicide. But according to Ian, Jay explicitly said he did not understand how anyone could take their own life. "Jay was dismissive of anyone who was suicidal," Ian said. "He thought it was stupid." Jay also told Ian that Jay himself planned to talk to Hiba about the murders. Perhaps Hiba would confide to Jay what she would not confide to Ian, at least that was Ian's thinking. Jay told Ian he was planning to meet with Hiba soon, and he would tell Ian what he learned.

After Jay met with Hiba, around 3:00 or 4:00 a.m., Ian said Jay sent him a text. Ian can't remember what the text said verbatim, but it was something along the lines of "I got some crazy shit to tell," and to call him back. Ian assumed the crazy shit had something to do with Hiba and the murders, because that was their last discussion. But before Ian could get back in touch with Jay, Jay was dead. Now Ian was really freaked out. Jay's death was ruled a suicide, but Jay had just told Ian in plain terms there was no way he would ever do that. Before Jay died, Ian did not take the suspicions about Hiba seriously. Now he did. But he and Hiba still kept in touch. After the bombing, she reached out to him on Facebook.

On May 20, 2013, at 9:48 a.m., Hiba sent Ian a message: "Hi Ian, Wow things just keep getting crazier and crazier huh? Im just gla[d] to know that Jay isnt involved as I originally thought. Hope you're well."

I wouldn't learn about Jay's cryptic last message to Ian or Hiba's stated suspicions about Jay until 2021.

In 2013, in the months after the bombing, stories about Hiba were in the back of my mind, but I had to figure out what happened to Ibragim first.

∼

In 2013, in the weeks after Ibragim was killed, reporter Maria Sacchetti wrote another report in the *Boston Globe*. Tatiana Gruzdeva, a nineteen-year-old woman from Moldova, had been living with Ibragim in the condo where he died. Five days before Ibragim Todashev's fatal interview, Tatiana was arrested for overstaying her visa. The article said Tatiana was still behind bars and was set to be deported to Russia on July 1.

I looked Tatiana up on Facebook. She had long blond hair and liked to pose for pictures with puppies and large bouquets of roses. I sent her a Facebook request, not expecting a response, and went back to scouring the internet for information.

CHAPTER
TWENTY-NINE
[Insert Kafka Reference Here]

Weeks, then months, went by, and not only were there no answers about Erik's murder or the shooting in Orlando, but it wasn't clear which agency was looking into the different parts of the investigation, where answers would come from, or whether we would have any answers at all. At first the FBI was the only agency reviewing Ibragim's death. Ultimately, a review of the shooting was conducted by the DOJ's Civil Rights Division. But a note on the report reveals that it was authored in association with "agents with the FBI Inspection Division." So it was not an entirely independent review.

Aria learned about the Orlando shooting in the news like everyone else. She called the Middlesex DA's Office after the story broke and spoke to a victims' advocate. The advocate could confirm that a man named Ibragim Todashev was dead, but Aria said they could "not confirm or deny" anything else, not even that Massachusetts state troopers were present for the shooting.

The Middlesex County District Attorney's Office, newly helmed by Marian Ryan after Gerry Leone stepped down, did issue a brief statement on the 2011 triple homicide after the shooting. The statement did not address the shooting in Florida or address Ibragim or Tamerlan by name. The office asserted only that the Waltham case was still "open and active" and that the office and their law enforcement partners had conducted a "thorough, far-reaching investigation" beginning in 2011. "This investigation has not concluded and is by no means closed," the statement read. The statement also noted that the Middlesex DA's Office was investigating the homicides in coordination with the FBI. The FBI was not mentioned in the district attorney's future statements. I later found out in internal documents I received via a federal records request that the Middlesex DA's Office would go on to block FBI agents reviewing the shooting from accessing the Waltham murder case files, and an assistant district attorney would refuse to answer agents' questions about murder evidence.

The district attorney's statement did, however, note the Massachusetts Rules of Professional Conduct, Rule 3.6, "Trial Publicity," at length. This was a rule that the office insisted prevented them from providing any information whatsoever on an open case. The press release did not cite the section of the same rule that also asserts that there are vital social interests served by the free dissemination of information and that "the public has a right to know about threats to its safety and measures aimed at assuring its security."

It should be noted that in addition to the Boston FBI agent, the interview team in Orlando included a Massachusetts state trooper assigned to the fugitive task force and a Massachusetts state trooper assigned to the Middlesex County District Attorney's Office. Although this was not made clear in any of the public statements, records I obtained later reveal the interview was apparently led by the Middlesex County District Attorney's Office. The trooper assigned to the District Attorney's Office led the questioning, and the three men in the room were taking orders from Assistant District Attorney Stephen Loughlin, who instructed the men not to cuff Todashev after he allegedly confessed.

For many years, I reported on this story with the naive optimism that one authority or another would eventually release an official report on the Waltham case. At the time of writing, that moment has yet to arise.

∼

Ibragim Todashev was killed in Orange County, Florida, a county that was then presided over by State Attorney Jeffrey Ashton—Florida's equivalent of a district attorney. Ashton is perhaps best known for prosecuting Casey Anthony for allegedly murdering her two-year-old daughter, in a widely televised six-week death penalty trial. Anthony was found not guilty of murder.

Ashton initially declined to conduct an independent investigation into Ibragim's killing. However, according to records of his communications obtained in a records request, he grew concerned there might be a "backlash from the public" once the medical examiner's report, which the FBI had initially blocked from the public, revealed Ibragim was shot in the back. In August 2013, more than two months after the shooting, Ashton announced that he would review witness and forensic evidence in the case. "The prosecutor's inquiry marks the first state investigation of a shooting that has been cloaked in secrecy," Maria Sacchetti wrote in the *Boston Globe*.

Ashton's decision to review Ibragim's shooting death was applauded by civil rights groups like CAIR and the ACLU. But how independent could Ashton's review be if he was receiving the forensic evidence and crime scene photos directly from the FBI? The Bureau had sealed off the crime scene immediately after Ibragim Todashev was killed and did not call the Medical Examiner's Office until two hours later. Would the Florida State Attorney's review include the events leading up to the fatal killing or the moment the agent pulled the trigger alone? And would he examine the veracity of Todashev's alleged confession? To do so, he would need access to the Middlesex County District Attorney Office's case files, which the district attorney would not supply.

Nor was the Florida State Attorney's Office aware that the FBI agent who shot Ibragim, Agent Aaron McFarlane, had a checkered past. McFarlane had been an officer in the Oakland Police Department, where he testified in defense of an infamous gang of Oakland police officers dubbed the Riders. The Riders were charged with making false arrests, planting evidence, and falsifying police reports. During the course of his testimony, McFarlane pleaded the Fifth to protect himself from self-incrimination, as was first reported by Maria Sacchetti in the *Boston Globe*. In the same story Sacchetti reported that McFarlane had also been the subject of two brutality lawsuits, and even though he had left the department in 2004 on disability due to an on-the-job leg injury he claimed prevented him from working, he still received an annual pension of $52,000 from the police department despite being employed by the FBI at the time of the shooting nine years later.

Martha Coakley was the Massachusetts attorney general, the state's top legal officer, at the time of the bombing. She was also campaigning, making what would be a failed run for governor. While district attorneys do not typically answer to the attorney general directly, the AG is supposed to oversee all district attorneys in the state. According to Massachusetts General Law statute 12, section 27, it appears Coakley could take over any investigation handled by a Massachusetts district attorney. The law states that the attorney general and the district attorney "may interchange official duties" and "the attorney general, when present, shall have the control" of all criminal and civil cases in the Commonwealth.

Shortly after Florida State Attorney Jeffrey Ashton announced he would conduct a review of Ibragim Todashev's death, Aria Weissman and Dylan Mess approached Attorney General Martha Coakley at a ceremony for homicide victims, where she had been slated to speak.

Coakley said that she did not have jurisdiction to investigate the Florida shooting herself, even though Massachusetts state troopers were involved. She said she had not been in touch directly with the Florida district attorney and did not have a timeline for when their report would be done. But she promised Aria and Dylan, "[If] you do not get the answers that you want"—and if Ashton's report wasn't satisfactory—"then I will do everything that I can to get it."

"How about a further investigation just on the Waltham triple murder, not so much what happened in Florida, but just what's going on here?" Dylan asked. "It feels like whoever is on it really is not up to the task. But it also feels like if the number one suspect is an American terrorist and the Boston bomber, it seems like it should be a focus of national security to look into that murder. Obviously he couldn't have done it by himself. Most like there are a few people out there still at large," Dylan said.

"It feels like it got swept under the rug," added Aria.

"I know that at the time they seemed very frustrated on leads, and until the bombing happened didn't make that connection at all," Coakley told Aria and Dylan. Coakley promised to be in touch with the Florida State Attorney and to make sure that Middlesex and Waltham were working together on the case. But she didn't. When I followed up weeks later, neither the Waltham PD nor the Florida office had been contacted. Documents would later show that the Middlesex office did not share case files with Ashton's office. Instead Ashton gleaned information about the unsolved murder from Wikipedia.

Coakley's chief of staff, Corey Welford, did get in touch with Aria about the Waltham murders. "We know the case is open. We're not sure if it's active," Welford told Aria when he called. Welford promised a victims' advocate from Middlesex would be in touch with Aria soon. But no one called.

∼

Officials would remain silent on the circumstances of Ibragim Todashev's death for ten months until, in a coordinated effort, the DOJ and the Florida State Attorney's Office released their reports and cleared the agent shooter of any wrongdoing. The reports found Aaron McFarlane fired in self-defense. This finding was based on the moment McFarlane pulled the trigger, not the decisions investigators and those above them made leading up to that point, which created a situation in which investigators confronted a trained fighter about an unsolved murder in his own home for three and a half hours.

In the Florida State Attorney's review, Jeffrey Ashton concluded that he found no evidence of misconduct, malice, or poor judgment on behalf of the agent shooter. He also made clear that his bar for such findings was high. He cited an appeals court decision that questions "whether a law enforcement officer should ever be, in the absence of intentional misconduct or some degree of malice, criminally responsible for using poor judgment."

In his open letter to FBI Director James Comey, Ashton wrote that Ibragim "was, at his core, a fearless fighter" who "simply didn't have any quit in him." Perhaps on this occasion, Ashton speculated, Ibragim "simply reverted to that basic aspect of his personality and chose to go down fighting."

The report written by the Civil Rights Division of the DOJ in collaboration with the FBI made clear that their finding was not based on whether or not there was wrongdoing. The review sought to determine if there was enough evidence of wrongdoing to bring charges. To find wrongdoing, the government would have to prove that a member of law enforcement willfully deprived a person of their constitutional rights or conspired to use unwarranted, unnecessary, and unreasonable force. The DOJ concluded that "the evidence does not reveal a prosecutable violation."

Days after the shooting reports were released, the Middlesex County District Attorney's Office issued another statement asserting once more that the investigation into the Waltham murders was "open and active." The office did not address allegations about Ibragim Todashev's or Tamerlan Tsarnaev's involvement in the crime. Instead the office stated that "identifying all parties for that terrible incident" remained a top priority.

CHAPTER THIRTY

Conspiracies

Erik's mother, Bellie, was furious when she learned of Ibragim's death. Through the nightmare of the bombing and the endless requests for interviews, she still believed there was a real opportunity to utilize the FBI's help and get answers. Now a man who could have provided answers was dead. And yet for all Bellie knew, Ibragim was innocent.

"The last thing the US government needs to do is fuel wild conspiracy theories by releasing too little information or investigating too slowly," the *Washington Post*'s editorial board wrote after Ibragim was killed. The paper called for the Obama administration to get involved and "move heaven and earth" to release an account to the public. Of course, that never happened.

Over at InfoWars, Alex Jones had claimed the Tsarnaevs were framed, disseminating the angle first put forth by *RT News*. When Ibragim was killed Jones's outrage reached a satisfied boil. "They want to secretly disappear us, secretly kill us, secretly torture us!" he railed. "They've declared national security on his autopsy and what the FBI did!" To the later point, Jones was actually right. The FBI had taken the unusual step of blocking the release of the medical examiner's report. Instead, information about Ibragim's bullet-ridden corpse came from Abdulbaki Todashev, Ibragim's father.

There was a press conference for Abdulbaki Todashev in Moscow in which the grieving father waved photos of Ibragim's corpse before the press. The photos were taken by Khusen Taramov at the morgue and appeared to show Ibragim had been shot seven times, including three times in the back and once in the top of the head. "They came to his house like bandits and shot him in cold blood," Abdulbaki said with the help of a translator. These were trained men, Abdulbaki insisted. Ibragim's death could not have been an accident. "Maybe my son knew something police didn't want to come out, and they killed him to keep him silent," he said. He did not elaborate on what Ibragim could have known.

What country do I live in? Bellie thought. She actually felt a kind of kinship with Abdulbaki. Here was a man who, like her, lost his son to a violent death and was desperate for answers. "It's like our own democracy is crumbling underneath us. We're killing a person, we don't know why, and we're not given any information about it," she said. "We're the family. I'm his mother. I gave birth to him! Tell me what happened to my son! Tell me what you know."

Before the bombing, Bellie focused on her son's life and tried not to dwell on questions about what happened. Now thoughts about Erik's death were inescapable. Every development would stir her anguish anew.

Aria was also tormented by questions surrounding Ibragim's death. "Why did he need to get shot seven times?" she asked. Grappling with her brother's death was hard enough, but now she was trying to process the fact that Erik's open murder case may have been connected to the largest terrorism attack on US soil since 9/11 and an FBI shooting in Florida. Or maybe Erik's death was not really connected to any of this at all. Maybe it was all a ruse. With no one officially confirming the reporting in the press, Aria didn't know what to believe. The thought that her brother's death might be part of a cover-up or conspiracy was terrifying. Were they pinning her brother's murder on "two dead guys" to take the spotlight off Waltham and halt the investigation? Nothing made sense. "How much crazier can it get?" she asked me. She found catharsis watching Kerry Washington on the political thriller *Scandal*. The fictional plotline revealing a maze of government secrets actually felt relatable.

After the marathon bombing, I was all thought and no action. Then Ibragim was killed. Either his death was a massive cover-up or federal agencies were not nearly as capable as I imagined them to be. If the latter was true, I thought there would be some sort of system to address those errors. But the Bureau's actions (and their inaction) gave credence to the growing body of conspiracy theories. It wasn't hard to believe that there was something sinister happening behind the scenes and that agencies and officials were working to save face, rather than serve the public interest and security. Was Ibragim killed because he knew too much? Knew too much about what? I had no idea. But I had to do something. Or at least try.

Journalists are supposed to hold systems of power accountable. So I figured that's how I could help. I discussed my concerns with my father, who is always game to get on the phone to talk through a homicide—or whatever else is on my mind. Reporters at the *New York Times*, Serge F. Kovaleski and Richard A. Oppel Jr., were calling him as well. They found his name listed in Erik's court documents. My father did not tell the reporters that Erik was his daughter's friend. He was patient, and he was also protective. He didn't want me to get involved.

So my doting father scooped me. He sent the *New York Times* reporters to Cambridge Lunch, but he didn't tell them why. When they got there, Dana gave Kovaleski and Oppel my number, along with my first name. When Oppel called, I told him I was the reason they went to the diner in the first place. I spoke with him and Kovaleski. I told them about my fears and the questions I wanted answered. Did police have Tamerlan's name back then? Did police question him?

The *New York Times* was the first to report that, in fact, several of Brendan's friends said they told police about Tamerlan before the murders, listing him as one of Brendan's closest associates. The *New York Times* spoke to another individual who said they alerted investigators again after Tamerlan did not show up to Brendan's memorial. It should be noted that an anonymous law enforcement source, quoted by the *New York Times*, flat out denied Brendan's associates provided investigators with Tamerlan's name. The *New York Times* was also the first to report that after the murders, investigators never went to the Wai Kru gym, where Brendan worked out with Tamerlan several days a week, which I would also confirm. They quoted me in the kicker: "Susan Zalkind, a friend of Mr. Weissman's and a freelance journalist who has been looking into the case since 2011, said she remains surprised how few friends of victims the police talked to. 'Despite being one of the most gruesome and unusual crimes of the year, I saw the least amount of public outreach,' she said."

The front page story caught the attention of Nazanin Rafsanjani, a producer for *The Rachel Maddow Show*. After a couple of phone discussions, Rafsanjani invited me on as a guest. I had two hours to tell my boss at the research center I was leaving work early to go to New York City to talk about my dead drug dealer on national television, pack, and hop on the train. I tried to straighten my one red silk shirt under the Amtrak bathroom hand dryer. My hair was still wet and in a braid when I got to the studio with about seven minutes to spare. The makeup artists coated me with concealer and blasted me with a blow dryer, and a producer ran me on set with Rachel, where I sputtered something about how Ibragim's alleged confession only raises more painful questions for the people closest to this case. I said *weird* a lot and made strained facial expressions.

Rachel Maddow, of course, spoke succinctly. "Since Ibragim Todashev was killed, it has been sewed up in the press. The national press has been sold the story that Ibragim Todashev confessed. It was him and Tamerlan Tsarnaev, case closed. Both the perpetrators are dead, and it is over. I am critical of the way the national press has picked this up because I feel like they bought this hook, line, and sinker as an anonymous tip from law enforcement sources that have told things about this case that haven't turned out to be true in the past."

"I have nothing but questions," I told her. "Knowing one of the victims, having those questions unanswered, it's really painful." Around this time I also began interviewing Erik's family. When I first sat down with Aria, she told me that meeting Erik's friends was always a gift. She treasured every anecdote and every memory of her brother. I noticed Erik's signature was tattooed on her wrist. I would speak to family members of all three victims, some more regularly than others, over the course of the next decade. These were painful conversations. They wanted answers. But ideally, these answers would not be coming from me.

Other reporters contacted me as well. I didn't mind helping. I didn't think I could investigate this story on my own, not all the way. One journalist who asked for help insisted that I could never report on this case myself because of my relationship to a victim. My best option, she said, was to give all my information to her and her partner, the senior reporter who hit on me after dangling a work opportunity. When I told her the story about her partner's behavior—a pattern with him, I would learn from talking to other young women—she said I was overreacting. All media men are like that, she said. Usually worse. I was embarrassed I brought it up. This case was bigger than me. If giving them all my sources was really my only option, I was determined to get over my unease about interacting with the senior reporter. Still, I hesitated before moving forward with the arrangement.

Another note I received was from a senior science reporter at a different prominent Boston news outlet. He informed me he was investigating the Waltham case and had information that might be of interest.

~

There is nothing inherently wrong or delusional about conspiracy theories. In her seminal book *Real Enemies: Conspiracy Theories and American Democracy, World War I to 9/11*, first published in 2010, historian Kathryn S. Olmsted asserts that a conspiracy theory is nothing more than a theory about collusion "that may or may not be true; it has not yet been proven." As Olmsted points out, conspiracies do happen, and fears about wrongdoings and cover-ups are not without precedent. The government propagates their own "conspiracy theories" too. Olmsted points to Watergate and the pretexts for the Iraq War, for example. The problem isn't the theories, writes Olmsted; it's the people who come to "believe in their theories the way zealots believe in their religion: nothing can change their mind."

Since the publication of Olmsted's book, conspiracy theories have come to play an increasingly significant role in political and public discourse. But in the summer of 2013, few were cognizant of the growing phenomenon or its potential harm. I read the news, and then I read blogs, dozens of them. The bloggers claiming the Tsarnaevs were framed seemed outlandish. There were offensive theories about the bombing victims being actors. But others who questioned the extent of the FBI's previous interactions with Tamerlan exacerbated my own creeping concerns. I was wary of outlets like *Russia Today* but perhaps not wary enough.

Over the course of my investigation, reading Olmsted's and other academic studies helped me cut through the narratives surrounding this case and informed the way I shaped my reporting into the story you are reading now. Brian L. Keeley is a professor of philosophy at Pitzer College, and in his 1999 paper "Of Conspiracy Theories," he argues that people latch on to theories out of a deep-seated desire to make sense of a seemingly chaotic world. "Conspiracy theorists are, I submit, some of the last believers in an ordered universe," he writes. It may be terrifying to imagine there is an evil cabal at the helm of world power—but it is scarier, maybe, to think that perhaps no one is in control at all. Keeley cautions us to watch out for conspiracy theories that tie together unrelated events and make sense of errant data. Another warning sign is when the theory becomes impossible to disprove. Belief in or attachment to a story can become so intoxicating they begin to construe facts that might undercut their beliefs as "evidence *in favor* of them," Keeley writes—more proof that a powerful entity is working behind the scenes on a counternarrative campaign.

And yet, as Olmsted also points out, officials actively corrode trust in the systems they govern when they are not transparent, deliberately obscure the truth, or sidestep accountability. Citizens are smart to be skeptical; it's logical to think there might be a cover-up, even if the facts are not immediately available. Cover-ups happen all the time. The danger is when these theories are reported as fact or when information is contrived to support sensational claims. Another overlooked risk Olmsted points out is that conspiracy theories can become distractions. People genuinely seeking accountability and justice can get stuck on these theories and end up asking the wrong questions and missing opportunities for reform.

But in the summer of 2013, the theories stoked my fears. Investigating a gruesome unsolved murder is one thing, but investigating a gruesome unsolved murder at the center of a massive federal cover-up in which a witness was shot to death execution style is quite another.

~

I was curious to hear what the science reporter had to say. Maybe I could help him push the story forward. He worked at one of the most credible outlets in town, and, in truth, I was also hoping for reassurance. Perhaps my fears weren't as warranted as they seemed. He called me back right away. Greeting me in a commanding baritone, the science reporter informed me that yes, I had stumbled into some sort of real-life spy thriller. I was in over my head, and yes, I should be very, very afraid.

I grabbed a yellow legal pad and started taking notes as he mentioned a string of crimes and mysterious deaths I had no idea were related. The less I said I knew, the more excited he got and the more eager he was to share his findings. Not only was Ibragim killed because he knew too much, but a fatal helicopter accident in Virginia in which two FBI agents were killed was also somehow related. I found the helicopter crash on bombing conspiracy blogs—there is no hint of any connection to my case that I have found. Had I heard about the "Chechen neckties"? That's when a person's tongue is pulled through a slit in their throat, he said. By this point I was standing outside a café, holding my cell phone to my ear as I wrote, wishing I had taken the call somewhere more private. An image of Erik flashed before my eyes. I looked down at the curb to steady myself, the shock burning an otherwise inane image into my mind: the sun flooding the sidewalk, covering the cement in neat squares of light. *No, I had not heard anything about Erik's tongue being pulled from a hole in his neck,* I told him, trying to maintain an even tone. I would never hear anything else about Chechen neckties. I have not seen the crime scene photos. The science reporter would never report, or explain how he came to believe, that Erik was mutilated in that way, though I would of course spend many hours trying to determine if it was true. My research indicates the practice is actually dubbed a "Colombian necktie" and is usually seen in the Latin American drug trade. I'm not sure if the necktie theory would bring me closer to figuring out who killed my friend even if it were true. The science reporter kept going as my heart raced.

The science reporter and I talked for several weeks. He wanted me to help him investigate the case, but he didn't want to give me a byline. Instead he suggested I write for a conspiracy theory blog—for women. I wasn't thrilled with the idea. But pursuing the truth outweighed my vanity, however great. It was the leaps he made that alarmed me. He once suggested that my own father could be tied up in the larger scheme—which is absurd. But even if it wasn't, why would he tell me that? Why would he tip me off? I was concerned about his method. When I eventually broke off our correspondence, he accused me of being a federal agent. He watched me in court; I didn't take enough notes, he claimed.

But over the course of our conversations, he pointed me to a growing body of blogs about potential connections between Tamerlan, the Waltham murders, and a string of crimes linked to Waltham and Watertown in 2011. There was an unusual amount of criminal activity in the area at the time. I was interested in a case involving a Massachusetts state trooper, who was arrested for extortion in connection to a Watertown gambling racket. The science reporter told me he was interested in the unsolved murder of a retired Watertown police officer as well as a former Watertown city councilor busted with two million dollars' worth of weed in a Waltham warehouse.

He also told me about Operation Blackstone and Safwan Madarati—the head of the Waltham and Watertown drug ring busted a few months before Brendan moved to town. His theories were complicated, and he talked about crime with an enthusiastic use of outdated slang. At the time, I didn't know that

Madarati had been one of Rafi's suppliers, although that was never on the list of theories the science reporter shared with me.

In the wake of the bombings, few people close to the Waltham murder victims spoke to the press. A couple of blogs about Madarati and the Waltham murders pointed to an Associated Press article quoting a man named Christopher Medeiros, who said he knew Brendan Mess and did not think Tamerlan killed him. Medeiros told the AP that Tamerlan and Brendan had always gotten along, and he believed the Waltham murders were actually drug related. He claimed that the Friday before he died, Brendan had confided to him and said, "Listen, I'm getting ready to make this big move."

But before the bombing, in the days after the murders, Medeiros and his roommate, Elizabeth Jason, pointed reporters to Hiba. They told a *Boston Globe* reporter about Hiba allegedly throwing bottles and knives at Brendan and a fight about houseguests. According to the story, which ran on September 16, 2011, Medeiros and Jason said they were unable to locate Hiba. I have not been able to locate Medeiros myself. Barbie Kerr remembered reading that story while Hiba was with her in Richmond. Hiba hadn't run away. *She's at my house,* Barbie thought. "I just felt like she was more or less being singled out because she's an outsider. She's a foreigner, she's Black, she's female, she's the new addition to his life, she's beautiful," Barbie said. All of those factors could lead to people being unfairly suspicious.

There was a bizarre national component to the Madarati case as well. *APTN National News* in Canada was the first to report that Safwan Madarati was connected to a prominent businessman named Michael Chamas. Chamas had been photographed with conservative Canadian politicians before fleeing to Dubai to escape gun and tax charges. Before he left the country, in an apparent parting gesture, Chamas had controversially lacquered the entire exterior of his Quebec McMansion with upside-down Canadian flags. It was quite a statement. If feds were going to make a dime seizing Chamas's property, they would have to chip away the insult. Chamas confirmed his relationship with Madarati to an APTN reporter, claiming that he had given Madarati $2,000 to procure a green card. "I have friends in the police," Madarati reportedly told Chamas, before allegedly absconding with the loot.

I like stories about international smugglers and wealthy criminal expats. The wide-reaching tentacles in Madarati's story were intriguing. I think the HSI agents were interested in these actors too. I could not reach Chamas, but I did have luck pursuing local angles. The facts of Madarati's case, as they appeared in court documents, were interesting enough on their own.

For example, agents would have liked to have monitored Madarati and his associates for a good while longer. But on April 20, 2011—a day that just so happens to be celebrated by stoners the world over—Operation Blackstone screeched to a halt. Listening in on Madarati's calls that afternoon, the agents learned that he had come under the impression that Watertown police detective John St. Onge and Waltham police detective Joe Connors, two detectives on the Suburban Middlesex County Drug Task Force, had robbed and beaten "the shit" out of a young marijuana dealer who worked with Madarati.

The agents said it was all a big misunderstanding. Madarati's attorney would later say that Madarati was misinformed. But I had questions about the mix-up and about Madarati's relationships with local law enforcement in general. Not only was Rafi associated with Madarati, but I was also able to confirm, via confidential records and sourcing, that Connors was directly involved in the Waltham murder investigation. He was called to the murder scene the day the bodies were found.

PART V

Ibragim's World

CHAPTER
THIRTY-ONE

The Girlfriend

Screw it. Fuck all, I muttered to myself, pacing up and down the banks of the Charles River. I made a pact with myself to do my best and to push this story forward as far as I was physically able. I did not think that would mean reporting this story on my own, but the local journalists were giving me a headache.

~

On September 15, 2013, shortly after the two-year anniversary of the murders, I emailed Carly Carioli and S. I. Rosenbaum, editors at *Boston* magazine. Carioli, the new managing editor, had been the editor in chief of the *Boston Phoenix*, a legendary alt-weekly I'd aspired to write for since I was a teenager. It was known for its voicey investigative journalism and shoestring budget. The shoestring had finally snapped, however. The *Phoenix* had gone defunct only a few months prior. Rosenbaum had also been a *Phoenix* editor.

Rosenbaum called me in to speak to them at *Boston* magazine the next day. I took an extended lunch break and stepped into the large, bright office by Symphony Hall. Rosenbaum gave me the once-over. They wore black and silver jewelry and had a kind of no-nonsense attitude I immediately respected. Rosenbaum looked at my clip with Rachel Maddow, my quote in the *New York Times*, and a feature story I'd written about the economy of Southern African beer in *Beer Advocate* magazine since taking the job at the research center. I brought a folder of my college newspaper clippings. It wasn't exactly a hefty résumé, but it wasn't nothing.

Carioli was still getting used to the luxuries of the *Boston* magazine office: the skylight and the white furniture, so different from the rodent-infested *Boston Phoenix* headquarters he had been working out of for the entirety of his career. He flashed me a canine smile. He told me he was interested, but I would need to write a formal pitch to get the story past the editor in chief.

The next two evenings after work, I sat down on our ugly red futon beneath a string of fairy lights and tried to write a pitch. I had so many questions it was hard to find a clear angle. At the time, I was not sure Ibragim had, in fact, implicated himself in the Waltham murders. Months later, reports of an alleged confession had yet to be confirmed by anyone on record.

I was just about to give it up for the night and go to bed when I saw I had a Facebook notification. Tatiana Gruzdeva, the woman Ibragim Todashev had been living with before his death and who had supposedly been deported back to Russia, had accepted my friend request. It was Wednesday, September 18, 2013, at 10:41 p.m.

My career as an investigative reporter had begun.

After exchanging a few messages, I got Tatiana on the phone. She was not well. She spoke quickly, in a thick Slavic accent, sobbing in between breaths.

She had not been deported as planned. Tatiana was released on August 9, 2013, and had moved back to the condo she once shared with Ibragim. For the last five weeks, one of Ibragim's friends, a twenty-three-year-old Russian speaker from Tajikistan named Ashurmamad Miraliev, who went by "Ashur," stayed with her. Earlier that very day, as she and Ashur drove past Universal Studios, they were surrounded by at least a half dozen unmarked law enforcement vehicles, and Ashur was taken away. This was her first night alone, she told me, sleeping in the room where Ibragim had been killed, and she was scared.

She said Ibragim was a good man—there was no way he could have been involved in a murder.

~

Why and when exactly Ibragim found himself in Orlando would become an increasingly important point in my investigation. But for Tatiana and many others like her, I would learn, Orlando just sort of happened. Walt Disney chose the city for his theme park in the 1970s because it was cheap and near an interstate. Similar factors have likely drawn others there as well. But once Tatiana arrived, she became committed to the Orlando dream, posing with photos of Mickey Mouse at Disney World and petting a fake alligator outside of Universal Studios. This is where everyone in America longed to go. This is where Tatiana wanted to stay.

Tatiana said she was raised in Tiraspol, in Moldova, a former Soviet republic in Eastern Europe. She first arrived in North Carolina in the summer of 2012 on a student work visa. She was eighteen years old and worked at a resort and restaurant before making her way down to Florida in the fall. When Tatiana met Ibragim in November 2012, she was couch-surfing and looking for a more permanent place to live. He told her he had a condo where she could stay.

"First it was just friends," she said, "and after, we started having a relationship and we were sleeping together like boyfriend and girlfriend."

Tatiana told me Ibragim treated her very well. "Everything was so nice. He never screamed at me. It was always *This is for you.*" However, he kept their love affair a secret. Ibragim told her he couldn't tell his friends because having a girlfriend was against his religion.

Tatiana said she supported Ibragim, working as a hostess at a pizza place, and she used to cook them meals, which Ibragim would eat at the kitchen table seated in a folding chair, the only chair the couple owned. Together they adopted a little black cat, Masia. "He was like a little baby for us." Tatiana knew Ibragim had been married before, to Reni. But Ibragim told Tatiana they were divorced.

Tatiana learned about the bombing in the news but did not dwell on it long. Though she did notice that around that time Ibragim seemed sad. At first he would not tell Tatiana why. Then he told Tatiana his friend was dead. He did not elaborate. Tatiana did not know the death of his friend had anything to do with what happened in Boston.

The morning after the Tsarnaev brothers were identified, a fleet of armed FBI agents showed up at Ibragim's front door. Tatiana was washing dishes when Ibragim stepped outside to stretch his leg. He was recovering from knee surgery. She heard shouting and turned off the water. She looked outside to see Ibragim on the ground, surrounded by strange men with guns. She had no idea they were

FBI agents. She ran to the loft upstairs and hid in the bathroom until an agent told her to come out. They were the FBI.

She opened the door to find Ibragim seated on a folding chair in handcuffs with six or seven FBI agents surrounding him. The agents began questioning Ibragim about the Boston bombing, asking him what he knew and where he was the day of the attack. Tatiana told the agents Ibragim was with her, and he didn't do anything wrong. Tatiana heard Ibragim tell the agents he had known Tamerlan Tsarnaev and they had once been "real good friends." In Boston they had trained together and gone clubbing together. Then he said Tamerlan had become more devout, and they had grown apart. Tatiana told me that this was the first time she had heard her boyfriend talk about Tamerlan. The agents asked Ibragim about a call he received from Tamerlan the month before. Ibragim told the FBI Tamerlan had asked about his knee surgery. They pressed him, asking why he had deleted the call from his phone's memory. "I was scared," he said.

~

The agents left with Ibragim and took his phones and his computers. They interviewed him at a local Orlando police station and took his DNA and fingerprints, according to FBI documents I obtained. When he returned six hours later, he assured Tatiana everything was okay. The FBI called Ibragim back for several more interviews. For the next three weeks, undercover agents followed the couple everywhere. Ibragim would point out unmarked cars on their way to work or when they went to visit friends. Then Ibragim was called to the station once more. By then these visits had become almost routine. Tatiana went with him and waited in the lobby. Then one of the agents beckoned Tatiana in for an interview. The investigators told Tatiana outright they suspected Ibragim of murder. "We think he did something else, before," they said. "He killed three people in Boston in 2011 with a knife."

"It's not true! I can't believe it!" Tatiana insisted. "I was living with him seven months, and we have a cat!"

The agents told Tatiana they wanted her to help them and spy on Ibragim and report back. "Can you tell us when he will do something?" they asked. Tatiana told the FBI she couldn't and wouldn't because "he wasn't doing anything, and I didn't know anything."

When Tatiana refused to inform, she said the agents threatened to involve Immigration. Her work visa had expired two weeks before. Tatiana was shocked. They already knew her visa was set to expire and had done nothing. "Now because you need me and I say I don't want to help you, you just call to Immigration?" she asked them. An agent told Tatiana that was exactly what they were doing. "And they called Immigration, and Immigration came, and they put me in the jail," she said.

When Ibragim was released, he had no idea where she had gone. He looked for her everywhere. "They stole you," he said, when she finally reached him on the phone. When Ibragim went to visit Tatiana at the detention center, she said he proposed. "He kissed me. He hugged me like never. It was so sweet, like always. And he tell me, 'I will marry you when you get out of here, or in the jail, whatever. If we can marry in the jail, we will marry in the jail.'"

Meanwhile, as I would later learn, FBI agents were camped out at the Hooters restaurant around the corner from the Windhover condo complex, where they lived. The agents contacted the property manager and asked to see a condo identical to Ibragim's.

One week later, on May 22, the evening of Ibragim's fatal interview, Tatiana was transferred from an Immigration jail to a cell in the Glades County Detention Center in Moore Haven, Florida, and placed in a medical unit alone. Tatiana asked why she had been moved. "We'll tell you tomorrow in the morning," a warden told her.

The next morning, they told her that her boyfriend was dead. "And I'm screaming. I have panic attack." As she told me the story on the phone, she began to weep. "And everything is flush in my heart. My heart was broken, because me and Ibragim, we had a plan. We had a plan to be together. We had a plan to have a family."

Tatiana was kept in solitary confinement in the medical unit for four more days, she said. She never knew if it was day or night. She saw visions of Ibragim's face behind her closed eyes and thought she would die of grief. Finally she was released to the general population women's dormitory. Though she originally was set for deportation, on August 8, she was released from custody after being detained for ten weeks.

In Florida, Ibragim had reestablished himself with another close-knit group of Chechen friends and Russian speakers. Ashurmamad Miraliev had been one of Ibragim's friends. Ashur picked Tatiana up from the detention center and drove her back to the condo where Ibragim had been killed. He told Tatiana not to worry; the condo was clean. It was clean enough, Tatiana found. But the cat, Masia, was nowhere to be found.

"Did Ibragim ever tell you why he left Boston?" I asked Tatiana.

"No, he didn't tell me why. I never asked him," she told me.

"Why do you think Ibragim was killed?" I asked.

"Because maybe he don't want to say what they want to hear," she said.

Tatiana told me she was still waiting for some immigration paperwork to go through. In the meantime, she wasn't sure what she was going to do. It was like a nightmare, being all alone in that condo where her boyfriend's blood once stained the floor.

When we got off the phone, Tatiana sent me a photo of Masia and a video she had taken of Ibragim on Valentine's Day walking through the aisles of a store. Tatiana was giggling and begging Ibragim to put on a silly party hat. It was all so strange, hearing the voice of the man who may have killed Erik. At the same time, they seemed like any other couple. "Do you love me?" Tatiana asked in Russian.

"What does that have to do with it?" Ibragim replied. He mumbled something about *kompromat*, but he eventually gave in and donned a pointed, purple polka-dot party hat, to Tatiana's audible delight.

When I first looked through Tatiana's Facebook profile, I wondered if she could be some kind of spy. At that point anything seemed possible. Were the photos of her posing with puppies a ruse? What, if any, role could she have played in Erik's murder? Now I just felt really bad for her. I wasn't expecting to feel so much sympathy for the loved ones of my friend's alleged killer. But I was not at all sure Ibragim did kill my friend. I was also surprised to hear that Ibragim had had so many interactions with the FBI. His relationship with investigators seemed almost cordial, at least until Tatiana was detained.

The story Tatiana told me about the fleet of undercover officers arresting Ashurmamad Miraliev was equally puzzling. I started looking into the case. There were three different branches of law enforcement working together—local, state, and federal. And they all had different accounts of what happened. The Orlando Police had the incident recorded as a routine traffic stop—with no mention of FBI involvement. But an affidavit from the Orange County Sheriff's

Office showed that Miraliev was arrested on an Osceola County warrant. He was accused of witness tampering for threatening a victim of an assault that had occurred ten months earlier, at a local club called the Ali Baba Hookah Lounge. The affidavit stated that, after, Miraliev was questioned by the FBI and held on a $50,000 bond. It was not clear what the hookah bar fight had to do with Ibragim's death, the bombings, or the homicide case. But there was a note on Miraliev's booking sheet: *ON TERRORIST WATCH LIST/PLACED PROTECTIVE CUSTODY AND HIGH RISK. HOUSE ALONE.*

I wrote to *Boston* magazine about the interview the next morning. Coincidentally, the editor in chief had stepped down that very day, and Carioli was assuming his role. I don't know what excuse I gave to the research center, but I went to the *Boston* magazine office that day instead of work. Carioli had me write a story about my interview with Tatiana and Ashurmamad Miraliev's arrest and ran it online. I never did finish writing that pitch. Carioli had *Boston* magazine buy me a ticket to Florida the next day so I could meet Tatiana in person. I gave the research center my two weeks' notice.

Carioli had never flown a journalist anywhere for a story before, he Told me before I got on my flight. "Good luck," he said.

CHAPTER
THIRTY-TWO

Orlando

The first time I spoke to Tatiana, she was scared and crying. Before the flight I sent her a link to the *Boston* magazine story I wrote about her interview. I also told her I knew one of the three men Ibragim was alleged to have killed, in case she did not read the article. Tatiana was not distressed; she did not believe Ibragim had killed anyone. She seemed excited by the prospect of my visit and asked me to bring my swimsuit. The condo had a pool.

When I landed it was raining, and Tatiana wasn't answering the phone. It was an hour drive from the airport to the hotel. I passed signs for Disney World, SeaWorld, Orange World, Souvenir World, and the Holy Land Experience. Where in the midst of these tourist traps, Spanish moss, and breakfast buffets was Ibragim's World? The lobby of the Comfort Suites hotel was full of families visiting Universal Studios on a budget, and a church group with matching T-shirts. I bought a microwave pizza, and heated it up in my room. Tatiana still had not called. The thick Florida air was making it hard to breathe. I took a puff from my inhaler, lay down on the synthetic blue bedcovers, and waited.

Finally, Tatiana sent me a text. "I want to see you," she wrote. But she was hesitant, she said. "Now I have more problems." However dark the circumstances, I believed so deeply in journalism as a power for good that I didn't think of how my reporting could have unintended consequences. Maybe she was involved in Erik's murder somehow. Maybe that's why she didn't want to talk to me. My stomach turned. If that were true, I really had to see her.

I pleaded with Tatiana to meet with me. I had come so far. She told me she was working in "New York–Style pizza" in Kissimmee, the next town over from Disney, and I could find her there. Nervous that if I asked for clarification she might change her mind, I visited three other Kissimmee pizza shops with *New York Style* in the name before finding the right one. There was a poster advertising Halloween Horror Night at Disney World by the door, and there was Tatiana in a white T-shirt studded in rhinestones, reaching for a hug. The restaurant was empty. All the tourists were at Halloween Horror Night, she explained. I sat down in a booth and ordered a bowl of spaghetti and shrimp. It was the wrong order, but at least it was the right restaurant. Over the course of an hour, Tatiana came back and forth to my table to chat while I swallowed down as much of the oily noodles as I could, smiled, and informed her that I had, in fact, brought a swimsuit as she requested. I wanted to get into that condo. She told me I could come by tomorrow.

The next day was overcast. I waited for Tatiana outside the condo, watching as lines of white ibis marched along the edges of the brown artificial pond. 6022 Peregrine Avenue has a large sliding door looking over the dark water. Neighbors said the blinds were always drawn. Inside was a single dark room with a lofted balcony-style bed area illuminated by an orb ceiling light. Tatiana asked me to take off my shoes when I stepped inside. The condo was still owned by an associate of Ibragim's who had moved to Texas and only asked that Ibragim pay utilities. He allowed Tatiana to stay under the same terms.

There was only the one folding chair, so Tatiana took me to the loft upstairs. We sat on her twin bed, beneath a Muhammad Ali poster, with her collection of nine teddy bears, one of which had been a gift from Ibragim. She started to cry. "I am here alone," she said. "I hope it never can be worse than this." She insisted that Ibragim was a good man. He could never have committed a murder.

Tatiana and I met a couple of times over the next two days. Inside the condo there was a large blue rug near the entranceway to the kitchen on top of the beige wall-to-wall carpeting. We sat on the rug and ate stale pastries the next afternoon. Did she know where Ibragim had been killed, I asked? Her face went white. That's what the blue rug was for, I learned.

Part of me wanted to protect Tatiana. She seemed so frightened and helpless, all alone in the apartment where her boyfriend was killed. Another part of me wanted to run. She was still talking to Ibragim's friends, trained fighters some of them, and from what I gathered, they didn't like that I was there. Tatiana was much more hesitant to speak now, in person, than that night on the phone. There was a part of me that wanted to turn Tatiana upside down, grab her by the ankles, and shake her until the truth came out like lunch money. But of course, I didn't. I listened and gently prodded her, collecting whatever pieces of information I could scrape together about Ibragim's life and death and tried not to cause any more pain.

What did he like to eat? I asked. Meat and chocolate, she told me. What music did he listen to? She told me he liked a Russian artist named Mr. Credo. Mr. Credo, I would later learn, styled himself as a Chechen crime boss, and sang in a fake North Caucasus accent about buying drugs from the Taliban.

On the second day it was pouring rain. I drove Tatiana to the store so she could buy credit on her phone and call Ibragim's father. It would have been Ibragim's twenty-eighth birthday, and Abdulbaki Todashev was feeding the poor in Grozny, in his son's honor. On the way back, we passed the spot where Ashur was arrested. "I don't want to be next," she told me. Then she told me her immigration agent was coming to drive her to his office, and I needed to leave before he came.

The story about the regularly visiting Immigration and Customs Enforcement (ICE) agent and Ashur's arrest was confusing to me. By then, I had spoken to members of the Florida chapter of the Council on American-Islamic Relations, who told me that Ashur had been denied repeated requests to an attorney during a six-hour interrogation with the FBI. (The FBI has declined to comment, but a public-affairs official from the Tampa field office told me it was their policy to question individuals "with their consent, or in the presence of their attorney.") Tampa CAIR–Florida executive director Hassan Shibly was already up in arms about Ibragim's shooting death. Now Shibly claimed the FBI had been systematically harassing and threatening Ibragim Todashev's friends and called on the US Department of Justice to investigate. I tried to reach Ashur myself, but had no luck contacting him while he was detained.

"Keep in touch," I told Tatiana before I left. "If something happens, please let me know."

"All right. I hope nothing," she said. "Because it's already a lot."

It is difficult to say how I felt on that plane ride home. Before the bombing, my journal entries documented dreams and lengthy emotional ruminations. After the bombing, I filled pages with lists, facts, observations, and evidence. I needed to talk to people who had been close to my friend's alleged killer. I remembered the walks I took alone at night after Lynn died. I knew I could set my feelings aside if I had to. So that's what I did, on and off for years.

~

Less than two weeks later, on October 1, 2013, I received a call from the Glades County Detention Center. It was Tatiana. "Do you remember me?" she asked. She said she had been arrested and was set for deportation—all because of her interview with *Boston* magazine. She said she had valid immigration papers and had been in the country legally, but the agents who detained her claimed her papers had been revoked because of our interview. I told her I couldn't believe it, that it was crazy. She said she couldn't believe it herself.

I had no idea someone could be deported for speaking to a reporter. I also wasn't so sure I trusted her account. Tatiana had been detained on the first day of a partial government shutdown. Everyone in ICE's media relations department had been furloughed. So it was a while before I could get a statement from ICE about what happened.

Tatiana was deported back to Moscow twelve days later with nothing but the clothes she was arrested in and a winter coat supplied to her by ICE.

When the shutdown was lifted, an ICE official released a statement that Tatiana Gruzdeva had been in the country legally; however, she was here under a somewhat unusual proviso called "deferred action." These agreements are drafted individually, and are sometimes written with unique terms. They can be revoked by federal agents at will for any reason and without ceremony.

Tatiana and I stayed in touch, but she no longer felt comfortable speaking to me at length. For more than two years, I had been dogged by questions about what happened that night in Waltham. Why was the FBI so concerned about my reporting that they locked up and deported a teenage girl? Not only did the FBI interfere with my interviews with Tatiana, but deporting her had a chilling effect on my whole investigation. People who knew Ibragim started to decline interviews because they were afraid of the repercussions. I had been trying to cut through the conspiracy theories surrounding Ibragim's death. But this really did look like a top-level orchestrated cover-up. There was something the FBI didn't want me to know.

Yet my reporting did seem to be pushing the story forward. A week after *Boston* magazine published my story about Tatiana's arrest, on October 7, 2013, Dzhokhar's defense team filed the first public motion citing Ibragim Todashev by name. It was a motion to compel discovery, legalese for forcing the government to turn over investigative material relevant to the defense. The defense wanted the FBI's interview notes, the 302 reports, from Ibragim's fatal interview. They also requested 302 reports from interviews with Ibragim's girlfriend and wife. This motion would mark the beginning of a nine-year legal battle over the Waltham murder evidence and the defense to save Dzhokhar's life.

The government fired back two weeks later, insisting that the defense's request was premature, the Waltham case was not relevant, and that disclosing information about the case "might jeopardize Middlesex's open and ongoing investigation into the triple homicide." Besides, the defense already knew every-thing they needed to know about the matter, the government argued, because the government had already informed the defense that, "according to Todashev, Tamerlan Tsarnaev participated in the Waltham triple homicide."

That line asserting in writing the government's account, that Ibragim impli-cated Tamerlan in the Waltham murders, was a big deal. Though this speaks more to the paucity of information than what the government actually said. Four and a half months had passed, and there had been no public statement from the FBI or the Middlesex DA's Office or *anyone* about what Ibragim allegedly said in that room, other than quotes from anonymous sources in news reports. The government included no information about Ibragim's alleged role in the killings, the motive, or the circumstances surrounding his death. But now at least the government had revealed some of Ibragim's account and linked Tamerlan to the Waltham murders in writing, albeit indirectly, by way of a federal prosecutor.

After Tatiana was detained, I started to fear this case was more than I could handle on my own, even with the help of *Boston* magazine. I was still in com-munication with the team at *The Rachel Maddow Show*. They brought the story to producers at *This American Life*. When I learned *This American Life* wanted to work with me, it gave me new life.

CHAPTER
THIRTY-THREE

History of Violence

The next few months were a whirlwind of interviews and research and trips to local courthouses. At first Julie Snyder and Brian Reed—*This American Life* producers—communicated with us remotely from New York while Carioli, Rosenbaum, and I brainstormed in Boston. Then Brian and I flew together to Orlando. I was, admittedly, starstruck. Getting on *This American Life* was like a lifetime career goal. Yet, here I was on my first big story, working for *This American Life* and trying very hard to look like I knew what I was doing. So hard that I nearly lost my suitcase in the airport. Eventually I settled down, and we got into a good rhythm. Brian was tireless and meticulous and surprisingly well dressed—he said his girlfriend was a stylist. I'd learn from him the importance of timelines and itinerary lists. We worked sixteen-hour days, and he showed no signs of slowing down, so I tried my best not to either.

The whole time Brian and I were investigating, we were also waiting for the shooting reports on Ibragim's death from the DOJ and the Florida State Attorney. That we ourselves were conducting a sort of third parallel investigation became apparent to the point of comedy. If that does not sound very amusing, well, for the most part, reporting trips are exercises in humiliation and despair. A twisted sense of humor is a necessity when you're spending most of your waking hours in rental cars you don't know how to drive, in places you've never been, going from door to door, ringing bells, leaving notes, loitering in strip malls, trying to get someone, anyone to talk to you while working your way through a list of names and addresses. These addresses may or may not be right and may or may not be relevant, but either way you are probably not welcome. For every interview you do get, there are about a half dozen failed attempts. Most interviews are not all that noteworthy. If you're lucky, they provide a little color—you learn that Ibragim gave candy to the neighbor's children, or that he didn't know enough English to write his own checks, or that investigators had been there before looking for the same person, but they don't live there anymore. Anecdotes about the other investigation gave me hope that the reports on Ibragim's shooting death might actually produce answers, however long the wait.

We focused on the mysteries surrounding Ibragim's associates. It appeared the FBI was working with local and state officials to systematically arrest and deport them. Deportations fall under the jurisdiction of ICE. In fact, FBI guidelines forbid agents from making threats or promises regarding immigration status. But an ICE agent told us that if we wanted to know why Tatiana was deported, we should ask the FBI. No one at the FBI would explain. Khusen Taramov, who went with Ibragim to the fatal interview and gave Abdulbaki the photos of Ibragim's corpse, had gone back home to Chechnya for Ibragim's funeral. Khusen was a triplet. He and his two brothers went to high school in America. All of them had green cards. But they weren't being let back into the country. According to Khusen, who messaged me on Facebook, the three of them were escorted off the plane when they tried to return.

Brian and I also found documents that showed the FBI had assisted in getting Ibragim's friends—including Ashur—evicted. We figured out Ashur was technically arrested for a verbal argument he had after Ibragim allegedly beat up a guy at the Ali Baba Hookah Lounge in 2012. After Ibragim was killed, a local detective and an FBI agent convinced the victim of the assault—a manager of a hookah bar—to press charges against Ashur for allegedly yelling at him after the fight. To Ashur his arrest was frightening, but the coordination was remarkable. It seemed like the undercover cars came at him from all sides. When Ashur asked them why he was stopped, they told him it was because his license was expired. Ashur was shocked. *All this for an expired license?* But he was also curious. "Let's go to the office—there's air-conditioning," one of the officers said to him. After some hesitation, he agreed. "I wanted to know what they want for me." He got in a car and went with them to the Orlando police station.

But when he got to the station, Ashur said FBI agents asked him about Ibragim and the murders in Waltham. They told Ashur they were certain Ibragim was involved in the Waltham crime, but they wanted to know more. *Do you know who was with him at the time of the triple murder? What do you know about the triple murder? What did Ibragim tell you about the triple murder?* they asked, according to Ashur. Ashur said he knew nothing about Ibragim's life in Boston, so he had nothing to say.

After hours of questioning, Ashur asked to leave. The agents told him he couldn't. He was headed to jail on a state witness-tampering charge. The charge was later dropped, but by then Ashur had missed an immigration hearing and he was deported back to Tajikistan.

The story for *This American Life* focused a lot on Tatiana, Ashur, and the fight at the Ali Baba Hookah Lounge. Later the DOJ shooting report would insist that although Ibragim Todashev's associates were subject to law enforcement interest and some were incarcerated and deported, these were unrelated matters: "Speculation that these persons were deported to conceal information is unfounded." That may be true, but it looked pretty suspicious at the time. And I still had questions. Was Ashur on a terrorist watch list simply because he was Muslim and knew Ibragim? Were agents really curious about a third suspect, and did they genuinely believe Ashur might have answers? Or were they questioning him in that way—staging synchronized stunts in unmarked vehicles and arresting him on bogus charges—because they could? Ashur was an immigrant without permanent residency. Ashur's arrest—ostensibly for an expired license and a ten-month-old verbal dispute—revealed a tangle of different law enforcement agencies following orders from . . . whom? The answer was often murky and not as it first appeared.

For many years, I only had a vague sense of where this reporting might take me. Information that felt significant then seems less so today. I followed hunches that never took form: medical transportation companies, mortgage schemes, precious-metal liquidation firms, shell companies, the Hells Angels. Too often, I was so caught up in one strand of the reporting, I neglected the undertow; the story was pulling me in a different direction.

In the beginning, I knew little about the slain Chechen fighter. I also spoke to Ibragim's family at length, including his father, Abdulbaki Todashev; his wife, Reni Manukyan; his mother-in-law, Elena Teyer; and his brother-in-law, Alex

Kovlenko. I made calls and sent messages on Facebook. I visited Ibragim's old apartments, I called his old employers and his old trainers, and I reached out to his friends. His friends were scared, especially after Tatiana was deported. I made desperate pleas. I told them we all needed to know the truth. Sometimes it worked, sometimes it didn't.

I didn't realize this at first, but figuring out when Ibragim left Boston was crucial to making sense of the story. Meanwhile, Ibragim's father, wife, and girlfriend insisted the allegations, then only from anonymous law enforcement sources, were false. Ibragim would never attack a federal agent. Later, Ibragim's family tried to sue the FBI for his wrongful death based in part on this premise. The judge did not order the bureau to turn over evidence that their lawyer, James Cook, said was necessary to build the case. But the information I found suggested that Ibragim was exactly the kind of guy who would attack an agent, or anyone who confronted him in that way. What was surprising was that law enforcement chose to confront a trained fighter with a hair-trigger temper about an unsolved murder—for more than four hours in his own home. The argument I wish James Cook could have made is that the investigators and those above them created a scenario that was dangerous to themselves and Ibragim. Albeit, this argument could not find traction in the legal system because, ultimately, the instigating variable is Ibragim's own proclivity to violence.

Ibragim's father and I seemed to reach an understanding about this at one point in our first conversation. He told me his son was like a scared animal in the hands of American law enforcement: "If you catch a mouse in your hands, it's in your hands. If it bites, you would squeeze it and kill it and say that it threatened your life."

～

Abdulbaki Todashev speaks in a classic Chechen accent, my translators told me, and in a slow earnestness that resonated through our translated calls. We would communicate back and forth in this way over the course of nine years. In our final conversation, in 2022, he told me his grief had left him immobilized and unable to work. Ibragim's mother, Zulay, had died of a heart attack due to her broken heart, he explained.

Ibragim was born in 1985, the eldest of Abdulbaki's twelve children. Abdulbaki had two wives. They used to live across the street from one another in Grozny. Ibragim had been a chubby child with a sweet tooth. When the First Chechen War began, in 1994, Ibragim was eleven years old. "We were always on the run," Abdulbaki told me. The family moved from place to place, trying to escape the violence. In 2007, the wars were over, and Abdulbaki got a government administrative job. The next year Ibragim left for America. He wanted to study English.

He arrived in June 2008 and joined a traveling carnival in Pennsylvania, he told the FBI, according to reports I obtained. He said he slept in the woods, was fired after a week, and went to Massachusetts, where he knew other Chechens. Ibragim would call his father and complain about the cold winters. Abdulbaki told him to drink warm milk and honey for his colds. When he wasn't training at local gyms, Ibragim worked sporadically as a driver for medical transportation companies, making a little under $200 a week.

∿

Ibragim and Reni met in May 2010. She was in town to visit one of Ibragim's Cambridge roommates and was immediately smitten. "I felt something good in him," she said. They were married in a religious ceremony in July 2010, two months after they met, though they were never legally bound. Ibragim then went to live with Reni in Norcross for a time. She said she supported him so he could focus on MMA.

Ibragim apparently told FBI agents that his relationship with Reni coincided with a period in which he was recovering from his knee surgery. In early 2011, he returned to Boston. On July 23, 2011, he had an official amateur MMA fight. He lost. I asked Reni about the fight. She said she went to see him and that Ibragim returned to Norcross, Georgia, to live with her in August of that year. She said she was certain Ibragim was not in Massachusetts in September, because she looked over their shared back account and there were no transactions in Massachusetts that month.

By February 2012, Ibragim was in Florida. He had another official amateur fight and won via ankle lock and submission. There weren't many fights in the Atlanta area, Reni explained. That's why he moved. Reni joined Ibragim in

Florida for a while, but in November 2012, she said they hit a rough patch. Reni was more family oriented and Ibragim wanted to focus on MMA. So she moved back to Georgia. But Ibragim still visited her once a month, they talked on the phone, and he spent money on their shared bank account, she said. Reni took care of him. "I had no choice," she said, laughing. "That's what love does." She told me she knew about Tatiana. She knew Ibragim and Tatiana lived together but she insisted Tatiana was never his girlfriend. Abdulbaki said he knew Ibragim had a girlfriend but did not know he had a wife. Reni said it was true, Ibragim's father did not know they were married, but Ibragim's mother did. They spoke on the phone. (Ibragim allegedly told FBI agents he divorced Reni by stating "you're not my wife" three times but that they stayed in contact, according to a partially redacted 302 report.)

Reni and I began talking after she flew to Chechnya for Ibragim's funeral. She did not return to America, she said she was frightened the American government might take down her plane. Reni has never turned down my request for an interview. She arranged for me to speak to her mother and her brother. She was courteous, no matter how prying or sensitive my questions.

A day after the Boston bombings Reni flew from Georgia to Russia for a cousin's wedding and stayed for two weeks. Before Ibragim was killed, Reni was skeptical about the narrative surrounding the 9/11 Twin Towers attack. She said when she heard the Boston bombing suspects were Chechen, she figured they had been framed. *Chechens are always getting framed.* She said she spoke to Ibragim regularly on this trip. They were close. But he neglected to mention being interrogated by the FBI. On her way home she was stopped at the airport and questioned for hours. She said agents wanted to know when she met Ibragim and a timeline of his movements between Massachusetts, Georgia, and Florida, among other questions. Afterwards she called Ibragim. "What's going on?" she said. Ibragim was absolutely calm, Reni told me. That was one thing she loved about him, his consistent demeanor.

"Just say what you know," he told her.

"Why you never tell me of what happened?" Reni asked.

"Why I'm going to tell you if you're back home having fun?" he said.

Reni found this answer to be satisfactory. Ibragim wasn't close to the Tsarnaevs, she said. Reni never met Tamerlan. Although later she said she recalled Ibragim knew someone in Massachusetts with that name. She said she had been following the #FreeJahar movement and did not think it was possible that a teenage boy and Tamerlan could have pulled off a bombing of that size.

After the airport interview, agents questioned Reni on several occasions. Her younger brother, Alex Kovlenko, bartended at a Holiday Inn where she cleaned rooms. Alex was surprised when two FBI agents came up to the bar and asked after his sister. Reni was at home, he said. He called Reni as soon as they left. "I was, like, 'What's going on? Why are the FBI agents here?' and she was, like, 'Don't worry about it.' And she, like, laughed a little bit."

When Alex got off work, he went to his sister's apartment to make sure she was okay. The FBI was there. He waited in another room but he could hear what they were saying and he didn't like the way they were speaking to his sister.

Reni said she told the agents she felt bad for the bombing victims, but thought the Tsarnaevs were framed. "And that's when one of the FBI agents actually blew up on me, start[ed] cursing," Reni said.

"Who do you think set the Tsarnaev brothers up?" I asked.

"Law enforcement," Reni told me.

"Why?" She said she wasn't sure. She was still thinking about it.

～

I was not sure when Ibragim arrived in Florida or when he started driving the white 1997 Mercedes-Benz sedan, but the vehicle was central to his life in Orlando while he was there. In the afternoons he could be seen outside the condo cleaning his car with a hose. Reni said the agents asked her about the white Mercedes on several occasions before we spoke. She said Ibragim drove it, but it was actually her car. I asked her about the car in two instances in our early conversations in late 2013. Reni told me she bought the Mercedes in Miami in October 2012—a year before we spoke and a half a year after she was repeatedly questioned about the car by the FBI. Which is why later I was surprised to learn later that what she told me about the car wasn't entirely true.

～

Ibragim spent his Florida afternoons rotating through a couple of area gyms and hanging out at a shopping plaza in Kissimmee. He passed his time in the parking lot leaning against his car while his friends went back and forth delivering pizza. Behind the plaza was a Cheers restaurant, where patrons drank beer in pajama pants at all hours of the day. But the plaza itself catered mainly to Arab and Muslim patrons. Business owners and regulars called one another "plaza friends." There was a mosque, a hair salon run by an Iraqi family, an Egyptian supermarket, and the Ali Baba Hookah Lounge where Ibragim and his friends sat on a pair of white leather couches, dubbed the "Russian Corner" due to their frequent visits. On weekends the hookah bar hired a DJ and a belly dancer, and the place was full of teenagers. Weekdays were quiet, and Ibragim and his friends smoked hookah and watched UFC fights on the flatscreen TVs.

According to Youness Dammou, a former manager at the hookah bar, Ibragim had a favorite waitress. On July 7, 2012, Ibragim wanted the waitress to serve him hookah. Dammou said the girl was not assigned to his table. So Ibragim allegedly asked Dammou to step outside, and proceeded to pick him up by the legs and throw him down on the ground.

I learned more about Ibragim's temper back in Boston at the Wai Kru gym. The gym owner, John Allan, at first tried to cut a deal with Ibragim, in which he would let him train for free if Ibragim swept the mats. But when Allan handed him a broom, Ibragim freaked out. Sweeping was women's work, he said. Later Allan tried to get Ibragim a job as the bouncer at a local bar. The first thing they asked him to do was sweep. "He lost the job before he began," Allan said.

Broomsticks were not Ibragim's only sticking point. The word *motherfucker* would incite in Ibragim an inconsolable rage. "He would lose it. He'd be ready to fight seventeen people and not care if he would win or lose. Sometimes it wouldn't even be directed at him," Allan said. "I tried to explain to him, like, *Listen, it's not a literal term in America. It's just a slang saying.*" Ibragim was not convinced.

In February 2010, Ibragim was charged with disorderly conduct and resisting arrest in Boston. Ibragim was driving for a company called Coco Transportation. According to the police report, Ibragim made an abrupt stop, and a man drove into the back of the van. When police arrived on the scene, they could hear Ibragim screaming, "You say something about my mother. I will kill you."

Ibragim also allegedly beat a man bloody over a parking spot a couple weeks after the bombing, Two men, a father and his grown son, Lester Garcia Jr. and Sr., were just about to pull into a space outside the Orlando Premium Outlet

Mall, when they reported a Mercedes-Benz sedan whizzed past and started backing into their space. "Park if you can!" the driver yelled, according to a police report. The men got out of their cars and Ibragim allegedly punched Junior in the face, knocking him unconscious and rearranging his teeth. Then he drove away.

Orange County officer Anthony Riccaboni chased after the white Mercedes. Riccaboni just so happened to be an MMA aficionado himself. According to the report, Riccaboni yelled at Ibragim to get out of the car with his hands raised and to lie on the ground. He wasn't going to take any chances with this guy. He saw that Ibragim had cauliflower ears, thick, puffy, and hard, the mark of a cage fighter who does not rest to let their appendages heal. Once on his feet, Ibragim told Riccaboni something unexpected: the vehicles behind them were FBI agents, and they were following him, according to the report. Sure enough, three vehicles with dark tinted windows slowly drove away. Riccaboni saw that one of the drivers had a computer on the dashboard and was talking on a radio. According to the DOJ and Florida State shooting report, they were FBI agents, and they were following Ibragim. The agents did not intervene when Ibragim beat a man bloody but they did film the violent melee. The Massachusetts investigators watched this footage before confronting Ibragim in his home.

CHAPTER
THIRTY-FOUR
Official Findings

The release of the DOJ's and the Florida State Attorney's shooting reports ten months after Ibragim was killed felt eerily akin to the conclusion of a game of Clue: it was Ibragim, running between the living room and the kitchen, armed with a coffee table and then a broomstick. Ibragim Todashev, who in his life was so vehemently opposed to sweeping, allegedly died with a broomstick in his hands.

Gary Lee Utz, the deputy chief medical examiner noted that Ibragim's body was that of a well-developed, well-nourished, white man weighing 159 pounds. His beard and mustache were closely trimmed, and there was a marked bone abnormality of the nose. *Both ears display cauliflower-type deformities,* he wrote. Ibragim was shot seven times, including three times in the back and once in the top of the head. The shot to the head would have been immediately incapacitating, he found. The wounds were inconsistent with the subject being shot from behind and turned away from the shooter. Rather, it appeared the subject died while falling toward the shooter with his head down. Utz found no evidence of close-range firing and concluded the manner of death to be homicide.

The Florida State Attorney's Office went to great lengths to account for the bullets in Ibragim's back and conducted a deep dive into Ibragim's MMA training—he was trained to stay low and go for the legs. According to the reports, Ibragim simultaneously lunged for the trooper's legs while wielding the broomstick over his head. No "prints of value" were detected on the red handle. Photos of the broomstick show the brush head was removed. The Florida report also states that there were no photos of Ibragim gripping the weapon when the corpse was turned over and removed from the condo. Both reports emphasize that the lack of prints does not "disassociate that source from having touched the evidence."

Working alongside my *Boston* magazine editor, S. I. Rosenbaum, we found that the photos on the Florida report were improperly redacted. I had a lead but they made the breakthrough removing the redactions on Photoshop. This error is how reporters were able to identify the investigators there that evening: the lead investigator Joel Gagne, a state trooper assigned to the Middlesex County District Attorney's Office, Massachusetts state trooper Curtis Cinelli, assigned to a fugitive task force, and Boston FBI agent Aaron McFarlane. Maria Sacchetti was the first to report on McFarlane's checkered past in the *Boston Globe*, a short time later.

One would think that if Tamerlan Tsarnaev were genuinely suspected to have played a role in the 9/11/11 murders, investigators looking into the bombing would have a vested interest in figuring out what happened in Waltham. But the shooting reports reveal that the Waltham murders were essentially an afterthought.

On April 21, 2013, shortly after the brothers were identified, FBI agents in Orlando were tipped off to the fact that Ibragim had previously communicated with Tamerlan by phone. The FBI questioned Ibragim about the bombing and his relationship to Tamerlan for three weeks. Then the DOJ report suggests the bureau basically handed the inquiry over to the Massachusetts district attorney.

McFarlane and Gagne flew down to Florida, on May 14, 2013, a week before McFarlane killed him. They did not contact Ibragim directly; Florida agents called him into the Orlando police station and questioned him while the Massachusetts investigators watched from another room. The agents asked Ibragim about his movements in and out of the Boston area around the time of the Waltham murders but the reports note investigators did not ask him about the murders directly. Gagne would later report that he thought Ibragim was being cagey; he didn't want to admit he was in the Boston area in early September 2011. Gagne said this was his first clue that Ibragim may have been involved in the murder.

But internal FBI documents note that Massachusetts investigators planned to confront Ibragim with "forensic evidence associated with the triple homicide." The DOJ report also says that Ibragim Todashev was deemed a *suspect* in the Waltham murder case prior to the fatal interview. Ibragim being an official suspect is an important distinction from the account of Massachusetts state troopers, who said that Ibragim was only a "person of interest." For example, in an interview with a Florida State Attorney investigator, Cinelli said that Ibragim Todashev was a suspect, prior to the May 21 interview. But an attorney representing the Massachusetts State Police was quick to interject, and Cinelli rephrased his statement.

Middlesex's account, as told by Gagne and Cinelli, with supervision by their attorney, was that Ibragim's confession essentially came out of left field. Gagne told investigators that prior to the fatal interview, investigators "didn't have anything concrete at that point that tied him into that homicide" other than his cagey answer about his whereabouts. They make no mention of obtaining forensic evidence beforehand.

FBI documents also indicate that Ibragim began to confess after he "was confronted regarding his involvement in the triple homicide." Did investigators have forensic evidence linking Ibragim to the crime? The Florida State Attorney report and records requests show that in the months after Ibragim was killed, FBI agents asked Middlesex ADA Stephen Loughlin about DNA evidence found at the crime scene in Waltham. Loughlin refused to provide the FBI agents with any information on that point, claiming that it "was not the District Attorney's Office's policy to comment or provide information on an ongoing investigation."

McFarlane, Gagne, and Cinelli insisted they were acting with a sense of urgency when they returned to Florida on May 21, 2013, to set up an interview. They were under the impression that Ibragim was about to leave the country. Ibragim had bought a May 24 plane ticket to see his family, whom he had not visited in five years. He had bought presents for eleven brothers and sisters—T-shirts and large bars of Toblerone chocolate—his father would later tell me. But by May 21, Ibragim had cancelled his flight. A supervising FBI agent in Orlando knew this. So did Chris Savard, the Orlando JTTF agent who helped the Massachusetts team set up the interview. It's unclear if this information was kept from the Massachusetts investigators. Nonetheless it appears they continued to pursue Ibragim as if he was about to flee.

In the past, Ibragim had been cooperative with federal agents. (A redacted copy of an FBI 302 report reveals that the FBI also conducted a "full investigation" into Ibragim on June 28, 2012, shortly before the hookah bar fight. The FBI has not responded to Freedom of Information Act requests for records pertaining to Ibragim's earlier interactions with the bureau.) After the bombing he provided them with his phones, his computers, and a DNA sample. He went voluntarily to the Orlando police station for interviews on several occasions. But after agents locked up Tatiana, he did not want to talk. The morning of May 21, 2013, Savard tried to set up an interview for the Massachusetts investigators. Ibragim said he did not want to meet them, but Savard said he was able to persuade him to talk over the course of three phone calls, according to his statements in shooting reports. The persuasive technique Savard neglected to mention is that while he was calling, undercover agents in unmarked cars were circling Ibragim and his friends like sharks.

Finally Ibragim relented and said they could meet at the Ali Baba Hookah Lounge. Savard said he didn't want anyone to overhear them. Was there somewhere else he would feel comfortable? Ibragim proposed they meet at the condo where up until recently he lived with Tatiana.

McFarlane, Gagne, and Cinelli were waiting at their hotel when Savard called. If they wanted to talk to Ibragim, now was their chance. The men jumped in their rental car and pulled into the parking lot at 7:35 p.m. Savard was there, and Ibragim had brought Khusen Taramov. The investigators allegedly discussed Ibragim's propensity for violence on the drive over and had agreed to have at least three men in the condo with Ibragim for safety reasons.

While the FBI stated that there was a plan in place to confront Ibragim with evidence, apparently they had not made any preparations in the event that Ibragim actually confessed. No operation or arrest plan was documented, the DOJ report explicitly stated. In addition, internal FBI documents obtained via records requests reveal there was no communications plan to provide operation updates to the appropriate FBI personnel on the progress of the interview.

The investigators in the condo were taking orders from ADA Stephen Loughlin, according to the shooting reports and FBI records. Loughlin was not in Orlando, nor was he waiting at the Middlesex office for updates. Three hours into the interview, Ibragim allegedly began to confess. Only then did Loughlin drive to the office to write a warrant. He ordered the Massachusetts investigators to wait until the warrant was prepared; meanwhile he told them to let Ibragim, a trained fighter who moments ago had apparently implicated himself in a gruesome triple murder, move freely about the condo.

~

Savard told Khusen he had questions for him and pulled him aside. Ibragim led the investigators up the walkway, cracked open the sliding door facing the pond, took a seat on a mattress that served as a sort of daybed, and lit up a Marlboro Red. McFarlane sat on the stairs leading to the loft. Cinelli leaned against the wall. Gagne took a seat across from Ibragim on the folding chair. He would lead the questioning.

Cinelli took video and audio recordings of some of the interview and the alleged confession on a home video camera and on his phone. Cinelli later claimed that he deleted earlier parts of the interview to free up memory. Gagne had an audio recorder in his shirt pocket with which he recorded one hour, fifty-three minutes, and forty-eight seconds of the four-and-a-half-hour interview. It's unclear why he did not record the entire interview. Crucially, no one recorded the moment when Ibragim allegedly attacked the men in the room.

"Like I said, I didn't kill nobody, and I need your help," Ibragim allegedly told the agents. The Florida State Attorney's shooting report did include a few phrases transcribed from these original recordings. Unfortunately, the fragmentary transcripts released in the shooting reports do not substantiate Ibragim's alleged confession. In fact, on their own, these statements could just as easily support an argument that under pressure, Ibragim told the investigators what they wanted to hear to make them go away. "Will you guys help me?" he said. Only later, after the "confrontation," did Ibragim allegedly admit to having gone to Waltham with Tamerlan in connection with a robbery.

"Okay, I'm telling you I was involved in it. Okay, I had no idea [redacted] gonna kill anyone," he allegedly told investigators at around 10:30 p.m., after three hours of interviews. At this point the records show Ibragim was read his Miranda rights. Cinelli texted Savard, who was waiting outside to be alert in case Ibragim tried to escape. Savard sent Khusen home.

According to the reports Ibragim said his motive was financial. Ibragim allegedly claimed he and Tamerlan took $40,000 from Brendan's apartment and split it between them.

The investigators alerted Assistant District Attorney Steve Loughlin as soon as Ibragim confessed. Thirty minutes later, Cinelli texted Loughlin again. "He will be in custody after interview," he wrote.

"Don't put him in custody until we get a warrant," Loughlin replied.

Inside the apartment Ibragim began to chain-smoke and twitch. Cinelli noticed he was stretching and making odd movements. An hour and a half went by. Cinelli, having seemingly grown bored, began to text a repeated jeer of "Whos your daddy" to an unknown recipient. "Getting confession as we speak," Cinelli wrote.

It was almost midnight. The Massachusetts investigators had yet to get permission from the Middlesex DA's Office to make an arrest. Gagne asked Ibragim if he would like to write out his account in his own words. Though the investigators had agreed to keep three men in the room at all times, when Ibragim began to write, Gagne stepped outside and gave Loughlin a call.

Loughlin would later tell FBI agents conducting the shooting review that he thought the investigators were doing a good job from a legal standpoint; they gave Ibragim cigarette breaks and bathroom breaks, and they allowed him to move around the room freely. Loughlin did not think anything of it when his call with Gagne ended abruptly. In his experience, many law enforcement calls of that nature end abruptly.

McFarlane took Gagne's seat in the folding chair in front of a white coffee table near the mattress, where Ibragim was writing on a pad of white, lined paper. Cinelli, who up until this point had been leaning against the wall, took McFarlane's seat on the stairs.

Ibragim asked the two men if he would be able to smoke in jail and how much time he would get. He asked for more cigarettes. He had a nearly full pack of Marlboro Reds right in front of him. Cinelli opined that Ibragim was looking for a way to get one of the troopers out of the room. Then Ibragim asked to go to the bathroom. Before Ibragim made it back down the stairs, Cinelli ducked into the kitchen, and hid the sword Ibragim kept hanging on the wall behind the shoe rack.

Ibragim sat back down on the mattress and picked up the pen as if to write. McFarlane had returned to his seat in the folding chair and was looking down at his notes. Cinelli had hoped to grab McFarlane's attention with a text. "Be on guard. He is in a vulnerable position to do something bad. Be on guard now. I see him looking around at times," Cinelli wrote. Cinelli would later say he was waiting for McFarlane's BlackBerry to "ding" to confirm he got the message. Cinelli did not hear the ding. Cinelli looked away and checked his phone to see that his message had gone through.

The story goes like this: There was a terrible "roaring noise." Cinelli looked up. The white coffee table was in midair. Cinelli screamed. McFarlane felt a blow to the back of his head. Ibragim ran to the kitchen. The investigators heard scuffling and clanging. "Show me your hands!" McFarlane shouted. McFarlane repeated the command again. Then Ibragim turned to face the men, wielding what looked like a "five-foot-long pole."

Ibragim "moved incredibly quickly, almost like something in a movie," Cinelli would later say. He raised the broomstick above his head and charged like he planned to impale someone. McFarlane drew his weapon and fired the first round.

Cinelli allegedly watched Ibragim twist, fall to his hands and knees, spring up, and lunge at Cinelli once more. Cinelli screamed. McFarlane fired a second round. This time Ibragim stayed down. The threat, McFarlane would later report, had been eliminated.

~

The Florida State Attorney's report also contained a photograph of a notebook; the white pages were speckled with blood. The text of the photo had been redacted, but this was one of the redactions that I was able to remove.

This is how I first read Ibragim's confession in his own words.

"My name is IBRAGIM TODASHEV. I wanna tell the story about the robbery me and Tam did in Waltham in September of 2011," he wrote. Not all of his writing is legible in the photograph, but he appears to say that he and Tamerlan had planned to "rob the drug dealers." He and Tamerlan went to their house, Tamerlan had a gun, and he pointed it at "the guy that opened the door for us." Ibragim then wrote that they went upstairs, into the house, and there were "3 guys in there." Then he writes that he and Tamerlan "put them on the ground" and "taped their hands up." The note stops there.

This was the first I had heard of a gun. If the victims were ordered to the ground, how did that account for Erik's bloody lip? Friends who saw Brendan's body said he had puncture marks on his temple and the top of his head, a mark on his ear, bruises on his face, and scratch marks down his neck. (Although multiple sources said they observed Brendan to have scratch marks down his neck in the days leading up to his murder.) Ibragim's handwritten confession did not address the victims' neck lacerations. Ibragim also introduced a new element: the victims had been bound. I called Hiba in Sudan to ask if this account aligned with what she had seen. "None of their hands were tied as I recall," she told me. That was the last time we spoke on the phone.

Even if the investigators entered that interview with the best of intentions, it was still possible that Ibragim told investigators what they wanted to hear. Mike German, a veteran FBI agent, told me the length of Ibragim's interview— four and a half hours—and the sweltering Florida night could have affected what he said. "You always have to worry about false confessions," he told me. "Particularly in an interview that's gone on for so long. The person is sometimes just trying to give the answer that you want." Brian Reed spoke to Jim Trainum, a former DC police detective and expert in false confessions. Trainum said that if the victims were not bound, Ibragim's claim that they were is especially troubling and potentially a sign of a false confession.

After reading the shooting reports, I did not feel like I was any closer to knowing if Ibragim was actually connected to the Waltham murders. But the DOJ report also included strong language suggestive of Ibragim's guilt. "According to Todashev's uncontroverted confession, Todashev was complicit in the triple homicide," the report read. This made me hopeful that we would learn more about the Waltham murders and Ibragim's confession in Dzhokhar Tsarnaev's federal death penalty trial. Little did I know that in the campaign to sentence Dzhokhar Tsarnaev to death, federal prosecutors were preparing to controvert the "uncontroverted" confession in the most forceful of terms.

BOOK TWO

PART VI

Arguments

CHAPTER
THIRTY-FIVE

House of Pain

Boston Harbor is busy. Cargo ships, whale watch tours, ferries, foul-smelling lob-ster boats, multihulls, and rental kayaks circle around the mouth of the Charles River. Planes fly low over the boats. The airport is across the channel. Along the shore, joggers weave between suits, tourists slurp chowder, and wedding guests spill out of hotels. The harbor walkway goes past the seal tank at the aquarium and ends at the turn to South Boston at the John Joseph Moakley United States District Courthouse, a towering redbrick sentinel of a building, with a five-story semicircular glass wall overlooking everything. Inside the Moakley, ocean light reflects off the sparkling white floors. Spokeswomen in stiletto heels, undercover agents in clean construction boots, and attorneys with rolling briefcases walk through the hallways before the undulating backdrop of the sea.

For more than fifty years, my father had an office by the aquarium, where he had established his own small firm. Every morning before trial, he would walk past the seals and along the harbor to court. My father calls the Moakley "the House of Pain" due to the steep federal sentences, and he calls the court marshals "Hug Judges" because they decide how long his clients can embrace their loved ones. The court marshals call him "Big Bird" in turn, which I have to admit is pretty good. He is tall and has wild, untamable hair that stands up on top of his head, not unlike the Muppet's plumage. We share the same distinctive beak, and he's sociable and warm. Despite the House of Pain joke, he usually likes going to court and catching up with his old colleagues, even the prosecutors he spars with in trials. I used to go to the Moakley to watch him argue. After the bombing, I started coming on my own, walking past The Daily Catch and chatting with the Hug Judges at security. In the months and years leading up to the bombing trial, I followed the case as lawyers squabbled back and forth in combative motions and pretrial hearings. There were also four trials involving the Tsarnaevs' associates that I was following closely as well.

The cases against Dias Kadyrbayev, Azamat Tazhayakov, and Robel Phillipos, Dzhokhar's friends from UMASS Dartmouth, played out like a dark stoner comedy or anticannabis PSA, depending on the day. Dias and Azamat were nineteen years old at the time of the bombing. They were roommates, from Kazakhstan, known on campus as rich kids. They shared a BMW with a novelty license plate that read "Terrorista #1." Azamat's father, who was a member of the city council of the oil-rich capital city Atyrau, told reporters that *terrorista* was a reference to the song "Harlem Shake" by Rotación Caliente, not a celebration of ideological violence. Robel Phillipos had no oil money ties. He was like Dzhokhar. He grew up in Cambridge. Robel's mother was from Ethiopia and worked with refugees. Like Dzhokhar, Robel spent a lot of time at Dias and Azamat's off-campus apartment, smoking weed. None of the friends were charged with helping the Tsarnaev brothers plan the attack or even knowing of their horrific plans beforehand. They were charged for what they did after the attack, when they recognized Dzhokhar in photos of the as-yet-unidentified bombing suspects and while, as their lawyers would point out, they were in a state of shock and very stoned.

It happened like this: Dias texted Dzhokhar after he recognized him in the photos. "Better not text me my friend," Dzhokhar wrote back. "Lol," he added. Then Dzhokhar texted Azamat that he could go to his dorm room and "take what's there," followed by a smiley face. Dias, Azamat, and Robel went to Dzhokhar's dorm. They found Dzhokhar's laptop and a backpack full of fireworks and Vaseline. Azamat and Dias removed the items. They threw the backpack in the dumpster; the trash was collected and released into a Cambridge landfill. The indictment would later say that thirty FBI agents had to search through the garbage for two days before they retrieved the backpack. Even though Robel did not take anything from the dorm room, when FBI agents questioned Robel later, he lied about going with Azamat and Dias when they took the items. Dias's attorney, ex-cop Robert Stahl, tried to argue that Dias did not understand English that well, and anything he said to federal agents should be suppressed in trial. To that end, he put Dias on the stand. "Sup," Dias greeted the court with a smile, pulling a full-on class clown act for the duration of his testimony. He told the court he was currently "chilling" behind bars and reading "hood books," by which his attorney explained he meant literature written in vernacular English. A jury found Dias guilty of taking the laptop and the backpack and throwing it away, and he was sentenced to six years. Azamat was sentenced to three and a half years for agreeing with Dias to go along with the scheme. Robel was sentenced to three years for lying. The trials did not reveal any new information about the Waltham murders, though they did give me some insight into Dzhokhar's social circle. Years later, I would learn that Stahl had tried to secure Dias a plea deal in exchange for his testimony in the bombing trial. The back-and-forth between Stahl and the prosecutors did pertain to the Waltham murders in part. But prosecutors did not take Stahl up on his offer, Dias never testified, and documents related to this negotiation would not be released for another four years.

Then there was Khairullozhon Matanov. Matanov was a cabdriver from Kyrgyzstan. He had eaten lunch with the Tsarnaevs and gone with them back to their Cambridge apartment in the hours after the bombing. Later, Matanov allegedly told his roommate he thought the bombing could have a just reason, such as being done in the name of Islam, and that he would support the bombing if the bombers had a good reason or it was done by the Taliban. The government also maintains that Matanov possessed videos with "violent content or calls to violence." He pleaded guilty to lying to investigators about his interactions with the Tsarnaevs after the bombing and to deleting violent material from his hard drive.

The feds surveilled Matanov openly for a year before arresting him. Matanov knew he was being followed. As an FBI agent testified later, they wanted him to know. At one point the FBI contacted his attorney, Paul Glickman, to ask Matanov to stop driving erratically. Matanov obliged. (When I was a teenager, I babysat for Glickman's kids on two occasions. Much to my dismay, Glickman did not deem this prior relationship reason enough to leak me any inside information or encourage his client to speak to me.) I first laid eyes on Matanov in a bail hearing. He walked into court in an orange jumpsuit. His eyes were half closed, and he rested his head on the table before crossing his arms on his chest. FBI agent Timothy McElroy testified on behalf of the government that Matanov had made 114 MoneyGram transfers overseas in the time period between September 2011 and April 2013, occasionally using an alias. He also testified that Matanov could speak seven different languages. Matanov was a flight risk, prosecutors argued. The judge did not grant him bail. I wrote to Matanov after reading an unsubstantiated report that claimed he had been beaten by guards in jail and noted the broad application of the Sarbanes-Oxley Act—normally reserved for corporate crimes—under which he had been charged for clearing his browser history, and provided him with my home address. "I don't support any kind of violence at all," he wrote back to me in a letter. "This whole case is a mystery to me. The FBI is trying to destroy my life." But in response to my second inquiry, Matanov wrote that his attorney had instructed him not to speak to me. My other letters were returned unopened. Matanov's dark bowl cut bobbed slightly when he pleaded guilty months later. "I signed a deal, and I found guilt most fitting for my situation," he told the court. He was sentenced to two and a half years. It would not be until years later, when documents in the bombing trial were unsealed, that I would discover that the MoneyGram transfers could be crucial evidence in the Waltham murder case and that Matanov had been Ibragim Todashev's roommate.

I would write dispatches of the court hearings for *Boston* magazine and *The Daily Beast*, as I tried to piece together what, if any, relevance this had to Erik's death. At the end of the day, I'd walk over to my father's office and go over what I had seen in court. My father and I follow criminal trials the way other families bond over sports. We'd review the play-by-play of motions, orders, trial strategy, legal history, records, and backstories of lawyers and judges while he rocked in his leather chair near a window overlooking the sea.

~

I also followed the pretrial motions and hearings leading up to Dzhokhar's trial. Death penalty cases are different from every other kind of criminal case. In capital cases jurors must be "death qualified," meaning that they must agree that the death penalty should be applicable in some instances. No anti–death penalty advocates allowed. The jurors must also reach a unanimous decision to execute the defendant. The defense only has to sway a single juror to win.

Death penalty cases are actually separated into two separate trials, each of which is argued before the same jury. In the first trial the jury is asked to reach a verdict on the defendant's guilt. Did they pull the trigger? Did they plant the bomb? Did they mail the anthrax? Did they drown their children? Did they do it? Yes or no? While the subject matter in these cases is as grim as it gets, the path to these verdicts, as opposed to, say, those reached in trials concerning date rape, bribery, or collusion, is straightforward. If the jury finds the defendant guilty, the court proceeds to the sentencing trial.

At this juncture, jurors are required to weigh less tangible factors: aggravating and mitigating evidence. The jury is essentially asked to decide who they believe the defendant is as a person and to measure that up against their own understanding of redemption and the limits thereof. The prosecution's task is to turn the jurors' attention to the horrific nature of the crime and brush off the defense's attempt to unearth a more forgiving psychological portrait. *The defendant will be able to watch TV behind bars and make phone calls to their family,* the government reminds the jurors. *The defendant will spend twenty-three hours a day confined in a cell, a fate worse than hell,* the defense tells the same panel. Arguments like these go back and forth.

Leading up to *United States v. Dzhokhar Tsarnaev*, pretrial hearings and motions made clear that the defense's mitigation argument would focus almost entirely on Dzhokhar's deceased counterpart, his older brother, Tamerlan. Meanwhile, the government prepared to argue that Dzhokhar played an equal role to his older brother in the conception and planning of this crime and in the act itself.

The defense wanted to argue that if not for Tamerlan, the bombing would never have happened. The mitigating evidence the defense was ultimately able to put forth included that Tamerlan had an undue influence in the family, due to traditions from the North Caucasus and his status as eldest brother, and that Tamerlan's size, age, aggressiveness, and domineering personality made Dzhokhar particularly susceptible to his influence. They wanted to show that Tamerlan became radicalized first, before Dzhokhar, and drew his brother into his ideology, and that Tamerlan planned, led, and directed the marathon bombings. They painted a picture of the Tsarnaev family with Tamerlan as the leader, doted on by his parents, whereas no one attended Dzhokhar's wrestling matches or paid for his school uniforms. Anzor, his father, was swirling in insanity behind closed doors. Then the parents divorced, left for Dagestan, and Dzhokhar, once a promising student, was headed off to school, with no one waiting for him at home, no other pillar of support than the deranged Tamerlan.

The government was preparing to argue that Dzhokhar set off a bomb at the finish line because he wanted to and because he saw himself as a holy warrior. The defense was preparing to argue that Dzhokhar had been manipulated by Tamerlan's special force of personality.

The Svengali defense has worked before, in the 2002 Washington, DC, Beltway sniper case. Lee Boyd Malvo and John Allen Muhammad were arrested for murdering ten people at random over the course of three terrifying weeks and were tried in two separate capital cases. Malvo was seventeen; his co-conspirator, Muhammad, was in his forties. Muhammad was sentenced to death. Malvo's life was spared because the defense was able to show that Malvo had been brainwashed by Muhammad. Malvo's attorney, Craig Coolidge, told me in an interview for a story I wrote in *The Daily Beast* that the defense was able to effectively show the jury that this was a case of "indoctrination." Coolidge cited a 2000 FBI report called Project Megiddo, which examines terror attacks and cultish methods of manipulation. The report shows how extremists are able to convince people to commit horrific acts they would typically find objectionable. The defense also had strong civilian witnesses to call to the stand, including one who had watched Muhammad train Malvo to overcome his hesitation to shoot the human form.

Dzhokhar's defense was trying to make the same argument, but in this case the alleged indoctrination regarded two brothers, and there were few outside witnesses to testify to what their dynamic was like behind closed doors. The defense could point to the radical materials Tamerlan sent to his younger brother, Tamerlan's role as the eldest in a Chechen family, his flouting of rules at the gym, like refusing to take off his shoes, his yelling at a store owner about selling halal turkey for Thanksgiving, and the possible abuse of Katherine Russell before he married her. But none of this evidence is in any way as powerful as the allegation that Tamerlan may have murdered three men, one of whom was his "best friend," in an ideologically motivated crime eighteen months before the bombing, independently from Dzhokhar.

For the defense, the Waltham murders could have been used as clear and concrete evidence to distinguish the brothers. Tamerlan's guilt in this earlier crime could show that unlike Dzhokhar, Tamerlan had a track record of violence. The motive for the murders was also important to the defense team. They wanted to argue that the brutal slaying on September 11, 2011, was an act of ideological violence, proof that Tamerlan's radicalization predated Dzhokhar's and that Tamerlan had a history of roping another individual, namely Ibragim, into his diabolical plans. If Tamerlan could kill his best friend, was it not an unspoken threat that he could harm Dzhokhar as well?

The problem for the defense was that the murder case was open and at that point the Middlesex County district attorney had never publicly connected Tamerlan Tsarnaev and Ibragim Todashev to the crime. The government fought tooth and nail to withhold evidence about the Waltham murder case from the defense and block them from introducing this evidence to the jury. In this way they effectively acted as Tamerlan's defense in the 2011 murders, bending over backward to argue that the alleged evidence linking Tamerlan to the homicide was not sound and, in any case, irrelevant.

The government did this by presenting a series of circular arguments. When the defense first requested this material in 2013, the government argued that the murder case was open and active, releasing information could jeopardize the investigation, and protecting the investigation trumped Dzhokhar's right to discovery on a mitigating issue, which they also claimed was not all that relevant. After months went by and there were no updates from the Middlesex DA's Office, the defense filed another motion, and the government made a different argument about jurisdiction. The Waltham matter was a state case, not a federal investigation, so federal prosecutors did not have access to the case files.

This was confusing, because an FBI agent was present at Ibragim's fatal interview, and it seemed like the FBI was involved in the murder investigation to some degree. Remember, after Ibragim was killed, Middlesex released a statement saying that they were investigating this case in conjunction with the FBI and Waltham police, though Middlesex dropped mention of the FBI in later statements. It was unusual that an FBI agent was present for an interview in a joint law enforcement effort but the Bureau was not the lead investigative party. For example, the Joint Terrorism Task Forces involve actors from state and local law enforcement, but their activities fall under the jurisdiction of the FBI.

It would be another eight years before an FBI spokesperson clarified the matter of the FBI's involvement for me on the record: "The Waltham homicide was never classified by the FBI as an act of terrorism," spokesperson Kristen Setera wrote to me in an email. This was interesting. My reporting would show that there are many reasons to believe that the Waltham murders were, in fact, a terrorist act, which the FBI defines as a "violent, criminal [act] committed . . . to further ideological goals." Had the Waltham murders been classified as an act of terrorism, which is a federal crime, then the murders would have fallen squarely into federal jurisdiction, and the government would have had a much harder time blocking the defense from accessing the Waltham evidence, claiming the case was irrelevant to the bombing trial, and keeping the murders away from the jury. But as it was, the FBI never took over the Waltham murder case and apparently never investigated this triple homicide as an act of terrorism, which left the prosecutors in the Tsarnaev trial free to point to Middlesex, claim the stat office shut down their inquiries and their hands were tied.

In the final months leading up to Dzhokhar Tsarnaev's trial, the defense argued that Middlesex could no longer claim investigative privilege since a year had passed and they had produced no new information about their investigation and Dzhokhar was about to stand trial. The defense wanted the reports and recordings of Ibragim's interview, which the government had to have access to because an FBI agent was present. The defense wanted the forensic evidence alluded to in the DOJ's Orlando shooting report as well. But federal prosecutors insisted "nothing has changed" in the course of a year, and the Middlesex investigation "remains active and ongoing." Federal prosecutors said they did not have information to substantiate Ibragim's confession and they had no idea if Middlesex had additional evidence because that information was not available to them. And because the government claimed they could not substantiate Ibragim Todashev's confession, they said there was no need to turn over the evidence they did have, namely the notes and tapes of Ibragim's interview.

The defense accused prosecutors of strategically keeping the evidence in a silo. "It is not true that the government has chosen to insulate itself from the Middlesex district attorney's investigation of the Waltham triple homicides. The Middlesex District Attorney's Office has decided to insulate us from their investigation," Assistant US Attorney William Weinreb argued in retort. At this point, Judge George O'Toole Jr. called the two parties to argue it out in person in a pretrial hearing.

~

When, in November 2014, I learned attorneys in the bombing trial were going to argue about the Waltham murders in open court, I made sure to be there. I was aware that there had been closed-door hearings about the case and was endlessly frustrated that I couldn't listen in on what the two sides were saying about Erik's murder. This was the moment I was waiting for. Once the facts of the case were aired, I figured my questions about Ibragim's confession would be put to rest. I waved to the Hug Judges and took a seat in the corner of the courtroom.

Instead, Weinreb exacerbated all my doubts. "We have no idea whether Mr. Todashev was telling the truth," he told the court.

O'Toole ruled in favor of the government and denied the defense access to notes and recordings detailing Ibragim's confession. Though this was crucial, O'Toole made his decision without listening to or watching the tapes himself. Rather, he reviewed some, and not all, of the FBI's 302 reports. O'Toole came to the conclusion that, contrary to the defense's speculation, the reports he looked at did not materially advance the theory that Tamerlan killed those three men in Waltham. "It would be a different matter if Todashev were available as a potential witness," he wrote in his order. He did not address the reason why Ibragim was not available to the court: namely that a federal agent killed him.

When O'Toole blocked the defense from introducing the Waltham murder case, I was in disbelief and, admittedly, denial. I thought that the trial would be the moment when we finally got answers about Erik's case. "It's a bit of a setback for everyone that the judge ruled against disclosing the Todashev evidence," I wrote in my journal. "Regardless, it's pretty clear this murder case will come up in the Tsarnaev trial, and when it does, will the prosecution again insinuate that Todashev may have been lying?"

Shortly thereafter, the government filed a motion to preclude any reference whatsoever to the Waltham triple homicide before the jury. O'Toole sided with the government again and said that introducing the murders would result in a "mini-trial" and would be distracting to the jurors.

My father advised me that aggressive, well-spoken prosecutors have an Achilles' heel. If the defense plays it right, strong-arm prosecutors are actually vulnerable when matched with a government-friendly judge who consistently takes their side. My father calls it "overarguing." When prosecutors fight the defense's every motion and every plea, and the judge always takes the government's side, the government may have an advantage going into trial, but it gives the defense extra ammo to work into an appeal. This strategy works especially well in federal death penalty trials because in capital cases the defense is automatically granted an appeals hearing, and fair trial standards are supposed to be set at the absolute highest bar. Wise prosecutors know this and are strategic about picking battles before judges they know they can win over.

But an appeal and potential retrial could take years, was not at all certain, and would inflict unimaginable agony on the bombing victims who testified—not to mention taxpayer money. So my father's insight did not comfort me, exactly. O'Toole's first ruling only held for the guilt phase of the trial; he said he could revisit the issue of the Waltham murders if Dzhokhar was found guilty—which everyone except the gaggle of #FreeJahar conspiracy theorists protesting outside the courthouse saw as an inevitability. Maybe O'Toole would rule differently before the penalty phase, when lawyers argued about whether Dzhokhar should be sentenced to death. That's when mitigating evidence actually matters, I thought.

In those days, I still visited Aria at Zoe's almost every weekend. Neither Aria nor Bellie believed Tamerlan was behind Erik's murder. They had not seen any evidence to that effect, nor had they been presented with any information from the Middlesex County District Attorney's Office. Aria had been especially skeptical about Ibragim's alleged confession, and now, I told her, prosecutors were too.

"Sometimes I feel like I'm losing my mind," Aria told me, wiping down the bar. "In your heart do you really think you're going to come up with some answers?"

In my heart of hearts? I had to try, I told her. But I stopped swinging by the diner after that. I kept investigating, stayed in touch, called every time there was a story in the paper, and years later showed up to Aria's baby shower with purple tulips after agonizing over the appropriate gift to show how much I cared—while maintaining journalistic boundaries. I made myself available anytime she wanted to talk. But my regular visits weren't a help to Aria anymore. I had to come up with answers, and Aria had a life to live.

~

Dzhokhar would be found guilty on all thirty counts, but I would not be privy to the sealed transcripts of the hearings on the Waltham murders leading into the penalty phase of the trial; the transcripts of these discussions would not be released for several more years. Nevertheless, behind closed doors Weinreb would insinuate in more forceful terms that Ibragim was lying. The defense had no evidence that Tamerlan killed those three men in Waltham, he argued. "The only thing that the defense has to offer is the uncross-examined and uncross-examinable statement of someone who was clearly somewhat unbalanced, if not deranged," he said of Ibragim.

I knew Weinreb's statements were part of his legal strategy. But unlike the defense or me, he could listen to the interviews, and he essentially said Ibragim pinned the murders on a dead guy. Weinreb said Ibragim told several different stories, and it wasn't until he was confronted with evidence that he himself had been involved in the murders that Ibragim admitted his involvement. The fact that Ibragim put all the blame on Tamerlan makes Ibragim's confession less credible, Weinreb said. Weinreb did not disclose the evidence Ibragim had been confronted with or why that evidence did not also substantiate the confession in the unsealed transcripts—although parts of these documents remain under seal.

Even though Judge George O'Toole Jr. banned mention of the triple homicide before the jury, I still had to watch the trial just in case a lead did break loose.

CHAPTER
THIRTY-SIX

The Trial

On the morning before the first day of Dzhokhar Tsarnaev's trial, I ran into Erik's mother on the train. It was Monday, January 5, 2015. It snowed a lot that winter, and I had tromped through the aftermath of a storm to the Central Square stop in a pair of heavy snow boots, my laptop over my shoulder and a notepad in my jacket pocket. Bellie was on her way to work.

The train from Cambridge to Boston was crowded, but after one stop I took a seat beside Bellie so we could talk above the rattle. She was recovering from knee surgery and had a pair of crutches at her side. She turned to me beneath the commuters in headphones, and asked about the role her son's murder case might or might not play in the death penalty trial. I went over the legal back-and-forth. Before she left she whispered in my ear, "There must be a cover-up" and planted a kiss on my cheek.

Outside the Moakley Courthouse there was a frenzy of TV cameras and protesters. I cut through the crowd and made my way to the jury selection room, where Judge George O'Toole Jr. gave instructions to two hundred prospective jurors filling out a questionnaire.

There were journalists there from the *New York Times*, the *New Yorker*, the *Washington Post*, NBC, and the *Guardian* to name a few. There were reporters I admired and wanted to impress. When the court broke for recess, I went to the bathroom to find I'd spent half of the day with Bellie's red lipstick smeared across the side of my face.

~

The halls of the Moakley Courthouse are bright, criminal defendants are not generally privy to the sea view. The court marshals escort them up from the bowels of the building to the windowless courtrooms in chains. For everyone else, walking out of the death penalty trial was like leaving a matinee. The harbor glare was blinding.

Rows of cameras lined up outside the Moakley Courthouse every day of the trial. Networks and newspapers are banned from photographing in federal courthouses, so they ran their stories with courtroom sketches, grainy surveillance videos, and photos of Dzhokhar taken when he was a handsome teenager with soft features. *Rolling Stone* magazine sparked a boycott when they published one of Dzhokhar's selfies on their cover. People were angry because they thought the cover story made the terrorist look like Jim Morrison. By the time I laid eyes on Dzhokhar, he was not so handsome anymore. His face was marred by bullet wounds, and his navy blue suit hung off his skeletal frame.

In court, Judy Clarke argued for the defense that Dzhokhar was in thrall to his older brother, Tamerlan. She held up a photo of the former boxing champion with his arm wrapped around Dzhokhar as a child, slight, smiling, dwarfed by his older brother. The defense called to the stand Tamerlan's old boxing coach, John Curran, who said Dzhokhar followed his brother around "like a puppy," and an expert who testified to Chechen social codes. They argued that the radical material on Dzhokhar's computer came from Tamerlan's thumb drive. There was a vacuum in Dzhokhar's life, and Tamerlan was the only one around to fill that void, argued Clarke. Without Tamerlan, Clarke claimed, "the horrific events of the Boston Marathon bombing cannot be told or understood in any degree of reality." Dzhokhar became convinced by Tamerlan's passion, Clarke said. The bombing was Tamerlan's plan; Dzhokhar followed. Not once did jurors in the bombing trial hear about the Waltham murder case or about Erik's death. The moment I'd been hoping for never came.

At the start of the penalty phase of the trial, the government called Bill Richard to the stand to tell the court about that terrible day. He spoke of how his wife and three young children had gone to cheer on runners and get ice cream cones; the confusion of the first blast; and the second that blew his life apart. He described what he saw when he came to: his daughter's leg, as if it was hacked with a meat cleaver; his youngest son, ribs exposed, bleeding onto the concrete; and his eldest, who witnessed it all.

After Dzhokhar was convicted, Bill and Denise Richard wrote an op-ed in the *Boston Globe* urging the Department of Justice to rest their case and refrain from pursing the death penalty. The Richards knew that capital trials are almost always followed by a lengthy appeals process, and they feared the prolonged anguish that pursuing capital punishment would entail. "We sat in the courtroom, day after day, bearing witness to overwhelming evidence that included graphic video and photographs, replicated bombs, and even the clothes our son wore his last day alive," they wrote. They wanted Dzhokhar to spend the rest of his life behind bars without the possibility of parole and for this case to fade out of the spotlight. Years later, it would be revealed that Dzhokhar actually had offered to plead guilty and accept a life sentence without parole if the government took the death penalty off the table. Had the government accepted this offer, there would have been no need for a trial, and no reason for Bill Richard to recount that day before an audience or for spectators to mull over images of his son's lifeless body.

I went to court day after day for the duration of the five-month trial. By the time the jury handed down a death sentence, the snow had melted and the magnolias were in bloom.

CHAPTER
THIRTY-SEVEN

The Appeal

I spent the next four and a half years looking into other leads, the findings of which I will detail shortly. Then on December 12, 2019, four and a half years after Dzhokhar Tsarnaev was sentenced to death, nearly six and a half years after the bombing, and more than eight years after Erik was killed, I found myself back at the Moakley Courthouse. Dzhokhar Tsarnaev's attorneys were appealing his death sentence.

In many ways my life had stayed the same. I knocked on doors. I made uncomfortable phone calls. I taught myself to write holed up on Cape Cod in the fall. I moved in and out of relationships, went skinny-dipping in Walden Pond, and in 2017, I landed a book deal. But there was still a lot of work to do, more doors to knock on, more people to call. My reporting was pointing me in some scary directions, and I was tired of being brave. I talked to my father about my work. My investigation had brought us closer together. But my father is after all a father and an attorney, not a journalist, who still calls my interview subjects "witnesses."

Which is why after some hesitation I agreed to produce a docuseries. My agents connected me to the production company Anonymous Content. I was afraid the show might go off the rails and filming could interfere with my reporting rather than help me move the case forward. Then I received a call from a screenwriter named Matt Cook. Cook lives in Texas with his wife and three children. He wrote *Patriots Day*. He's the son of a preacher, and he likes his whiskey neat.

I tried to turn him down on our first call, like I had turned down others. But my tough-girl schtick didn't work with Cook. He is a combat veteran. He did not intend to go to war, his first day of training was September 11, 2001. He was a staff sergeant and did two tours in Iraq. I read his war reporting and memoirs in *Texas Monthly* before our call. I had to admit, he had seen some things. And he knew what it was like to lose a friend. I asked him if he wanted to knock on doors with me, and he said he did. I started to think that maybe it would be useful to have a guy like him around. Matt interviewed bombing survivors and members of law enforcement before he wrote *Patriots Day*. The film is about the bravery of those impacted by the Tsarnaev's violence, including hardworking cops. He took a close look at members of Watertown PD, who faced down the Tsarnaevs in a shoot-out. Those stories are important but they aren't what my investigation is about. I asked Matt if he was prepared to follow leads that might make law enforcement look bad. He said he was and he had other questions about the case too. Cook's writing is sharp and clear. He kept me focused. He told me that navigating the TV industry might make me emotional and that I should call him if I got upset, before going to anyone else. I didn't know what he meant. And then I did. He listened to me bitch and scream for a solid five years. Maybe it helped that his hearing is partially shot from so many close encounters with explosives. We talked over every new break. There were big ups and big downs, but eventually we teamed up with the production company Story Syndicate and sold the show to ABC New Studios, and it aired on Hulu in September 2022. While we were filming, the two of us spent hours in the car driving around Massachusetts, Florida, and Virginia, seeking the answers to the questions that had haunted me for so long. In addition, his wife Lauren, while not an official part of the production team, is an uncannily good researcher. She found things I missed. Some of what we found ended up in the series; a lot did not.

I texted Cook and called my father on my way to the Moakley, then parked my car in the basement of a newly minted pharmaceutical building, braced myself against the cold, salty air, and made my way back to court.

∼

Dzhokhar's appellate team was trying to overturn the death sentence. Victory for the defense would be Dzhokhar living out the rest of his natural life behind bars—with no chance for parole. Unlike the original defense team, the appellate attorneys were able to review the FBI interview notes and the video and audio recordings of Ibragim's fatal interview.

In written arguments, the defense put forth that Tamerlan killed those three men on September 11, 2011, and that the Waltham murders were part of a jihad. They argued that blocking the defense from accessing the reports and recordings of Ibragim's confession violated Dzhokhar's right to a fair trial and so the capital sentence should be made void. If the government insisted on seeking the death penalty, that option was still available to them. But the government should be forced to try the sentencing phase again under fair conditions.

Dzhokhar did not return to Boston for his appeal. He remained detained in his cell in a "clean version of hell"—one ex-warden's description of Terre Haute, the Rocky Mountain maximum-security prison. But there were still a few familiar faces. Outside the courthouse stood a protestor in a knit cap, silently displaying a "Death Penalty Is Murder" sign, as he had done throughout the entirety of the trial, sometimes with company, sometimes alone. Opposite the capital punishment protestor stood a man wearing a fur ushanka with his shirt unbuttoned halfway to his navel, holding a sign on which he'd scrawled "Free Jahar, FUCK THE USA." Adrianne Haslet, who had been a professional ballroom dancer before the Tsarnaevs blew her leg off, approached the courthouse behind me and flipped him off as she walked in the door. I squeezed onto a wooden bench with the rest of the press pool and waited for the appeal to begin.

I had paid close attention to developments in the appellate case in the five years of legal back-and-forth leading up to this hearing as well as documents and transcripts of closed-door hearings that were quietly unsealed. There are 1,779 entries in the docket listing in *United States v. Dzhokhar Tsarnaev*, and many of these entries are hundreds of pages long. I scrutinized every page I could get my hands on.

In the appeal the defense harped on a newly revealed claim that Dzhokhar had learned about Tamerlan's involvement in the Waltham killings when Dzhokhar came home from school over winter break in 2012, a few months before the bombing. They argued that the moment Dzhokhar Tsarnaev found out his brother was a killer was a crucial turning point in his own radicalization.

Yet the prosecution questioned and scrutinized every piece of evidence that the defense put forth and added new claims to muddy the waters. Even if Tamerlan had been involved, the Waltham killings stemmed from a drug rip-off and had nothing to do with Dzhokhar or the bombing, they countered.

The drip, drip of new information would occasionally catch the attention of other reporters, and it made an especially sensational splash in the headlines in the weeks immediately preceding the hearing. The court had released a copy of a 2013 FBI warrant. Though much of the warrant was redacted, it did include new details about what Ibragim allegedly said before he was killed, like that he and Tamerlan doused the corpses with bleach.

Aria and Bellie got wind of the news. "Is the case closed?" Bellie asked when I called to check in. I had contacted Middlesex earlier in the afternoon. They gave me the same open-case-no-comment line they'd been giving me for the last six years. "No," I told Bellie. "It's not closed."

Though video cameras and recording devices are banned in the Moakley federal courthouse, journalists with media passes are allowed to use computers and phones. Many of us took to Twitter throughout the trial in 2015, noting Dzhokhar Tsarnaev's rare gestures, jury reactions, and tears from the witness stand.

The First Circuit Court of Appeals is also in the Moakley building, but it follows different rules. No one in the gallery is allowed to use electronics of any kind, there are no clocks on the walls, and few of us wore a watch. "It's like a casino in here," a reporter grumbled to me, as we waited for the hearing to begin. Neither of us knew the time without our cell phones.

In the years since the bombing trial, I'd covered other cases and defendants—mobsters, gangsters, wealthy parents charged with bribing their kids into college, women who texted their boyfriends to death—with more or less the same group of journalists squeezed into the hard benches beside me: TV news men and women with their immaculate makeup and pressed suits; radio, online, and print media like me, in our unofficial uniform of blue oxfords. A spokeswoman from the Massachusetts US Attorney's Office walked up to the reporter sitting behind me and whispered for him to find her later, adding, "I've got some juice." I braced myself; if the attorneys brought forth new information about Erik's death like I read in the warrant, I would have to digest it here in this pin-drop-quiet room.

"All rise," the bailiff commanded as three appellate justices, William J. Kayatta Jr., O. Rogeriee Thompson, and Juan Torruella, took their seats above the court and adjusted their black robes. A hush filled the room.

Kayatta wore round glasses beneath his thick brows. Thompson wore barrettes and spoke, I would learn, in a refreshingly frank tone. Torruella had gray hair and magnetic glasses that he snapped together in front of his face to mark the start of the proceedings, a more subtle approach to the traditional gavel.

Daniel Habib, a public defender from New York, was presenting the appellate argument for the defense. Habib did not try the bombing case itself. In addition to his relative youth, he was not shadowed by the same cloud of despair that came to hang over Dzhokhar's original legal entourage. Opposing Habib was William Glaser, from the appellate section of the Department of Justice, in a navy suit and a boyish blond buzz cut. The justices seemed sympathetic to Habib's first two arguments—separate from the Waltham issue—about the defense's denied request to move the case outside of Boston. Not changing the venue made it all the more important to question the jurors who made contradictory statements about their media exposure. "Is there any more iconic event than the Boston Marathon? Let's limit it to New England," asked Torruella, pressing Glaser on whether there was a reason the government fought to hold the trial in Boston.

"Your Honor, none that I'm aware of. But the Boston Marathon is a national marathon," Glaser said, in an increasingly nervous lilt.

The justices were even harsher on Glaser in regards to Judge George O'Toole's decision not to question jurors about indications they had lied in voir dire. "If the juror is not being totally factual with you, how are you to probe the extent of her emotional impact?" asked Thompson. Did the government really need to seat jurors who engaged with social media posts calling Dzhokhar a "piece of garbage" or "scum" and "trash" or saying that he belonged in a "dungeon"?

"It's just very puzzling. You've got a defendant who is clearly guilty of this heinous crime, but you then stretched and don't try to follow the rules," added Kayatta.

In response to what Torruella described as the "jihad situation," Glaser said, "The evidence does not indicate that Mr. Todashev was involved in committing the murders and certainly was not forced to commit the murders by Tamerlan."

He again classified the murders as related to a drug rip-off not jihad and suggested there was more information to back up his point in sealed files.

I wanted to look at those sealed files, and I wanted to watch and listen to the video and audio recordings of Ibragim's confession so badly. Learning what he said in pieces, from second-hand accounts, was endlessly frustrating.

I would update Matt Cook when I got out of court. But not before giving my father a full briefing first. We had been yammering back and forth on my drive to the Moakley. The appellate court had few questions about the premise of the defense's arguments; rather they asked Habib specific questions about the implications of taking his side. I took this to be an indication they were inclined to rule in the defense's favor. Habib had given the justices assurance that Dzhokhar would remain locked up for life no matter what, and Glaser looked uneasy. "They overtried it," I barked.

~

Six months later, in the summer of 2020, the First Circuit Court of Appeals vacated Dzhokhar Tsarnaev's death sentence. The justices had reviewed the interview tapes, and they were unanimous in their decision to vacate on the grounds that Judge George O'Toole Jr. had failed to question jurors about prior media exposure to the case. The majority, Justice O. Rogeriee Thompson and Justice Juan Torruella, also found that O'Toole and the federal prosecutors violated Brady—a discovery rule—by not turning over the recordings of Ibragim's interview to the defense. In the appellate motions, the government had argued that withholding information on the Waltham murders was in any event harmless. But the First Circuit Court of Appeals found that this was simply not true. At least one juror could have found that because of what had happened in Waltham, Tamerlan was not just "bossy" but rather "a stone-cold killer who got a friend to support his fiendish work," the justices wrote in their ruling. If Tamerlan could influence Ibragim, who the justices described as "a mixed-martial-arts bruiser," Tamerlan could surely influence Dzhokhar as well.

President Donald J. Trump was furious. He raged against the appellate court on Twitter. "Death penalty!" he wrote. Rather than seek the death penalty by retrying the sentencing phase, the Trump DOJ took the highly unusual move of going over the appellate court's head and petitioned the United States Supreme

Court. Supreme Court experts were surprised and skeptical that the court would take up the case. This was not a typical Supreme Court case; there were no cross-circuit rulings to clarify. Brady violations and jury vetting are two common grounds for appeal. Trials are overturned for reasons like these all the time. But these were unusual times, and this was an unusual court.

~

In March 2021, the Supreme Court did, in fact, agree to take the case and review the First Circuit's ruling. Before stepping into office, in what was supposed to be a purposeful turn from his predecessor, President Joe Biden vowed to abolish the death penalty. Yet rather than circumvent Trump's Hail Mary to the United States Supreme Court, the Biden administration promptly picked up the torch and marched the DOJ onward with the quest to sentence Dzhokhar to death.

I talked to Aria when the news broke that justices at the highest court in the country would, albeit indirectly, be weighing in on Erik's murder. The path her brother's case had taken through the court system, constantly confronting the story in the news, with no real answers, and no apparent interest from prosecutors or anyone in law enforcement to find the truth, had been a seven-year roller coaster. Though Aria, as ever, tried to look on the bright side.

She was glad the appeal process helped shake loose some new information and was hopeful the Supreme Court case might reveal more. Perhaps there would be renewed pressure to get to the bottom of what actually happened. Because she is fundamentally against the death penalty, so if her brother's death helped save Dzhokhar's life, well, she could find some kind of peace in that. What Aria did not expect was for the Supreme Court justices or anyone else to treat the victims, or her family, with respect. "At the end of the day they're just three drug dealers, so we're not going to get the justice or attention that we would want," she told me on the phone.

Unfortunately, she was right.

In a brief filed in the lead-up to the Supreme Court arguments, Biden's deputy solicitor general, Eric J. Feigin, distinguished the Waltham crime, in which the victims were described as "drug dealers," from the bombing, in which "innocent people" were killed. In addition to picking up the narrative of the two previous prosecutorial teams and casting doubt on Ibragim's confession, Feigin was also preparing to categorize the murders as an unplanned killing, not ideologically motivated, and not terrorism. Feigin was strategic; he sought to win the argument put before him by the Biden DOJ. The truth of what happened in Waltham and the reason the case remained open all these years later were irrelevant to the DOJ's thesis. Feigin was arguing to sentence Dzhokhar Tsarnaev to death in the name of justice. But at what cost?

The Supreme Court hearing was held on a clammy day on October 13, 2021. I was in DC with the film crew. Though I was initially slated to attend the hearing in person, COVID derailed that plan. The director, Jesse Sweet, instructed me to walk purposefully back and forth in front of the courthouse while the camera crew followed me around. "The Waltham murders are like a pawn in this case," I said, in what I hoped was a convincing tone. Then I was released to a hotel room, where a camera was set up by a small desk, where I was to sit as a room full of people watched me listen to the live audio recording. I tried not to be self-conscious of my frizzy hair or my hangnails as the camera zoomed in on my hands while I scribbled notes to prepare. Once the hearing began, I forgot they were there. Nothing else mattered. The highest court in America was talking about Erik's murder, and as I had feared yet expected, the facts of the Waltham case were being brushed aside and distorted again.

The answers behind the mystery of Erik's death were unknowable, Feigin told the court. "We'll never know how or why three drug dealers were killed in Waltham in 2011," he said. But was that a fact? Or a self-serving command to leave this stone unturned? As Feigin put forth, "This investigation had hit the end of the road. There was no way to figure out what happened."

Was this death penalty case part of the reason why the case was still open at the Middlesex County District Attorney's Office? I wondered. It certainly did not help. The death penalty meant that the government had a vested interest in not getting to the bottom of what happened in Waltham.

Ibragim Todashev was "unhinged," and his confession was inherently unreliable, Feigin said. Ibragim had every motive to pin the murders on Tamerlan. "The only people who might have known what happened in Waltham were Todashev, who admitted to some participation, and possibly Tamerlan, and both of them were dead," said Feigin. This gave me pause. If the only people who might know something about the murders are Ibragim Todashev and Tamerlan Tsarnaev, then isn't that statement itself conceding that they did it?

I could not see their faces, but apparently a majority of the justices were nodding along. The court was divided along political lines, and in a 6–3 verdict the court upheld the death sentence, mistruths, and a decade of hypocrisy.

CHAPTER THIRTY-EIGHT

Evidence

The government is wrong. Tamerlan Tsarnaev and Ibragim Todashev did it. They killed those three men in Waltham. The basic facts of what happened are not "unknowable." The evidence of their guilt is readily available for anyone invested in seeking it. I don't know with certainty who slit which man's throat. But by all indications this was a cold-blooded, premeditated murder. If Tamerlan and Ibragim had lived, their respective attorneys would likely try to downplay their involvement. They would point fingers at one another, and if the attorneys were good, one of them might be able to reduce the charges to accessory. That is, if their attorneys were really, really good. I don't see any possible path to an acquittal. Tamerlan Tsarnaev and Ibragim Todashev are guilty of the 2011 triple homicide. This is not an accusation I make lightly. If there were holes in this theory then I would be duty bound, by my own conscience if nothing else, to reveal them to you. That was the whole point of turning this book into a memoir, the reason I inserted myself into this narrative in the first place. This story could end with me banging my head against the wall, no closer to the truth than when I began. It could end with my failure, but at least I would not have to warp the facts to fit a narrative that isn't true. But the truth is Tamerlan Tsarnaev and Ibragim Todashev did it, and this killing was more brutal, horrific, and depraved than anything I dared let myself imagine.

At first there were holes in the theory of Tamerlan and Ibragim's guilt, a lot of them, and few reliable, verified facts holding the theory together. It has taken more than a decade of research and investigation to piece together this story. I looked at alternative theories and suspects. I spent months and years trying to build other narratives. I collected fact after fact and followed them like stepping-stones. I imagined the other directions this story might go if one more piece of information lined up, though in its telling I have refused to take any leaps.

I am not a prosecutor. I do not have a police badge or the power of a grand jury. I cannot write up a warrant or request cell phone records. I was not privy to those first interviews with people close to this case. But unlike the officials tasked with this investigation, it seems, I actually want answers. One could come up with a counternarrative or an explanation other than Ibragim Todashev and Tamerlan Tsarnaev's guilt, but are these counternarratives reasonable? No. They are not.

The Court of Last Resort, a collection of stories by defense attorney Erle Stanley Gardner, first published in 1952, is often pointed to as the first original work of true crime. Gardner's work became the basis for the *Perry Mason* television series. He wrote these stories, thought of as unusual at the time, on behalf of his clients, whom he believed the court system had failed. Tackling this investigation on my own, producing a docuseries, and writing this book is truly a last resort. That we are in this position at all, that the answers to an unsolved murder case linked to a landmark act of terrorism have been left to an investigative journalist, not to mention a friend of a victim, is a testament to the failure of local, state, and federal law enforcement, the state court system, the federal court system, local politicians, and those in national office. But here we are, and in this court, the court of last resort, the only arena of accountability I have available to me, I can say with certainty that Ibragim Todashev and Tamerlan Tsarnaev killed Brendan Mess, Raphael Teken, and my friend, Erik Weissman.

There is no smoking gun or singular piece of evidence that on its own points definitively to their guilt, as might make for a satisfying twist in a fictional detective story. In real life, defendants are often convicted without a singular linchpin piece of evidence. Cases that rest on a sole testimony or clue, however damning it may seem at first, have made the career of many a skilled defense attorney. In such situations the defense has a clear target—a witness to discredit, forensic evidence to undercut—and if they can do that, they win the case. My case against Tamerlan Tsarnaev and Ibragim Todashev is more like a snare or a web. Even if one were to raise questions or reasonable doubt about a handful of facts, or cut through a number of threads, Ibragim and Tamerlan are still stuck. The logical conclusion remains the same: they did it.

Though I do not myself have access to the video and audio recordings of Ibragim Todashev's last interview, I was able to obtain new details about this confession from the order issued by the justices in the First Circuit Court of Appeals, who reviewed these tapes. I have also obtained a redacted copy of the FBI's 302 report of his final interview via a public records request, gleaned information from the shooting reports, a partially redacted copy of Ibragim Todashev's A-File (or immigration file), also obtained by records request, Dzhokhar Tsarnaev's trial, the trials of two Tsarnaev associates, and of course the unredacted copy of Ibragim's partially written, blood-splattered confession.

~

While all of these documents inform my findings, the circumstances surrounding Ibragim's death were so questionable and the answers, such as they were, took so long to be released—and did not include a review or accounting of the murder evidence itself or the decision not to arrest Ibragim after he confessed—that I could not take anything I found in these documents, filtered as they were through law enforcement and the courts, at face value. I needed to find primary source evidence on my own, independent from these secondary sources. Which I did. At the same time, I must address this secondary source evidence as well.

Let's start with what we know from these secondhand accounts about the hours leading up to Ibragim Todashev's confession. The crickets were screaming. Chris Savard, the Florida Joint Terrorism Task Force officer who had been acting as the liaison to the Massachusetts investigators, stayed outside with Khusen Taramov. Ibragim Todashev led Boston FBI agent Aaron McFarlane, Massachusetts state trooper Curtis Cinelli, assigned to the fugitive task force, and Massachusetts state trooper Joel Gagne, assigned to the Middlesex County District Attorney's Office, into the apartment. Ibragim commented on an AK-47 sticker decal as he ushered them inside. This was his friend's apartment, he said. He did not know how to remove the welcoming illustration of an assault rifle from the front door, though he assured the investigators that he had tried. Ibragim asked the three investigators to remove their shoes. They complied. Thus the interrogation began with all four men in a small, dark room, without shoes on.

Ibragim launched into an explanation of the fight outside the mall two weeks prior, in which, need he remind them, in a dispute involving a parking space, he beat two men bloody, sending one of them to the hospital in a stretcher with rearranged teeth. It was self-defense, he said. Meanwhile, Ibragim's three-foot sword hung near them on the wall, along with a Chechen flag, as they spoke. Ibragim appeared to have been under the impression that the investigators were there to talk to him about this parking lot brawl. Investigators apparently let him entertain this false pretext for a while, and according to a partially unredacted copy of the 302 report of this interview, even after they began questioning him they did not immediately reveal that the intended subject of their questioning was the triple murder in Waltham. In all his prior interviews, the overt focus of the questions had been about Tamerlan and the bombing, not the Waltham murders. Agent McFarlane began the interview on a similar tack, asking Ibragim familiar questions about his relationship to Tamerlan and his time in Boston, warming him up for Gagne.

Ibragim told the agents that he and Tamerlan were never close. They had a falling-out. Though the redacted 302 report does detail what this disagreement concerned it appears he told them that they were involved in some kind of fight. After that, Ibragim said, they ran into one another from time to time, usually at Friday prayer at the mosque, but did not have a personal relationship. Investigators asked about a woman in Tamerlan's life, potentially Katherine Russell, who Ibragim said he did not know.

Then Gagne took the wheel and began asking Ibragim about his movements in and out of Boston in September 2011.

According to the partially redacted 302 report, Ibragim appeared to have recited for the men a timeline of his life since arriving in America in 2008. He said he lived in Chelsea, before moving to Watertown and Cambridge. Then, according to the 302 report, he told the investigators that he left Massachusetts and moved to Georgia in 2009 or 2010.

This is not true. Ibragim was in Boston in 2011. He was arrested for a road rage incident in February 2010 while driving a medical transportation truck and appeared in Suffolk Superior Court on August 10, 2011, where the charges were dismissed. I obtained paperwork documenting this infraction at a local court-house, separately from the documentation released in the shooting reports, and talked to his boss at Coco Transportation, Victor Ten, who fired him.

The investigators interjected. He left Massachusetts in 2010? Was he sure? Ibragim recanted. Perhaps the move to Georgia was not so permanent. He tried again.

In the second telling, Ibragim said he left Atlanta and moved back to Boston in May or June of 2011. He had grown tired of Atlanta, he explained. When he first moved to Atlanta, he was not training or working because of a knee injury. When his knee had healed, he wanted to go back to Boston and resume training.

The investigators asked about his means of transportation. Ibragim said he never owned a car when he lived in Atlanta, so he must have taken either a bus or a plane back to Boston, he said. That summer of 2011, less than two years prior to the Orlando interview, Ibragim said he lived near the Wai Kru gym in an apartment with "a bunch of students." Then he said his memories were coming back to him; in the beginning of September 2011, he left for Atlanta. Ibragim had lost an amateur MMA fight, he had lost his job, and it was time to go.

He took a bus from downtown Boston, he said. Afternoon, morning, he was not sure. But it was daylight. He traveled alone, paid in cash, listed the ticket in his own name, and took a bus—he believed it was a Greyhound—all the way back to Georgia. Ibragim said he was not sure when he left Boston exactly, but he was only in Boston for "the first ten days" of September, he said. That, he was sure of.

Ibragim appeared to have given a somewhat detailed account about this Greyhound bus ride back to Atlanta. He said they made several stops. He believed they stopped in New York City and one other location that he could not recall. When he arrived in Atlanta, he said he called someone. Actually, he said, this person was waiting for him. The name of the person is redacted, though it's my guess the person he said he called was Reni. Ibragim said he stayed in Atlanta for a couple of weeks; after that, he left for Orlando. Ibragim did not seem to remember how he got to Florida. He said he probably took another Greyhound bus. He wasn't certain, but the bus was gray, and he paid in cash. When he got to Orlando he was met by "a bunch of guys."

Then, according to the FBI 302 report, the questioning turned to the matter of Ibragim Todashev's cell phone. Ibragim said he'd had the same phone number for a long time. The investigators did not seem to have made a point of this at first. The conversation returned to the summer of 2011. Ibragim said that he saw Tamerlan from time to time but that they never met at the Wai Kru gym; they worked out at different times.

Then investigators turned the conversation back to cell phones and what he knew about a phone number with a 617 area code. Ibragim said he did not remember the number, but it could be his old number, if that's what his friends said.

At this point one of the troopers confronted Ibragim with a form from the Massachusetts Department of Transitional Assistance (MDTA), the state's food stamp program, dated August 19, 2011, with Ibragim's name and the same number listed in his contact information. Ibragim said that another person—whose name is redacted—would fill out these sorts of forms for him. Then a trooper showed him a form from the International Institute with his signature, dated September 7, 2011. Ibragim said that it was his signature, but he was not sure about the date. He said he gave his EBT card to someone else a week before leaving Boston. I have not been able to independently obtain documentation confirming this food stamp form or the documentation from the International Institute, a nonprofit for immigrants and refugees. The program officer declined to comment, citing client confidentiality. But I do have a document from the Massachusetts State Athletic Commission dated July 15, 2011—Ibragim registered as an amateur fighter. He lists an address near the Wai Kru gym, on Gordon Street, and the same 617 phone number, and that he was unemployed.

Ibragim told the investigators that he was forced out of the Gordon Street residence in September, but he continued to live there for several more days. He wasn't sure when he left Boston exactly; it appears the investigators circled back to this point again, and it could have been a Sunday or a Monday, but he thinks he left on September 10, 2011. Seeing the food stamp documents helped his recollection, he said. Once he arrived in Florida, he got a new phone number with a 407 area code. He said he switched to the Florida number because it was cheaper, only $40 a month.

Then a trooper—the 302 report doesn't specify which one, but it was likely Gagne—took out a receipt from Boston Wireless that allegedly showed he paid

$40 a month for his previous 617 number, exactly the same rate. Investigators asked if it was his receipt. "Could be," Ibragim said.

At this point, I imagine the interview took a turn. Ibragim was caught in a lie or perhaps another error of memory. But if the notes from the 302 report are correct, it was looking more and more like Ibragim was deliberately misleading investigators. How else might one reasonably explain the discrepancies between his account and the facts? One might muddle up where one was when, even though the dates in question were not so long ago, and Ibragim had been questioned about his whereabouts and his time in Boston in at least a half dozen interviews within the previous month. It's surprising Ibragim had not sorted out his biographical information despite so many opportunities to review it, but people do have trouble with dates and numbers all the time. Yet the reason he gave to investigators for switching his phone number was more than a numerical error. He provided them with an explanation that did not make sense. This error appeared more significant and concerning as the interview went on.

Ibragim tried again. He said he last saw Tamerlan Tsarnaev at Friday prayer at the mosque, two or three days before he left town. Ibragim said he left Boston on a Greyhound bus on September ninth or tenth. Or perhaps he left on the eleventh.

The investigators asked Ibragim about a call he made from the 617 number on September 12, 2011, at 12:25 a.m.

Where was he when he made that call?

"I guess Atlanta," he said.

Why did he stop using the 617 number on September 12, 2011?

Ibragim said he wasn't sure.

I do not have independent documentation confirming that Ibragim Todashev stopped using his phone number a few hours after the three men were killed. Though I can independently confirm that he did switch to the 407 number.

Investigators let his story stand for a short while longer. They asked him if he read the news. Ibragim said he only read Chechen papers. Did he know Brendan Mess? He said that he did. Ibragim said he saw Brendan at the gym. Ibragim said he hadn't heard anything about Tamerlan and a triple murder.

At this point the 302 report notes that investigators confronted Ibragim on his story. The 302 report does not detail what information Ibragim was confronted with. But internal FBI documents obtained via records request and the Florida State Attorney shooting report state that the intended plan for this interview was to confront Ibragim with forensic evidence. Defense attorneys often try to undercut the significance of forensic evidence in trial, but when investigators present an individual with forensic evidence during questioning, almost universally the message they are trying to send is that it's an open-and-shut case. Whether or not that's true is a different story. Reni told me that after Ibragim was killed, investigators presented her with photographs from the murder scene and insisted that they had DNA evidence linking Ibragim Todashev to the crime, in an apparent effort to induce her to offer incriminating evidence. My guess is that they played the exact same game with Ibragim. Though that doesn't mean that the evidence actually exists.

The account from federal sources, that there was a plan to confront Ibragim Todashev with forensic evidence, and that Ibragim was a "suspect"—a term that carries more weight than *person of interest*—also paints in a different light the statements made by the state troopers to the Florida State Attorney investigators reviewing the shooting. Joel Gagne, the lead investigator tasked to the case over at Middlesex, told the investigator at the Florida State Attorney's Office conducting the shooting report that prior to this interview, they did not have anything "concrete" linking Ibragim Todashev to the Waltham murder investigation. According to Gagne, Ibragim's confession essentially took the investigators by surprise. A surprise confession might theoretically make the slipshod events leading up to the interview and the fact that there was no arrest plan somewhat more excusable—that is, if that was actually the case. But it's hard to argue that the confession was a surprise if there was a plan in place to confront Ibragim with forensic evidence in addition to records that he stopped using his phone and changed his number hours after the murders. Perhaps they were not certain he would confess. But wasn't this exactly the outcome they were trying to induce?

For my purposes, I am assuming that the forensic evidence does not exist. If Ibragim Todashev changed his cell phone number hours after the murder, that would be damning evidence. But I have nothing to back this allegation up other than the FBI's 302 report. If Ibragim Todashev left Massachusetts on a bus immediately after the murders, that would also be damning evidence indeed. But I could not confirm this detail either, at least not at first, and I could not trust the 302 report on its face. The extremely unusual nature of Ibragim Todashev's fatal interview and the conflicting accounts of investigators in the room raise questions about this account in its entirety.

∼

"Okay, I'm telling you I was involved in it, okay," Ibragim allegedly began to confess after he was confronted with evidence. He told investigators that the plan was to rob the men of $40,000 in drug money and that he and Tamerlan divided the cash between themselves, implying they each took home $20,000. He said he had no idea that Tamerlan "was gonna kill anyone." He thought it was only going to be a robbery. As he was explaining this to investigators, Ibragim began to chain-smoke. He told investigators that Tamerlan first approached him about the robbery during Ramadan, which in 2011 began on July 31 and ended on August 30.

In the lead-up to the bombing trial, federal prosecutor William Weinreb would latch on to this detail, claiming that Ibragim said things that seemed "fairly, if not wildly, implausible." He pointed to Ibragim's account that Tamerlan approached him about a robbery during Ramadan—"despite the fact that Tamerlan had just become very religious"—as a prime example of Ibragim's unreliability. As if the bombing wasn't evidence enough to prove that Tamerlan's interpretation of his faith was totally deranged.

There is additional evidence strongly indicating that Ibragim and Tamerlan did begin to discuss this crime during the aforementioned time period, though Ibragim seems to have left out the apparent ideological agenda in his discussions about the robbery with investigators. According to defense attorney William Fick, in the weeks leading up to the murder—during Ramadan—Tamerlan was reading material authored by al-Qaeda organizer Anwar Al-Awlaki about "stealing or taking or seizing the property of infidels." Al-Awlaki apparently asserted that stealing money from nonbelievers to support jihad conformed to Islamic precepts. According to Fick, there are records of extensive Skype communication between Ibragim and Tamerlan discussing this issue. The pair also exchanged "links to various radical, one might say jihadist, images and videos on the internet," according to Fick. They were conferring "with each other about religiously motivated violence and why that may or may not be justified." Thus, despite the protests of federal prosecutors, Ibragim's account that Tamerlan approached him about a robbery during Ramadan checks out exactly.

~

Some of the most significant evidence about the Waltham murders to come out of the Moakley federal courthouse actually originates in the trials and charges against two Tsarnaev associates, not the bombing trial itself. Dias Kadyrbayev, Dzhokhar Tsarnaev's college friend who took Dzhokhar's backpack and laptop from his dorm room, tried to cut a deal with federal prosecutors before his own trial. Dias, through his attorney, Robert Stahl, asked for a reduced sentence if he pleaded guilty and testified on behalf of the government in the bombing trial. Exchanges like these—plea deals—happen all the time. For better or worse, they are an intrinsic part of the justice system. This back-and-forth took place in 2014 in the lead-up to the bombing trial, although the documents detailing this exchange were not unsealed until 2019. Robert Stahl provided the government a list of points that Dias could testify to, if the government was to provide him with a beneficial arrangement. This list included the fact that in the fall of 2012, Dias learned from Dzhokhar that "Tamerlan Tsarnaev was involved in the Waltham murders" and that Tamerlan had a knife collection and at one time had access to a gun. Dzhokhar also allegedly spoke to Dias about his brother's ideological motivations in committing this horrific act, according to the proffer. Allegedly, Dzhokhar told Dias that Tamerlan "had committed jihad" in Waltham.

Dias noticed a change in his close friend's demeanor and behavior during this time, according to Robert Stahl. Dzhokhar stopped drinking and smoking, began praying more, started regularly watching Islamic videos on YouTube, and stopped socializing as often with his college friends, according to Dias's observations.

If Dias's testimony had helped the government's quest for the death penalty, the government could and probably would cut Dias a deal. Had that been the case, both sides would have been given the opportunity to investigate and challenge his account. But unfortunately for Dias, none of his proposed testimony was helpful to federal prosecutors. The government was trying to actively distance Tamerlan from the murders; they claimed there was no evidence linking Tamerlan to the crime. Dias's claim that Tamerlan called the Waltham murders an act of "jihad" would be especially damaging to the second prong of the government's Waltham argument—classifying the killings as part of a drug rip-off, not terrorism and not important to the story of the bombing. The government's third point was that Tamerlan's theoretical involvement in an earlier killing could have no impact on Dzhokhar unless Dzhokhar knew and was affected by Tamerlan's involvement. Dias's testimony could potentially undercut that too. The government was arguing that the brothers were equal partners in the bombing attack. Testimony of Tamerlan's involvement in an act of ideological violence that predated Dzhokhar's radicalization and was committed independently of Dzhokhar would have undermined the government's whole argument. Potentially, Dias could have been the defense's star witness. But defense attorneys cannot cut plea deals. Only prosecutors can. Because Dias did not testify, prosecutor William Weinreb was able to write off his proposed statements as third-party speculation and dismiss his account as "simply a red herring."

∼

Another reason why Weinreb said that Ibragim Todashev's confession was implausible was because in his handwritten note, Ibragim claimed that Tamerlan entered 12 Harding Avenue brandishing a gun. Weinreb pointed out that the Tsarnaev brothers had to seek out a gun prior to the bombings because they did not have a gun of their own. "All of the evidence points to the fact that Tamerlan Tsarnaev did not own a gun," said Weinreb. The gun question was another reason why Dias's testimony could have hurt the prosecution. Dias claimed Tamerlan had a gun but got rid of it. Ibragim's handwritten confession was the first I had heard of a gun. Ibragim stopped writing before getting to the murders themselves and made no mention of throat-slitting in his writing. I was also concerned because Ibragim said that he helped bind the victims with tape, and Hiba told me the victims were not bound.

I noted earlier that I interviewed Homeland Securities Investigations agents P. J. Lavoie and Mike Kroll at ICE headquarters about Safwan Madarati and Operation Blackstone. Lavoie said that although he had not been directly involved in the Waltham murder investigation, he saw crime scene photos in the initial stage of the investigation. "It was horrible," he told me. "I've never seen so much blood in my life." One of the victims had the imprint of what looked like the butt end of a gun on his skull—he didn't remember which victim. But it appeared that at least one of the Waltham murder victims was pistol-whipped and at least one of the victims was "hog tied." This meant that their wrists and ankles had been taped together. He saw the markings from where the tape had been. But the killers did not leave the victims in that state. "They were smart enough to take all the stuff, all the wrappings and stuff, off of them," he told me. Removing the tape also removed potential DNA evidence and fingerprints, Lavoie explained.

Ibragim's account of the gun and his taping up the victims checked out, according to Lavoie. Additional information from the First Circuit Court of Appeals also supported the account that the victims had been bound and that the tape was later removed.

~

There are many indications that the Waltham killings were ideologically motivated: Dias's account that Tamerlan considered the killing an act of "jihad," material on Tamerlan's computer about the justification for stealing from "infidels," which he shared with Ibragim, firsthand accounts of Tamerlan's anti-Semitism, including arguments he had with Brendan and Rafi about Israel, Tamerlan's study of the anti-Semitic conspiratorial touchstone *The Protocols of the Elders of Zion*, and his reading of publications fixated on the Rothschilds and on claims that Israel plotted 9/11. Then there is the fact that the murders took place on the tenth anniversary of 9/11, that two of the targets were Jewish with ties to Israel, and finally that there was a ritualistic nature to the homicides. Perhaps Ibragim was not aware of Tamerlan's ideological agenda. Perhaps he was. Ibragim told investigators it was his intention to help Tamerlan with the robbery for financial gain. But monetary and ideological motives are not mutually exclusive. In fact, many federal terrorism charges are centered on financial and material support alone. Moreover, financial strain is a contributing factor to all sorts of homicides even when financial gain is not a direct motive. For example, it is my belief that Tamerlan's eviction in January 2013 from the apartment where he had lived for a decade, a few months before the bombing, and before he started purchasing parts to build the bombs, was likely a tipping point for him—though clearly he was already teetering on the edge. Likewise, in the lead-up to the murders Tamerlan and Ibragim were in dire financial straits.

But do we believe Ibragim when he says it was a robbery? And what about the $40,000 that he said he split with Tamerlan? Do we believe that he gave investigators the correct figure? Of course, we cannot trust this account on its own. And even if we are to believe the gist of his confession—that he was there—it is also possible that Ibragim downplayed his role in the crime, the motive, and the amount taken from the apartment. Then again it's also possible that Tamerlan did rope him into this homicide and ripped him off.

Though the killers left $5,000 behind, it appears that at least some cash was taken from 12 Harding Avenue. As I previously established, multiple associates told me that Brendan Mess would regularly keep around $100,000 cash on hand at the Harding Avenue apartment. Associates also told me that Rafi did not keep as much cash at his apartment but would likely have at least $10,000 there in addition to the cash he carried on his person. My estimate is that the killers likely took around $112,000 from Brendan's place alone.

When I first heard FBI agent Timothy McElroy testify in the bail hearing of Khairullozhon Matanov—the cabdriver from Kyrgyzstan who had lunch with the Tsarnaevs after the bombing—about the MoneyGram transfers Matanov allegedly made overseas sometime between September 2011 and April 2013, I noted the dates.

Later I would obtain transcripts of closed-door hearings in Dzhokhar's trial, unsealed years afterward, that reveal that Ibragim and Khairullozhon had been roommates and that Khairullozhon was questioned about the money he wired overseas, occasionally using an alias, in connection to the Waltham murders. According to defense attorney Miriam Conrad, an FBI 302 report presented to the defense showed that Khairullozhon was "questioned at length" regarding the Waltham murders. She said he was specifically asked about money he wired to Russia, which the FBI wrote in the report was "in the amount of the proceeds of the robbery." She also provided exact information about the timing of these transactions. Matanov began transferring money on September 22, 2011, less than two weeks after the murders, the same day that Tamerlan, who had been fiscally strapped in the beginning of the month, purchased a new computer.

There were 114 transactions in all. Curiously, between November 13, 2011, and July 7, 2012, Matanov made no transactions at all. These dates also correspond to the period in which Tamerlan was in Dagestan. It appears Matanov began making these transactions again shortly after Tamerlan returned.

I went back and reviewed the transcripts from Khairullozhon's bail hearing. The wire transfers added up to about $71,000. Through his attorney, Matanov claimed that much of that money went to his family and that he used an alias to avoid paying taxes. Still, that was a lot of money for a cabdriver to send over in less than a year and a half.

I also found that the amount of money Matanov transferred roughly matched the $70,000 Anzor Tsarnaev transferred between bank accounts on March 22, 2012. Where did that money come from? There could be any number of explanations that aren't necessarily nefarious. Also, I can think of several explanations that are.

In any case, whereas before the murders the Tsarnaev family was struggling financially, at the end of the month, they could afford to buy a new computer, and a few months later, Tamerlan could afford a flight back to Dagestan. Meanwhile, Anzor, who for the previous two years allegedly could not find steady work due to his head injury, was moving large sums of cash around.

∼

In the months after the murders, Ibragim Todashev's financial predicament also took a notable turn. I first spoke to Alex Kovlenko, Reni's younger brother, on December 1, 2013. I did not think much of the interview at the time. Alex, like his sister, spoke to me to vouch for Ibragim's innocence. I was in the early stages of my investigation, and I had yet to consider a potential financial motive for the murders. Nor was I aware, as I would be later, of the significance of Ibragim's 1997 white Mercedes sedan.

Years later, I listened to the interview again. Alex told me that at the end of 2011, he believed sometime in November or December—he was not sure of the date—Ibragim returned to Atlanta flush with cash and had acquired the Mercedes. Ibragim having money and a car was a big deal and cause for celebration for Alex and his mother, Elena, who had been frustrated that Ibragim was relying on Reni, who juggled two jobs. But in late 2011, it was Alex's understanding that Ibragim had turned his life around after he "got a really good job opportunity in New York."

This was the first I heard of Ibragim living in New York. I asked Reni about the job. She said her brother was mistaken; there was no job in New York. Reni said she filed all of his paperwork and had intimate knowledge of his financial affairs, and later she sent me a copy of a 1099 from the medical transportation company, which showed Ibragim made $3,565 that year.

In 2013, Reni said Alex was also wrong about the Mercedes. It was her car, not Ibragim's. Remember, Reni told me she bought the car in October 2012, a year later than Alex recalled, and only one year before our first interviews. She told me without hesitation that she had bought the car in Miami. She was clear on this point. We discussed it twice.

But Alex was adamant about Ibragim returning to Atlanta in late 2011. He was sure of this detail. He emphasized this point; he was trying to tell me that his brother-in-law was not a deadbeat. He was a good guy. He even tried to give Alex cash. "Like, he would offer me money to pay for my gas. Like, whenever I come over to see my sister at her apartment," he told me. Ibragim wasn't lazy, he said. He was a hard worker, he just had trouble getting a job at first. "That's when my mom didn't really like him, but after that, after he got a job, I mean he got his life straightened out. He got a car, and he got everything. He had his own apartment. So everything was going well with him," he told me. "He made, like, none, none at all, and after that job, like, he just completely went up. Like, he stood up, and he took care of everything," Alex said.

Ibragim's A-File, his immigration records, include documents that show he claimed to live in Allston near the Wai Kru gym—the same address he mentioned to investigators in his final interview—between July 2011 and September 2011. The next month the records indicate he moved to an address in Kissimmee, Florida. He did not list an address in Atlanta between those times. But it's not clear if the records are an entirely accurate account of his movements.

But I also found tax documents in his A-File that show Ibragim made more money in 2011 than in any prior year. Ibragim claimed to have made more than $29,000 in 2011, about $26,000 more than he had made in any of the years since he arrived in the United States. This amount also roughly matches what Ibragim allegedly claimed to have stolen from the victims in Waltham—subtracting what he made in medical transportation.

When I pulled up the records of the 1997 Mercedes, I found that according to the Florida Motor Vehicle Department, someone named Youness Dafri bought the car on September 12, 2011, in Orlando, the day after the murders. Then it was sold again and registered in Reni's name on November 16, 2011, in Georgia.

The car was registered in Reni's name, but people who buy cars with illicitly earned funds often register cars in their wives' and girlfriends' names. And the November 2011 purchase date did not match what Reni told me at all. And what to make of this Youness Dafri character and his purchasing the car one day after the murders? I wasn't sure. I needed to talk to Dafri myself. It took me eight years to get ahold of him. In late 2021, as we were filming the documentary, I found an address linked to his name. Matt Cook met me at the Orlando airport. We pulled off our masks, jumped in the rental, and went off to find Youness Dafri. There was a Mercedes parked outside the address. His girlfriend got him on the phone and he agreed to a film interview later that evening.

Mercedes, Dafri told me, "last you forever." He fell in love with the cars as a young boy in Morocco, bought the vehicle in question after seeing a "For Sale" sign outside a Taco Bell, and had immediate buyer's remorse. The car vibrated funnily, so his girlfriend helped him list it on eBay. A short time later, a man with a mushroom cut and a crooked nose met him outside his apartment. Dafri said he sold the car for about $2,500 and that the man, who had a male friend with him, drove off without a license plate. Dafri was not sure of the exact date of this exchange since his ex-girlfriend, not him, posted the listing on eBay, but he believed it was sometime in the later part of 2011. After a series of intense WhatsApp exchanges, the girlfriend provided documentation that shows he sold the car in the later part of 2011.

Dafri recognized Ibragim from news photos after he was killed. He said a woman was not with him, but the FBI knocked on his door, shortly after the shooting. The agents also asked him about a woman and showed him photos of Reni.

So Reni was not there when Ibragim bought the car. I had asked her twice about buying the car. Was it a deliberate omission? And why did she get the year she purchased the car wrong? She had been asked about this car multiple times before I questioned her. She was clear and exact when I asked her about other dates. Maybe it was an honest mistake.

But I was not the only one who had questions about Reni's credibility. On September 20, 2016, Reni was indicted in the Northern District of Georgia for "knowingly and willfully making a materially false, fictitious, and fraudulent statement and representation, in a matter within the jurisdiction of the Federal Bureau of Investigation." Lying to an FBI agent is a crime. The indictment stated that Reni lied to FBI agents on May 21, 2013, before Ibragim was killed. The alleged lie centered on "a named individual with whom she associated." Reni allegedly told agents that this person returned to Atlanta, Georgia, on a bus after his employment in Massachusetts ended in or around August 2011. That was the same story Reni told me about Ibragim leaving Massachusetts. But according to the indictment, this individual did not return to Atlanta by bus in August; "As the defendant well knew, the defendant met that individual in the State of New York on or about September 13, 2011, and drove him to Atlanta, Georgia." Allegedly, this individual left Massachusetts two days after the murders and stopped in New York on his way back to Atlanta. Could this bus trip be where Alex picked up the story about New York? Did Ibragim leave Massachusetts two days after the murders flush with cash?

When I spoke to Gretchen Fortin, spokesperson for the US Marshals in Atlanta, shortly after the indictment was handed down, she informed me that the FBI was currently trying to locate Reniya Manukyan. Several days later, I was able to contact Reni via phone in Russia, where she had remarried and given birth to a boy. "I'm not going to make any comments, not to make it any worse or any of this. I'm just going to let it be as it is," she told me. "I have no idea what's going on with the case . . . I'm far away from that story." She alluded to the fact that her new husband did not like her talking about Ibragim. Shortly thereafter the line cut off.

After tracking down Youness Dafri, I called up Reni. It was six years since we last spoke, and I asked her again about the indictment, the car, and her claim that Ibragim was with her in Atlanta at the time of the murders.

"Did you pick up Ibrahim Todashev at a New York bus stop on September 13?" I asked. She told me that actually yes, she did. Reni told me that it was not that she lied; she simply couldn't remember when it was that she drove to New York to pick up Ibragim. She said she spoke to FBI agents about a year ago over video call with her attorney, Charles Swift. (Swift informed me that the indictment against Reni was still outstanding; however, the United States and Russia do not have an extradition agreement. He said he could not comment further.) Apparently, she got a parking ticket on that trip, the agents showed it to her, and it clarified her memory. Reni told me she was traumatized. "I lost my husband." But Ibragim was alive when she allegedly lied to FBI agents.

She told me that when she picked him up from the bus stop, Ibragim was coming from Massachusetts. She said she could not remember if Ibragim changed his phone number or when exactly he called to ask her to pick him up. He didn't tell her why he was leaving, and he was calm. He was always calm. He never showed his emotions even when he was mad or nervous. Nothing was unusual.

She also asserted again that she bought the white Mercedes. "I gave him my own money, and that's how he purchased it," she said. She did not think that her not being there and not driving the car was significant. "I couldn't remember exactly the year, but I believe it was 2012," she said. "Was I wrong?" I told her she was and asked if she was trying to distance the purchase of the car from the date of the murders. She told me she just mixed up the day.

"You told me that you had bank statements that proved Ibragim was in Atlanta on September the twelfth. But now you're telling me you picked him up at a bus station on September the thirteenth in New York?" She told me that this was an honest mistake. Ibragim never talked about a robbery and she never heard about a murder until after he was killed. I asked her if she thought it was possible he might have done it. At this point, she said she didn't know. I said I have evidence that strongly suggests he did. She hadn't heard about the tax records and did not know where he got that money. "He never did taxes," she told me. He never worked. He didn't have a separate bank account. Everything was under her name. "I put him on under my bank account, and my bank account was clean. I never had twenty-five grand on it."

"Do you think he could have been hiding it from you?" I asked.

"Doubt it," she said.

She told me this didn't make sense. How stupid can you be to list the money you stole from the victims of a triple homicide on your tax records? "It's kind of ridiculous." I told her I had thought about this as well. I emailed her the tax records, she told me she had never seen this paperwork before and didn't know where he got the money.

~

I do not have the recordings of Ibragim's confession, but I have learned much more about what he allegedly said from information gathered from records requests, details in the appellate ruling, and trial documents. Ibragim told investigators that on the evening of September 11, 2011, he and Tamerlan met on the street in Brighton "near the Wai Kru gym." The 302 report includes this detail followed by what can only be surmised to be paragraphs of text. All that is visible to me are blank white rectangles signaling redactions peppered with tantalizing phrases like *as soon as* and *while this was going on*. This is where the details from the First Circuit Court of Appeals ruling come in. Based on their ruling, we know that Ibragim allegedly said that they drove together in Tamerlan's 1999 gray Honda to 12 Harding Avenue.

Brendan Mess welcomed them inside, because Brendan was Tamerlan's close friend, Ibragim said. Tamerlan brought a gun. Together they held the men at gunpoint, beat them, and tied them up with duct tape. Ibragim said he only bound one of the victims—Tamerlan tied up the other two. They left the men like that, alive and bound, for a period of time. It is unclear how long. Meanwhile, according to Ibragim, Tamerlan beat Brendan Mess until Brendan told them where he hid his cash. After they located the money, Tamerlan told Ibragim he also planned to kill the three men and slit their throats. He did not want to leave any witnesses. That's when Ibragim said he began to shake. He had signed up for a robbery, not a murder, but he felt there was no way out. He told investigators he had no idea this was Tamerlan's plan and wanted no part of the throat-slitting. Ibragim told investigators he stepped outside while Tamerlan slit their throats. When Tamerlan was done, Ibragim went back into the apartment to help clean up the evidence. Tamerlan, who had taught himself English by reading Sherlock Holmes books, had come prepared. Ibragim said he brought everything: the gun, the duct tape, and some cleaning supplies. They used bleach and other chemicals to clean the surfaces and even poured some bleach on the victims' bodies.

At this point in the 302 report, there is a little more unredacted text stating that Ibragim claimed he disposed of his phone and got on a Greyhound bus at Boston's South Station Bus Terminal the next day after booking a ticket using a "Russian or Chechen name," the implication being he used an alias. At which point the 302 report duly concludes, "Todashev attacked the interviewing agents and was shot and killed in a violent confrontation."

There is no reason to take Ibragim Todashev exactly at his word. He might be telling the truth. He might be downplaying his role. But it is extremely unlikely that he is overstating his role in the crime. Ibragim confessed. He confessed under extremely unusual circumstances, but confess he did, and his confession matches the details of the crime. It is possible that these details were fed to him by investigators—which is why we need more evidence than this confession alone—but it's also possible that his confession matched what happened because he was there and committed the crime.

The story Ibragim told investigators makes sense. Tamerlan Tsarnaev knew all three murder victims, and he and Brendan had been close. It also makes sense that the killer was close to Brendan; there was no sign of a break-in at the apartment, and the victims were seemingly caught off guard. Tamerlan had recently gotten into arguments with Rafi and Brendan about Israel. And Tamerlan Tsarnaev is Tamerlan Tsarnaev, an anti-Semitic terrorist who was obsessed with Sherlock Holmes books and the eccentric, elaborate crimes detailed therein, read propaganda claiming Israel did 9/11, and went on to bomb the Boston Marathon. Tamerlan is exactly the kind of person who might murder these three men on 9/11/11 and hang around to stage the murder scene. He fits the very particular profile.

Few would like to admit this, but style matters. Criminals leave imprints or identifying markers of their indiscretions much in the same way artists do. One can analyze a rap sheet the same way one might study an artist's body of work. As with artists, there are few true originals. But Tamerlan was indeed unique. Unlike most terrorists who fall under the umbrella of "radical Islam," Tamerlan did not immediately make the motives and the message behind the bombing clear. The brothers did not have a typed manifesto to leave behind. Dzhokhar did not write that seemingly impromptu message in the boat until the jig was most definitely up. Conceivably, there could have been another outcome in which the brothers were never caught—unlikely but an outcome that Tamerlan and his bloated ego may have entertained. If Dzhokhar had not made it to the boat where he scribbled the one and only note about the brothers' intent, then we would be left on our own to guess at their motives. This is all to say that there are indications the Waltham triple homicide had clear ideological markers, but the identities of the perpetrators were not immediately clear, and the ideological message was kept obscure, which matches Tamerlan Tsarnaev's methods.

And for those who still aren't convinced that Tamerlan Tsarnaev and Ibragim Todashev killed three men in Waltham, my investigation into law enforcement, the potential reasons investigators may or may not have pursued this case as they did, and the criminal environs in which these matters took place would lead to my uncovering additional evidence linking Tamerlan and Ibragim to the crime. However, how I came upon this information and its significance will require additional context and explanation than this point-by-point argument, which I wrote beside my father's hospital bed. Two weeks after *The Murders before the Marathon* docuseries aired on Hulu, just as the last wave of publicity was starting to die down, the doctors found a 22-centimeter tumor in my father's stomach, and he was diagnosed with lymphoma. He took my arm and marched me around the hospital wing in circles, insisting that I could not lose my focus. I had to write. Meanwhile, he was going to fight cancer like he fights his murder trials, with every fiber of his being. At the time of writing, it appears he won.

CHAPTER THIRTY-NINE

Middlesex

Despite the arguments put forth at the United States Supreme Court that the investigation had reached a dead end, the Middlesex County District Attorney's Office continues to maintain that this investigation is open and active. Dzhokhar Tsarnaev's trial and appeal were argued and tried in federal courts. But the triple homicide remained in the jurisdiction of Middlesex County; it is a state case, a Massachusetts matter, and officials there categorize the Waltham murders on completely different terms from their federal counterparts.

I had been calling and emailing the Middlesex DA's Office for updates and information, or at the very least a comment, on the potential connection between these murders and the Boston Marathon bombing since 2013. I spoke to various spokeswomen and filed a records request through the nonprofit MuckRock. The answer was always the same: the office does not comment on open investigations.

At the time of the Supreme Court hearing, the Middlesex DA's Office had yet to issue a statement mentioning Tamerlan Tsarnaev and Ibragim Todashev by name. The Supreme Court hearing was in October 2021. In November 2021, I approached the Middlesex office again. I was no longer working independently. I presented my questions in my capacity as a producer with Story Syndicate and ABC News Studios and filed another records request. Now that I had a little more heft, I was hoping I might get some answers.

In my request I wrote that if the office planned to respond that they could not release information because the case was open and active, then they needed to prove that they were actively investigating. I also wrote that Tamerlan Tsarnaev and Ibragim Todashev were dead, so releasing information about those two parties could not impact a future trial about their role in the crime.

The office got back to me and at long last issued a statement linking Tamerlan Tsarnaev and Ibragim Todashev to the crime. "Over the course of the investigation, two people of interest, Tamerlan Tsarnaev and Ibragim Todashev, have died," the response issued by Assistant District Attorney Daniel M. DeBlander read.

Again, there is no legal definition of the phrase *person of interest*. It does not carry the same weight as *suspect*, which explicitly implies there is potential evidence of criminal involvement. Yet to call someone a "person of interest" demonstrates the office's belief that there is a direct connection between this individual and this crime.

Basically, the office was saying yes, Ibragim and Tamerlan may have been involved. But even if they were, they still can't close the case. DeBlander went on to say that the office continues "to investigate the potential involvement of additional undisclosed person or persons in connection with these homicides."

So there could be others out there, the office said. There could be additional assailants or accomplices still at large. But did they really believe there were others there involved in the crime? And was the office looking for them?

DeBlander claimed that they were and that investigators had interviewed a "material witness" within the last year. In addition, he stated that "as recently as November, 2021, we have identified new potential sources of physical evidence." I found it interesting that this latest breakthrough took place exactly one month after the United States Supreme Court hearing in which a government attorney declared, "This investigation had hit the end of the road." Was the office searching for these "potential sources of physical evidence" all along? Or only after the Supreme Court hearing had concluded?

I appealed the office's response with the Massachusetts Secretary of the Commonwealth. Rebecca Murray, the supervisor of records, ruled in my favor and found that the office "had not met its burden to withhold responsive records, in their entirety" and ordered the office to turn over the records to the Secretary of the Commonwealth for inspection. This was the first time, to my knowledge, that an outside agency reviewed any of the case files.

The Secretary of the Commonwealth's review of Middlesex's case files did not include all of the records, and the focus of the review was not an analysis of the investigation itself over the course of the last decade, but rather an examination of whether the Middlesex DA's Office could legitimately claim that it was active at the time of my records request.

The Secretary of the Commonwealth concluded that based on what they reviewed, the Middlesex case was, in fact, active. On January 5, 2023, the Middlesex DA's Office issued another response stating that in November and December of 2022, the office interviewed another material witness and identified a new source of forensic evidence. "The need to safeguard the investigation continues," DeBlander wrote. He claimed that releasing information could assist potential suspects by tipping them off; these potential suspects might destroy evidence, or the new information becoming public could impair future interviews.

DeBlander also provided additional information about the office's investigative files. He said the office collected 68,000 individual records, including state police reports, municipal police department reports, FBI reports, forensic examination reports, cell phone records, crime scene photos and videos, and handwritten notes. We don't know how substantive these records are. More to the point, they did not provide data on when this material was collected. That was the information I really wanted and thought they could disclose to me. The dates would track the actual activity of the investigation, when they were working, and to what extent. And, if redacted properly, the information would be unlikely to interfere with the open case. There is other information I wanted but respectfully understood I would not get. For example, details about to whom investigators did or did not speak, who the other potential suspects are, what role investigators believe those individuals may have played in the crime, and whether a future arrest is feasible. Are these individuals in the United States, or a country the United States has an extradition agreement with, and are they alive?

Maybe there was a third person there the night of the murders slitting throats and this person is just as guilty as Ibragim and Tamerlan. Maybe this individual is completely off my radar and the Middlesex DA's Office is hot on the chase. But my best guess is that when the district attorney says they continue to investigate the potential involvement of additional individuals, they are implying that Tamerlan and Ibragim may have had assistance before or after the fact. Accessory to murder is a serious charge. It is very plausible that Ibragim and Tamerlan had help. But how closely is the Middlesex DA's Office looking into these matters? And is the case against a potential accessory reason enough to leave the matter of Ibragim's and Tamerlan's guilt unaddressed? Over the course of my investigation I also saw how the Middlesex office might easily put forth to a reviewing body like the secretary of state that there could be just such an accessory, simply by showing a few handwritten pages. What I don't know is if there is any truth to this allegation.

CHAPTER FORTY

Jahmare

Hiba and her string of dead lovers sounded like something out of a campy noir. Yes, she and Brendan allegedly had a tumultuous relationship fueled by drugs and violence, but Brendan also played a role in that dynamic. People made judgments and assumptions about Hiba's behavior after the fact, but how is one supposed to react after opening the door of one's home and finding three dead bodies inside? Who were they to judge her reactions? Yes, three of her past lovers died in a short period of time. Yes, after Hiba threw a knife in an argument with Rafi, he stopped visiting Brendan's apartment when she was home. And, yes, Erik was trying to avoid her too. It seems unlikely that the triple murder would have occurred as it did, that all three men would have been at Brendan's, or that Rafi's apartment would have been robbed, if she had not left that weekend. But coincidences happen. Her trip to Miami was crucial to how the events unfurled. But that does not mean she intended any of this to happen.

For many years, I thought Hiba's dead lovers were a stroke of bad luck and nothing more. But additional reporting led me to investigate these deaths as well, just to be certain.

Ten days before the murders, on September 1, 2011, at approximately 8:30 p.m., Jahmare H. Smith was found in the driver's seat of a blue Honda Prelude with a bullet in his head on Staples Mill Road in Henrico County, Virginia. He was thirty-three years old. Hiba told me that she and Jahmare had not spoken in a while. "I'd seen him at a gas station maybe a year or so before that. That was the last time. We said hello, I gave him a hug, and we didn't talk. I didn't, like, have his phone number," she said.

Jahmare's murder appears fairly straightforward. A man named Jeffrey Runion was arrested on September 12, 2011. Runion pleaded guilty to second-degree homicide charges and was sentenced to fourteen years. In his plea hearing the state reviewed the evidence they would have presented had the case gone to trial. The story they put forth was that Jahmare tried to rob Runion.

Apparently, at around 7:15 p.m. on September 1, 2011, Jahmare was at a barbershop, when he got a phone call and ran out with product in his hair. Over the phone, Jahmare and an associate made plans to buy marijuana from Runion at a nearby apartment complex. Jahmare pulled out a gun and told Runion to give him the weed. Runion also had a weapon, hidden in his shoe, and he chased after Jahmare and shot him dead. A couple of hours later, Runion told a childhood friend he killed a man, and the friend told police.

Matt Cook and I went to visit Assistant Commonwealth Attorney Michael Feinmel at his office in Henrico County to take a closer look at the evidence. Investigators matched the shells at the murder scene to a Glock Runion owned. Runion had the box to the murder weapon in his house. Feinmel said that the Glock company test-fires their weapons and includes the shell casings in the packaging.

Feinmel had not heard of Hiba. Investigators never approached him about the Waltham murders. "She would have to be pretty Machiavellian to set this thing up," he told me. After all, it was Jahmare, not Runion, who allegedly instigated the violent encounter.

I also called Runion's defense attorney, Andrew Wood. Runion, Wood told me, was "an otherwise decent guy." But he said, "He did it."

Unfortunately, I could not get ahold of Jahmare Smith's family. But I wrote to Runion at the Buckingham Correction Center and he called me a short time later.

"You killed Jahmare Smith. That's correct, right?" I asked.

"Yes, yes," he told me. He didn't miss a beat.

"Can you tell me what happened?" I asked.

He told me more or less the same story prosecutors put forth at the hearing. He said he followed Jahmare in his car to get his phone back, saw Jahmare pull out his gun, and was first to pull the trigger. "It was something stupid," he said. He told me he had never met Jahmare—the deal was set up by Jahmare's associate. I asked him if he knew Hiba. He told me he did not, and sounded confused. I said that she had been a girlfriend of Jahmare's. He tried to be helpful. He mentioned the name of a woman he believed to be Jahmare's girlfriend who he saw at court. It wasn't Hiba. Then he said he had no idea what I was talking about. His story was all about him and Jahmare being in the "wrong place, wrong time, doing the wrong thing." It wasn't complicated.

Runion had done nine years at Buckingham, and he had five more to go. We talked a little after that, about how he had gotten his GED and was working on getting his plumbing license. And that was that.

CHAPTER
FORTY-ONE

Jay

My questions concerning the death of Hiba's late husband, Johnson Aimie "Jay" Edosomwan Jr., proved more difficult to resolve. The death certificate shows he died on Friday, October 7, 2011, in his home in Richmond, Virginia. According to a transcript of the 911 call, Richmond police were called to a gray brick multifamily home on West Leigh Street at 11:07 p.m. by a male caller who identified himself as Jay's roommate. The roommate had returned from out of town, could not get in contact with Jay, and had locked himself out of the apartment.

A public information officer at the Richmond Police Department, Officer Phon Hoosan, informed me that at approximately 11:13 p.m. police responded to a report of a person down. Jay was pronounced dead at the scene. "At the conclusion of a thorough investigation, the medical examiner ruled the death a suicide," Hoosan said. She added that anyone with information about Jay's death should contact Detective Jeffrey Crewell or submit a tip anonymously by way of Metro Richmond Crime Stoppers, a nonprofit designed to protect the identity of tipsters and that offers cash rewards for tips that result in an arrest. I found images of the wide-eyed homicide detective standing beside families of murder victims at news conferences and in the 2008 show *Crime 360*, reconstructing crime scenes, working his connections in the community, and fielding tips in response to news stories to solve murder cases.

Matt Cook and I had questions about Jay's communications with Ian McCleod. Before his death, Jay seemed to imply that he had something he wanted to say. He was pretty clear on that point. It was eerie. Almost too eerie.

Then we got ahold of a book Jay's mother, Rev. Dr. Mary I. Edosomwan, published about her son's death in 2020. In *Broken Hearted: A Mother's Journey to Wholeness*, the reverend and theologian shared her researched reflections on faith and healing. In the book, she also suggested that her son was killed by someone else. She wrote that investigators informed her that an investigation would be forthcoming as there wasn't forced entry; but the person who he opened the door to "was no stranger to him." She made a cryptic observation that Jay had sold his car a week before his death; some of that money was found at the apartment, but most of it was missing.

Matt Cook and I traveled to Richmond in December 2021. When I spoke to Rev. Dr. Edosomwan by phone, she told us her son "was very, very intelligent, very, very insightful, and very kind." He had a generous heart and a photographic memory. But she tried not to dwell on who may have killed him. She was leaving justice up to God. Yet she also seemed to blame Hiba, whom she disliked long before Jay's death in part because she wanted her son to marry a Christian woman. "I know that if my son had not invited her back into his life that Thursday, my son would still be alive. I don't know what role she played. I don't know who else was behind her. I don't know what she was into. I have no idea," she said.

It was Rev. Dr. Edosomwan's understanding that in the weeks before Jay's death, Hiba called him so often that he had to change his phone number. Hiba "was looking for him every which way."

The Thursday before he died, he called his mother and said, "You're not going to like this." He told her that Hiba had come to his home. "I'm just tired of running away from her," he said. Jay told his mother he was upset because Hiba had left a plastic hotel key card in his apartment.

The next day, her son was dead. "That woman was bad news all along," she told me. "Bad news."

A note: If Jay did die by suicide, it's extremely unlikely that Hiba or anyone else is criminally responsible for this tragedy. Commonwealth of Massachusetts v. Michelle Carter, colloquially known as the "texting suicide" case, in which a young woman from Plainville was convicted of murder for texting her boyfriend to kill himself, is widely considered an anomaly. Carter was found to have consulted with Conrad Henri Roy III as he procured the means with which to take his own life, and instructed him to "get back in" when he had second thoughts. I covered this trial in 2017 for *VICE*. In 2021, a young woman named Inyoung You pleaded guilty to involuntary manslaughter charges, accepting guilt for the verbal, physical, and psychological abuse that led to her boyfriend's death, much of which was documented in text messages. Crucially, You was also reportedly present at the time of his death. She received a suspended sentence and agreed to undergo mental health counseling. But there appears to be no such legal precedent in Virginia.

Criminality aside, experts say that simplistic explanations for death by suicide are, by and large, inaccurate. Even if it appears as though a single precipitating incident triggered the tragedy, one event is rarely the sole or primary aggravating factor. Suicide is best understood as a complex public health issue and by examining multiple risk factors that may have impacted a person's ability to cope in the time period leading up to their death.

But several of Jay's friends and family members remained unconvinced that Jay had died by suicide, despite findings from law enforcement. I wasn't trying to reach a conclusion as to *why* he might have taken his life. I needed to confirm that he did and what, if any, connection his death had to the Waltham murders.

~

I asked Hiba about Jay's death when we spoke in 2014. Hiba noted Jay's "financial issues" and disagreements with his family. But she also said that by late 2011, her relationship with Jay was a thing of the past. They had already been separated for "a year and some change" when she started seeing Brendan. They were in touch now and then but "not very often."

In regards to their final encounter, shortly before his death, Hiba said that she and Jay had not seen each other in a long while, and Jay contacted her *out of the blue*. "I think he knew he was planning on doing something like that and was maybe saying goodbye to me without letting me know, you know?" she said.

"What makes you say that?" I asked.

"Because we hadn't seen each other for a long time, and he was kind of just out of the blue, *I'd like to see you*. And so I was, like, *okay*. And I was, like, so wrapped up in my own pain that I didn't really notice that. I didn't really notice that he could have been going through some issues. I just kind of thought that my problems were the biggest problems in the world at that point, and I didn't really appreciate that he might have been going through something." She said they met up at his apartment and had a talk.

I asked her if Jay left a note. She said he did. I asked her what the note said. "He said that . . . I didn't read the note. I haven't read the note so, like, I couldn't read the note. I didn't have the power, like, the energy, like, I couldn't even face reading the note," she said.

Hiba's account of Jay's financial struggles adds up. Jay was losing his legal battle over the past due rent on his office space. There was a hearing scheduled for October 5, 2011—two days before his death. The hearing date was pushed back, but Jay was running out of resources to fight the landlord's claim. And Jay was on the line for a lot. The landlord was suing him for $153,094.

Officials at the Richmond Police Department declined my calls and email requests for additional comment. But while we were in Richmond, Matt Cook was able to get Tracy Walker, the director of public affairs, on the phone. Walker said the reason the department could not share any more information was because of the "potential connection" between Edosomwan's death and the Waltham triple homicide. She did not say what the connection was, but the only link that I could find between Jay's death and the triple homicide was Hiba.

∼

In contrast to Hiba's account that she could not even conceive of how one might go about carrying out such a plan like the events in Waltham, she did not have a motive, means, or contacts to coordinate or execute such an atrocity. While reporting in Richmond, I learned of three separate instances from three separate accounts in which she and Jay allegedly orchestrated robberies. None of these alleged robberies resulted in arrests. And again, Hiba denies plotting or engaging in any robberies or criminal activities.

In one alleged robbery, a victim was pistol-whipped, in another an individual was unknowingly recruited as a decoy, and in a third Hiba and Jay allegedly carried out an elaborate scheme to exact revenge on a roommate.

Ian claimed to have intimate knowledge of this third robbery. According to Ian, the plan was devised after Jay's roommate said something about Hiba that Jay didn't like. The roommate apparently talked about Hiba "sideways." It was Ian's understanding that the robbery was all Jay's idea, not Hiba's. It wasn't a violent altercation, but it was still "an example of him being malicious and looking to, you know, exact revenge in some form," he said. The way Ian saw it, Hiba was essentially victimized by Jay, and she more or less passively went along with his plans. Jay was tricky, Ian said. He respected that about Jay, actually. Interacting with Jay was like playing a game of chess. Ian didn't trust him, and he didn't like the way Jay spoke about women. But he was always curious to see what move Jay would make next. Nonetheless, he said, Hiba played a key role in the robbery. Jay allegedly took the roommate out of the house to a gun range. Meanwhile, Hiba and an accomplice allegedly went into the apartment and took all the roommate's belongings. Later, Ian said Jay reported the incident to the police to collect insurance money from the robbery.

I found a police report that may match this account or may be from a separate incident. On December 18, 2007, Richmond Police responded to a home on West Cary Street for a report of a burglary that had taken place the day before. Police noticed a camera monitoring the front door. The thieves apparently removed the doorknob at the back entrance and dropped it in a bucket of water so it could not be fingerprinted. Police also noted that three tenants lived in the building and only two tenants were missing items.

Jay initially claimed that watches, cash, a laptop, a desktop computer, radios, TVs, VCRs, and DVDs had been taken, totaling $9,350. But the officers tasked to the case had concerns. "For several reasons I am skeptical about this report," one officer wrote on December 22, 2007, shortly after the crime was reported. Investigators were curious as to why the residents had a high-tech security camera monitoring the front door but had not worried about a broken door handle on the rear door and why the victims waited more than twenty-four hours to call police. Also the investigators noted that the victims "run an illegal gambling ring out of their apartment" with a poker table and bar downstairs and brought more than a hundred people in their apartment each week. "The gambling could be the reason for the burglary, if in fact a burglary took place," an investigator wrote.

Six days later, an officer filed another report after receiving a call from Jay's insurance company. The report noted that before the robbery Jay's insurance policy was about to be cancelled due to nonpayment. Now Jay was filing a claim listing $30,000 worth of items stolen, far exceeding the initial estimate made to police. Investigators ultimately concluded that Jay's report of a robbery was "unfounded."

PART VII

Dirty Water

CHAPTER
FORTY-TWO

The Lake

In Lake Talk *quister jival* means pretty girl. *Cuya moi* means shut up or go to hell. If "the man is the eerie," the man is listening. *Chabby* is a child. Of course, the most important word is *mush*. A *divya mush* is a mush who is crazy, someone who doesn't play by the rules, is unpredictable, hotheaded, not to be trusted. Though *divya mush* can also be used endearingly as well. Lake Talk, like all good slang, is crude. Men use it to exchange thoughts on the female anatomy and their own, at the top of their lungs in greetings at street corners and bars.

For several years, before I landed a book deal and started work on the docu-series, I lived in Newton. My reporting on the case for *Boston* magazine and *This American Life* was well received. Rachel Maddow hailed the magazine story as "blistering," and it was listed as one of the top magazine stories of the year. I was invited on CNN, MSNBC, and a handful of other television and radio shows to discuss my work, and I walked back through the doors of the NECN newsroom, not as a lowly freelance overnight production assistant but as an on-air guest. My career progressed steadily from there. I covered the bombing trial for *The Daily Beast* and worked as a New England correspondent for the *Guardian* and *VICE*. But I couldn't let the Waltham story go. I never applied for a full-time job or investigated any other story in the same depth; the Waltham murder case remained my top priority. In the beginning, my freelancing work did not pay well or on time. It was also distracting. So I drove for Uber and Lyft late into the night and moved back in with my parents.

Back then, the majority of the evidence that would later convince me of Tamerlan Tsarnaev's guilt was not yet available. I took theories of alternative suspects seriously. It wasn't just word of mouth, bloggers, and errant articles. In the 2015 book *The Brothers: The Road to an American Tragedy*, *New Yorker* journalist Masha Gessen gave credence to theories suggesting Tamerlan may have been a federal informant or that Safwan Madarati was connected to the Waltham murders. After outlining the police corruption allegations in Madarati's case, Gessen suggested that the cops could have been behind both the Waltham murders and Miles's death on December 3, 2011, "which is one explanation for the similarity to the later killing of former policewoman Gail Miles."

Miles was hired in 1984, and she was the first Black female officer at the Watertown Police Department. She later accused the Watertown Police Department of racial and gender discrimination. The suit was settled in 2000 and Miles was awarded $150,000. She left the department in 2004 but had paid a visit to the department the day before she was killed and had gone out for drinks with her former colleagues at a bar, according to a 2015 WBUR story about her unsolved murder.

The initial news reports on Miles's death stated that she was beaten to death. I obtained a copy of her death certificate confirming her cause of death, and it also listed "lacerations to the neck," as was first reported by WBUR. WBUR also reported that according to Miles's sister, investigators informed her that the crime scene had been wiped of fingerprints.

Gessen detailed several theories but cautioned that while many of the contradictions and inconsistencies surrounding Tamerlan Tsarnaev, the Waltham murders, Madarati, and Gail Miles could be explained by "incompetence, ignorance, and fear," some of these connections could provide "useful leads." I followed these leads for close to a decade and found no evidence to support these theories. But I'm glad I did because what I found was useful, as Gessen predicted.

The events and crimes all circled back to a one-year time span in a small pocket of a suburbia I called home. I had a feeling there was another factor at play, an element that seemingly eluded the agents and other reporters, but I could not quite put my finger on it and articulate it. My familiarity with this area, specifically Nonantum, the village of Newton closest to the Watertown and Waltham town line, framed the way I understood almost every aspect of this story. I needed to see if my hunch was right, if it was more than a sentimental notion, so I conducted a deep dive into the criminal ecosystem surrounding my childhood home.

The Lake is home to Newton's first synagogue. People here still nod to this heritage with drops of Yiddish, though the culture is primarily Italian and Irish. Irish families came here first, for the factory jobs. In 1935 Italian immigrants formed the St. Mary of Carmen Society to gather funds to take care of the elderly and preserve Italian feast ceremonies. The society commissioned a large statue of their patron saint, which has been rolled through the winding streets of Nonantum in an eight-hour procession on the second weekend of July every year since—save for interruptions due to the pandemic. In preparation for the event, the fire hydrants and broad lines of Nonantum's streets are painted the colors of the Italian flag. More particular to this area, they also paint green, white and red shamrocks on the street. The Virgin Mary—La Madonna del Carmine—is wheeled through the streets as prayers are sung, with the help of a brass marching band and a seemingly endless supply of fireworks. Tribute is paid to the homes of prominent community members, and the dead are honored. People in the Lake walk alongside the idol, wave to her from barbecues, and adorn her with cash and jewelry. The money is later collected into a college scholarship fund. At the end of the night, the people in the Lake treat the idol to a ground-trembling firework display in the parking lot of a Catholic church. A young girl in a white dress and gold angel wings is hung by her waist on ropes tied between the branches of two tall oak trees and swung above the onlookers as she showers the statue with rose petals. The evening concludes with Mass.

In addition to the language and the festival, the Lake also has a long tradition of bookmaking and loan-sharking. This actually goes hand in hand with the more celebrated components of this culture. People here have an aversion to banks for good reason. This dates back to a 1929 bank robbery that was dressed up as a white-collar rip-off. The bank receiver made off with the funds. Some families lost a lot, some families lost everything. The robbery was part of the reason the St. Mary of Carmen Society was started in the first place, to pay for funerals and hospital bills. The people rallied together to support others in times of need. People here maintain an oral history of favors exchanged by grandparents and great-grandparents, and the 1929 bank robbery is still hailed as the origin story for the Lake's bookmaking and loan-sharking rackets today. This element of Lake culture is not advertised to outsiders. For example, Anthony "Fat" Pellegrini's bookmaking career was largely overlooked when he passed away in 2004. Fat is featured in a 1988 edition of *Yankee* magazine showing the writer around Newton's hidden tomato gardens and swearing. The writer was told this was the guy he needed to talk to if he wanted to see tomato gardens. Also the guy to talk to in order to get the roof of the synagogue fixed. I'd heard of Fat; everyone in Newton had. Fat also supported the local boxing gym, and his son "Fatty"—a short, slim Italian man like his father—would come to the high school and drill the boys' wrestling team. I joined the team my freshman year, along with three other girls. Fatty would scream at us as we ran up and down five flights of stairs. We'd come close to blacking out or vomiting from exhaustion. I loved it. But when I started falling asleep at the kitchen table, my mother encouraged me to quit. Nonetheless, my run-ins with Fatty were formative. I learned to get up after a beating and push myself long past what I believed was my physical limit.

Fat and his wife were known for helping organize local charities and fund-raisers, but he was best known for orchestrating a Christmas celebration every year, helicoptering in a statue of Santa Claus two stories tall and bedecking an entire park with decorations. He would collect funds for the disadvantaged children in the neighborhood. There was a box where neighborhood children could send their letters to Santa. I was one of those children. Santa always wrote back.

The Pellegrini family also helps put together the days-long carnival in Pellegrini Park, tangential to the St. Mary of Carmen ceremony, complete with a Ferris wheel and other dizzying rides, prizes, sausages, clams, and deafening renditions of Sinatra. The late Fat is honored as a local Robin Hood figure. His photo, with added angel wings, flutters above the fair on street flags.

In 2017 I went to the festival with my audio recorder and a microphone and asked people to explain the language and the culture. Waltham mayor Mary McCarthy's arrival at the celebration was announced on the speakers with cheer by a Sinatra impersonator. As housing in Newton has gotten more expensive, many people from the Lake have moved to Waltham and Watertown. Police officers from Watertown, Waltham, and Newton are especially welcome at the fair. That year, the Newton Auxiliary Police sold T-shirts reading "Watch out for the muskar" which means "Look out for the cops" in Lake Talk.

On the fairgrounds, I ran into my childhood friends and my old wrestling coach, John Staulo, who greeted me with raspy warmth and introduced me to his acquaintances with an extremely generous account of my abilities on the mat. He told me the story he tells me every time I see him, about when the Newton North wrestling team was up against Cambridge Rindge and Latin, back when Dzhokhar was captain. I was also reunited with Fatty, whose voice was almost entirely shot from swallowing clams with hot sauce all day. He didn't remember me, but his energy was the same. He told me he loved having girls on the wrestling team, because they worked hardest of all.

I stumbled into the front lawn of a party at a house dubbed "Mush mansion," inhabited by several men in their early twenties. The hosts pulled over their other buddy, covered in tattoos and flexing his considerable muscles, and had him turn around so I could take in the outfit. He was wearing sunglasses, a backward baseball cap, camouflage shorts, a T-shirt with the sleeves cut off that said *The Lake* in the colors of the Italian flag, adorned with a St. Mary pin. This guy right here was a mush, they informed me. "Motherfucking family," one guy interjected.

I made my way through the streets to a group of men hanging out on a front stoop sometime after the parade had passed. It was a relative's place. The men told me they lived in Waltham. I asked them to tell me what Lake culture was all about, and they started calling out to a gentleman across the street that they said was a police officer. "Mush, lock me up! Lock me up, mush, please. Put me in the cruiser! Please! I'll stay two days there!" one man yelled. The man who was allegedly an off-duty officer waved him away. "They wouldn't lock us up," another man said after some shushing and whispers of who did or did not have warrants.

Despite the plethora of Boston crime movies, save for a singular allusion in a *Boston Herald* story, there is little reporting about organized crime operating out of Newton, Watertown, or Waltham that I've found. Which is why I was surprised to learn the code was more than a custom. The local rules and criminal boundaries in these parts were explicit and had been enforced for decades.

When I ran into Joanne Pellegrini, Fat's daughter, at the festival I asked her how the Lake was or was not like the North End, what we call Boston's Little

Italy. I meant culturally, in regards to the influence of Irish and Jewish culture, distinct to Nonantum. Joanne told me they were all part of the same organization, and she meant the mob. The New England Mafia to be precise, which in Fat's prime was run by Raymond Patriarca in Rhode Island. Beneath him was Jerry Angiulo and his brothers in Boston. She told me this as if it was common knowledge. "Everybody has their own group of bookies, and they all answer in to the North End," she told me. The territory between Waltham, Watertown, and Newton is strictly divided. "Like, Watertown had their goodfellas, Newton had their goodfellas, Waltham had their goodfellas, who worked gaming and football games and numbers," she said. The rules about territory were strict. "Like, you weren't allowed to go book numbers in Watertown. That was their territory. It was very territorial, and everybody respected the others' territory, and if you didn't, there was a problem," she said. These rules extended to what kind of racket you could operate in these areas as well. Certain captains had their territory for football, others had their territory for numbers, and others could loan money. "You had to earn it, and you had to keep respecting to keep it," she said of the privilege to do business in these parts. Though, she insisted, no one ever got hurt, and they worked to keep the drugs out of the neighborhood. Out of Newton, at least. Waltham and Watertown were a little different—you could run drugs there. Just not in Newton. It still works like that, she said. "They're still here," she said with a laugh.

~

The agents working Operation Blackstone told me they had not heard of Lake Talk and did not know anything about the culture in Nonantum. I wondered if Madarati was familiar with these territorial lines. I still had questions about the allegations Madarati made about Waltham detective Joe Connors and Watertown detective John St. Onge robbing a drug dealer. Even if it was all a big misunderstanding, I was confused as to how such a misunderstanding might occur. Rafi had been an associate of Madarati's. In the Waltham murder investigation, some of the key leads investigators apparently overlooked also linked back to Rafi. Like the robbery of Rafi's apartment, for example. Then there was the fact that investigators did not seem interested in Rafi's father's assertion that

Rafi had had a recent argument with a Chechen friend, and they apparently did not contact everyone Rafi spoke to on the phone in the hours before his death.

The misunderstanding all boiled down to this one 4/20 drug rip-off. The victim of the violent home invasion was a twenty-one-year-old marijuana dealer named Bobby Johnson. Federal agents identified Bobby as one of Madarati's key buyers. "You deal with kids, I deal with monsters," Madarati told Bobby when Bobby was late on a payment, emphasizing to the young dealer the importance of paying on time. Bobby lived with his mother, and the agents had set up motion-sensor video cameras outside the Stoughton home to monitor Bobby's comings and goings. The assailants who approached Bobby's door that afternoon managed to do so without triggering the motion-sensor cameras. When Bobby called Madarati about the attack later, he described the assailants as "two older guys."

According to Bobby, and court documents, the men knocked on the door and claimed to be from the Department of Public Water and said that they needed to check the pipes. Bobby opened the door and invited them in and as soon as he turned his back, they pulled a gun, then gave him two black eyes before zip-tying his wrists. Bobby told me he had never seen the men before. He does not know who they are, and he does not want to know.

According to court documents, after he escaped, Bobby called Madarati. Then Madarati called a number he had saved under the name George Diamond. In the indictment, prosecutors said George Diamond was actually Roberto Velasquez-Johnson, who had been an officer at the Watertown Police Department for sixteen years but was fired a few months prior for improperly issuing and reporting a restraining order, the details of which Roberto disputes.

Roberto Velasquez-Johnson pleaded guilty to charges that he tipped off Madarati to the federal investigation in 2011 and lied to federal agents about his communications with Madarati after Madarati was arrested, but Roberto was never charged with profiting from Madarati's criminal endeavors. Roberto told me he and Madarati were friends, and he was complaining to Madarati on the phone about racism at the Watertown Police Department. But she says he isn't George Diamond, and that wasn't him on the phone, at least not that day.

I do not have transcripts or recordings of Madarati's calls with Bobby or George Diamond in their entirety. But according to the indictment, Madarati described Connors as having a goatee. The indictment claims that George

Diamond concurred, said Madarati's assessment was likely correct, and that Connors and St. Onge were "dirty." Then he provided Madarati with their home addresses. The agents then watched in horror as Madarati began circling the detectives' houses in his van. So they swooped in to arrest Madarati and his associates and bring the officers and their families to safety.

Here is the thing. Madarati's case also drew my attention to the Suburban Middlesex County Drug Task Force. This task force is how detectives from two different departments, Waltham and Watertown, could be partners in the first place. This is also the task force that officials from the Middlesex County District Attorney's Office said they consulted with regularly after the murders.

The direct involvement of this task force in the homicide investigation means that allegations of police corruption in Watertown could potentially have impacted the Waltham investigation, since they worked together.

It wasn't just this one allegation about Connors and St. Onge. Although Roberto Velasquez-Johnson was the only officer named and charged, the indictment against Madarati alleged that he had infiltrated the Watertown Police Department and accused him of having "connections" with "members" of the department—plural. Agents had subpoenaed and analyzed Madarati's phone and found that he had "frequent calls with several police officers from the Watertown Police Department."

～

At the height of his reign, Safwan Madarati, with his thick, manicured brows and angelic curly dark lashes, had shoulders so wide it was a wonder he fit inside his black Mercedes-Benz. (Although he drove a red plumbing van with a roof ladder most afternoons, to keep up appearances.) He went by Sammy, and until his arrest he maintained the trappings of his prior profession—plumber—while he went about the day-to-day tasks necessary for keeping up a semiorganized criminal fiefdom. These duties included delivering garbage bags full of weed and receiving suitcases full of cash. In between these errands, Madarati typically placed phone calls to work associates from a variety of unlisted prepaid burner phones, and from his listed number checked in on his wife, with whom he lived in a pale-blue bungalow. Madarati put in the hours developing his intimidating physique at the gym, where he plotted against those who sought to steal from or betray him. Hired hits were executed from rental cars.

The Lake is known for celebrating its Italian and Irish heritage, but across the river Watertown is home to the third-largest Armenian population in the country. Many of the men who allegedly stored Madarati's drugs and cash were part of Watertown's long-standing Armenian community. These men grew up playing soccer together on teams affiliated with the three local Armenian churches and eating buffet-style meals together at festivals. Madarati crashed some of the church lunches too and spoke Arabic with these men, but he wasn't Armenian. He was a newcomer to these parts, immigrating to Boston from Syria in 2000, before settling in Watertown. While his friends and enemies had roots here that went back generations, Madarati shot quickly to the top of this little-known criminal terrain.

I knocked on doors, wrote letters to Madarati and his associates behind bars, and tried to get Madarati and his associates to talk. People slammed doors in my face. One man was so angry, I watched as his biceps began to vibrate before he shut the door. I was treated to intimidating phone calls from attorneys. But sometimes I got lucky. I chatted with Vartan Soukissian, aka Wolf, who was essentially charged with being Madarati's gofer. With a monitor on his ankle and a sparkle in his eye, Wolf told me, "Not every cop is an angel" when I asked about the corruption allegations. Though he wouldn't tell me much more.

I made my way past the row of pink and red roses that wrapped around the outside of Madarati's home. His wife, Kim Dickert, a night-shift nurse with large doe eyes and short blond hair who was from the South Shore, spoke to me through a crack in the door. "My husband is a wonderful person," she told me. He made a mistake, was all. Madarati was in prison in Texas, and Kim was lonely. "The people were around us a lot, and I thought they were his friends. They don't knock, they don't call," she told me. I asked Kim about Madarati's friendships with local officers. Kim said she didn't know any names, but she assured me that he was friends with a number of officers before any of this happened. "They used to work out at the gym and stuff," she said. She was with Madarati on numerous occasions when he made small talk with local cops. She said they stopped to chat from the windows of their cars when they were on patrol.

Safwan Madarati chose not to answer questions for this book. I wrote to him in prison in 2014. He never wrote back. I called him in 2022. He told me, "I don't know what you are talking about, *ma'am*," and hung up the phone. In 2023, I texted him a detailed list of reporting and asked if he wished to provide clarification or comment. He texted me back a couple days later and wrote that he still had the letters I wrote to him in prison. "It's been all these years and you still don't know how to get the right story," he wrote in the text. He asserted that I was not "smart enough" to be an investigative reporter and alleged that I publish *nothing but lies*. Madarati did not respond to a follow-up text requesting that he specify reporting of mine he believed to be inaccurate so I could address any potential inconsistencies. But he did inform me of his plans to "write the real story from A-to-Z" and make my book "seem foolish." So perhaps further clarification is forthcoming.

CHAPTER
FORTY-THREE

The Waltham Warehouse

Operation Blackstone was not the only case I looked into. Thomas "Gus" Bailey was a former Watertown city councilor who was busted five weeks after the murders with millions of dollars' worth of weed in a Waltham warehouse after an anonymous tip was called in to law enforcement. I had ruminated on Bailey's case for years. I drew a cartoon illustration of him in cuffs and pinned it to my bulletin board. He chose an unlikely location for a grow operation, the same street as the Waltham Police Department, Lexington Street, in a warehouse less than one-fourth of a mile away from the department.

The investigation into Bailey was helmed by Waltham detective Joe Connors, which makes sense—Waltham is a small town, and Connors specialized in marijuana and drug raids. In early court filings, Bailey's defense attorney, Kevin J. Mahoney, took issue with the Suburban Middlesex County Drug Task Force and with Connors's ambiguous role as a local officer working with federal agents, calling Connors a "pseudo-DEA" agent and "cagey." It is a defense attorney's job to make such claims. Mahoney tried to get the evidence implicating Bailey thrown out. He said that Connors did not have a warrant when he busted down Bailey's door. Mahoney also argued the anonymous phone tip was suspicious.

Bailey's first problem was the evidence itself. Warrant or not, there was a lot of it: more than 198 kilograms of harvested weed, plus 1,063 plants and $33,942 cash.

Bailey's second problem was his mistress. According to court documents, Mary Coman told police that Bailey and his wife had been selling weed for fifteen years and that Bailey had been having Coman launder money for him, depositing the cash in five-thousand-dollar increments, which he'd spray with Lysol to hide the scent of the weed from the bank.

I finally got Bailey on the phone in 2022. He had served four years' time. When he was released, weed was legal in Massachusetts, and the state was giving special preference to nonviolent would-be dispensary owners and growers with prior cannabis convictions. Bailey opened up a legal grow house with his son, a Dartmouth graduate, and their website invites customers to "stop and smell the flowers." That's why Bailey got into this business in the first place, he told me. He really liked good bud.

On the phone, Bailey described the strains he's grown and loves, and interwove the story of his life. He knew Erik, which didn't surprise me, since he is exactly the type of grower Erik would try to seek out. Bailey said Erik was the "coolest, nicest" guy. He also remembered Erik was "pro-Israel," which came up because Bailey's wife was Israeli as well. "Be careful out there," Erik advised Bailey as Bailey was starting his grow operation. But Bailey didn't know Erik's last name, and when Bailey lost his phone to a pickpocket at a concert in 2008, he lost Erik's number.

Bailey served as a city councilor from 2001 to 2005; he had a campaign to introduce bike lanes, he said. That was the full extent of his political ambitions. Once he got the bike lanes set up, he was done with politics. He picked the Waltham warehouse because he liked the basement. He didn't think about it being so close to the police station. In fact, cops weren't the people he was most afraid of. He was more scared of getting robbed. He said he never used his prior political position to benefit his drug operation. "I wouldn't even know how to do that," he told me.

Bailey told me his arrest was almost a spiritual experience. He was tired of keeping secrets and tired of living in fear. He had been robbed on several occasions, though luckily it never got violent. When he saw Waltham detective Joe Connors outside of the warehouse with his goatee and a battering ram, he was terrified. He had never seen this man before in his life. To Bailey, Connors looked "like this biker from hell." When he realized Connors was a cop, he thought to himself, *Thank god.* Relief washed over him. "I really thought I was going to die." Officers zip-tied his wrists, but Bailey felt free for the first time in years. He was done. His secrets were out. *I have nothing to fear anymore,* he thought.

CHAPTER
FORTY-FOUR

The Russians

I was also curious about John Analetto, a Massachusetts state trooper with a scar on his face. Analetto was arrested in an FBI sting on New Year's Eve 2011 for threats he made in a Watertown auto shop. He was convicted on charges that he tried to extort a gambler. He was also caught on video, in a series of December 2011 auto-shop recordings, raving about how easy it is to get away with murder and threatening to kill a bookie.

Analetto went on trial three weeks after the shoot-out in Watertown and nine days before Ibragim Todashev was killed, which is likely why I and many others did not pay as close attention to this case as we might have otherwise. In the spring of 2013, Watertown became a national symbol of American bravery, an inspiring counterbalance to the Tsarnaevs' terror. First responders and the Watertown police force especially, whose officers faced down the Boston bombers in their final hours, were celebrated for their resilience and grit. Analetto's story didn't exactly jibe with that narrative.

Analetto was busted with the help of a bookie wearing a hidden camera on his jacket zipper. In the grainy black-and-white recordings, Analetto is heard threatening to hire "heavy-hitting Russians" to collect a gambling debt. Who were the Russians this wannabe mafioso state trooper had on speed dial in 2011? The Russians were not the only disturbing anecdote on these recordings. Three months after the Waltham murders, in an auto shop only a few miles away from the murder scene, Analetto was holding court. If police did not have video evidence or DNA, "they ain't gonna fucking get caught," he said. Analetto said he wanted to drive to the gambler's house and have Russo jump out and "slash a few fucking tires" and together they'd drive away. If the police pulled them over, Analetto would tell them: "What are you talking about? We're having a fucking sandwich. State police, get the fuck out of here." He told Russo it would be no problem. "You have a sixty-five percent chance of killing somebody and getting away with it. We're talking about puncturing a few fucking tires with a knife."

~

Analetto's facial scar was a focal point of his defense. He was born with a birthmark. The kids used to call him Fudge Face. The cruel words, psychiatrist Dr. Roger Gray claimed, left a mental wound. A plastic surgeon tried to remove the abnormality when Analetto was four years old. He was left with the scar instead. It would become Analetto's most distinguishing feature, offsetting his less memorable attributes—he is bald and has a medium build. The trauma, humiliation, and resentment Analetto endured in his Fudge Face days is unresolved, said Gray, who suggested Analetto would be better served by therapy than incarceration. The trial also revealed the more flattering nicknames Analetto gave himself. When he wanted a favor, he referred to himself as Trooper Analetto. When he bet on sports, he went by Big Red.

Four dozen family members and longtime friends wrote tender, desperate letters to Judge George O'Toole Jr. in an unsuccessful bid to get him released on bail. Analetto lived with his wife, Ellen—she was his middle school sweetheart—his son, daughter, and dog, Butkus. At family weddings, he was the king of the dance floor, grabbing Ellen to do the slide or the chicken. He had a Mrs. Doubtfire impersonation he practiced liberally.

The bookie, Robert Russo, was the star witness. He said Analetto threatened to kill him too. When Russo took the stand, at thirty-two years of age, he had seventeen years of experience in the bookmaking business under his belt. He started selling parlay cards in middle school. Analetto had placed bets with Russo for some time. They conducted these transactions at the Watertown transmission shop, which belonged to a mutual friend. From what I can tell, some of these Watertown auto shops essentially serve as men's social clubs.

In the summer of 2011, Russo was not doing well. He was 350 pounds and had a hernia the size of a human head—his own description. He was "polluted," he'd later tell the jury, which in his trade meant he was deeply in debt. Since the bookmaking game went digital, his gambling addiction had taken control of his life. Everyone knew it. His customers knew it, the loan sharks knew it, and so did the organization he worked for, which he referred to only as "the Office."

Russo met with Analetto in the transmission shop on a Friday afternoon in August 2011, as was their routine. Exchange days are always on Fridays. There was money to be paid, money to collect. On Fridays, Russo worked late, until the early hours of the next day.

There are videos Russo took that show Analetto amidst the clank of car parts, blowing smoke rings beneath rows of cars on lifts and a crooked "No Smoking" sign, drinking Johnnie Walker Black from a plastic cup. Russo can be heard but not seen. He says *fuck* in almost every sentence, using the regional pronunciation "fack," long and sharp, like a duck quacking.

Russo would later describe his state of mind that Friday as suicidal. Analetto knew of Russo's troubles and gave him the once-over. "What if I offered to help?" he said.

Thus, Russo and Analetto entered a complicated financial arrangement. Analetto became a sort of zealous self-help guru, preaching a mobster's version of *The Secret,* demanding Russo shave, exercise, accentuate the positive, and stop being a "negative fuck." He was also a bully. "Can I tell you what your problem is?" Analetto asked Russo and took a drag of a long cigarette. "You're fat." It was one of his gentler taunts. The loan made them business partners and Analetto's aspirations were big. He dreamed of one day taking over the Office so Russo would answer to him. Functionally he was also acting as a loan shark; he expected Russo to make regular payments on the $24,000 loan. He also expected a cut of Russo's bookmaking enterprise for life. On Analetto's end, he was supposed to bring in new clients. But he never did. Russo said Analetto's demands were unpredictable and unreasonable, and he couldn't meet them. Analetto was scarier than the loan sharks, Russo said.

Russo made money putting Analetto away and no longer had to make good on what he owed him. Russo also collected money from the FBI for his assistance in other investigations, according to court transcripts. Russo used this money to get a gastric bypass. Two years later, when Russo took the witness stand and confronted Analetto for the first time since his arrest, he had lost 150 pounds.

When I spoke to Russo in 2023, he told me he didn't "rat on anyone but [Analetto]." Some people got questioned, but "no one got in trouble." While it was true that he continued to work with his FBI handlers, he only did so for a few months in the capacity of "a consultant." He said he did not inform on any other individuals or organizations and that the FBI hired him to teach the agents the local bookmaking slang. "They needed the lingo," he told me. He was living a dangerous life, but he says he has since turned things around, gotten married, is a stepfather to three great kids, and works in hospitality. Meanwhile, he said his FBI handlers retired, are working in Hollywood, and have asked him to write a film treatment.

~

There are several instances on the recordings Russo captured in which Analetto mentions hiring a "Russian" to collect from the gambler who wasn't paying up. After Russo pushed back on Analetto's plan to slash tires, Analetto took a sip from a plastic cup, said that the next day he had plans to meet with someone of Russian descent who would help fix the problem.

In the recordings, Russo seems to direct Analetto away from discussing the Russians on tape. Russo swerved away from my questions about the Russians as well. When I asked Russo if other members of law enforcement placed bets with him and his office, he told me he would "rather not say."

This was not the first time Analetto allegedly proposed calling up "Russians" to make good on a threat. Analetto had allegedly gone so far as to put an individual with a thick Slavic accent on speakerphone, to demonstrate the seriousness of his intention to an individual, who reported the threat to the state police.

There were over twenty accounts in Analetto's Internal Affairs (IA) file, incidents in which individuals reported the trooper's behavior to the Massachusetts State Police. According to prosecutors, several investigations were closed because witnesses were too scared or intimidated to go forward, and two investigations were still pending. Many incidents detailed in this file concern Analetto's interactions with women. In one instance, a woman claimed Analetto followed her home after pulling her over for a traffic stop. She reported that she felt "as though the trooper would be following her in the future." On another occasion, Analetto allegedly pulled a woman over and "harassed her before allowing her to leave." Another account shows that a woman reported he had twice harassed and intimidated her on her way to her job at a sporting venue, first stopping her car and then, on a separate evening, following her inside to her place of employment. The report also said that Analetto once paid for two women to perform sex work "for himself and some friends." Analetto then had a dispute with the sex workers "over the lack of sexual services and money" and threatened them. Days later, he pulled one of the sex workers over in his cruiser, took her keys, and pulled out his gun, according to her complaint. He demanded his money back, and made her go to an ATM to get cash.

He also allegedly had an extramarital affair and threatened the woman's ex-husband, saying, "You don't mess around [with the] Irish, you don't mess around with the Italians, you don't mess around with the police." Analetto allegedly threatened to sexually assault the ex-husband with a broomstick, "take a sledgehammer" to the ex-husband's brother, and "fuck up" his brother's wedding the following weekend. Apparently, that weekend police did show up to the brother's bachelor party in response to a call about a disturbance.

The psychologist Dr. Roger Gray, hired by Analetto's defense team, testified that he thought Analetto might be cured from his gambling and alcohol addictions and other internal demons if he was released to inpatient treatment. Then, in cross-examination, the prosecution presented Dr. Gray with Analetto's IA file. Gray read the papers over and thought for a moment. He still believed Analetto could be healed if his issues were addressed. "This is a man who has been very troubled for a lot of years, who kept his troubles in some ways significantly hidden from his family. They apparently weren't hidden from his employer, who failed to make an intervention," he added (his employer being the Massachusetts State Police). "I was fascinated to read the litany of accusations and found myself asking, *Well, why was there no intervention?*"

Analetto's attorney, Gary Pelletier, said that he knew of no connection between his client and the bombing investigation and there were no heavy-hitting Russians. His client's threats were merely "puffery" and "bluster."

I also spoke to John Analetto over the phone briefly in 2022, after he had been released. I asked him if he knew Tamerlan Tsarnaev. "I'm not going to respond to those questions," he told me. I also asked if he had been involved in the Waltham murder investigation. Analetto did not respond to that question either. He did, however, speak at length about his deeply held belief that felons should be able to get their Second Amendment rights back. The case against him "wasn't fair," the very mention of the FBI made him want to "vomit." But he still felt like a cop at heart. "I'll bleed blue," he told me. Shortly thereafter he cut off the call, and that was all that came of that.

CHAPTER
FORTY-FIVE

Beat Da' Wrap

Prosecutors pegged Hagop "Jack" Sarkissian as Madarati's number-two man in the indictment, a categorization Jack refutes. He told me he had only known Madarati for a few weeks before his arrest. I wrote to Jack in prison and gave him my phone number. We started talking on the phone and kept up a correspondence for several months before I paid him a visit him at Fort Dix Federal Correction Institute in New Jersey.

The prison guards wouldn't let me into Fort Dix wearing an underwire bra or a long-sleeve white oxford shirt. The white oxford was deemed too risqué. So, after a humiliating ordeal, I met Jack in an undershirt and a moldy floral sweatshirt I had in the back of my car, a gift from the family I once nannied for. Jack has bright blue eyes, elfish ears, and the well-worn palms of a mechanic. He was waiting for me in the visitor room wearing a beige jumpsuit, concerned that the guards had given me a hard time. Jack is Armenian-American. He grew up in Watertown and has lived there his whole life. He owned a used car shop on Galen Street, in the little corner of Watertown on the Newton side of the Charles River near the bridge and a few blocks away from the Lake. Another mechanic who worked out of Jack's shop was also arrested in Madarati's case for conspiracy to sell marijuana.

Jack vehemently disagreed with the government's categorization of him. He said he only knew Madarati for a short time before he was arrested. But he says he made mistakes. He did not know introducing drug dealers to other drug dealers was grounds for a conspiracy charge, or that if Safwan Madarati discussed plans to commit crimes in his auto shop, prosecutors could argue Jack was complicit in them. He thought he was innocently conveying an informative message to a local nemesis in an attempt to deescalate the situation. Though in retrospect he realized that on a wiretap his words could be misconstrued to sound like extortion, he said he was never armed, even though those were the charges he pleaded guilty to. When we spoke again years later, after he had been released, he said he was being more selective about the kind of company he kept. On that end, he made mistakes. And he learned his lesson.

Jack told me stories of his life in Watertown. He knew Analetto from the auto shop circuit. Jack used to see Analetto at the gas station in Watertown Square, and he said Analetto would antagonize him, roll the window down and ask, "What's going on?" Jack said Analetto elongated the words to the point of sarcasm. "Staying out of trouble?" Analetto would tease.

He was also a cousin to Watertown officer Jean Sarkissian. Jean Sarkissian pulled Madarati over on a traffic infraction at the request of federal agents in the early phases of Operation Blackstone, on June 14, 2020. During this stop, agents seized $70,000 from a shoebox in the trunk of Madarati's Mercedes. According to court documents, after he was pulled over Madarati began listing names of local officers he claimed to be friends with. The officers were not named in the documents. Jean Sarkissian's brother, Artine Sarkissian, was also named in court documents in the Madarati case and was alleged to have participated in a "delivery of marijuana." He was never charged.

Then there was Zohrab Sarkissian (no relation). Zohrab and Jack had known each other since they were kids, playing soccer on teams affiliated with the Armenian churches. Jack and Zohrab had had a long-running feud over a gas station property across the street from Jack's auto shop, documented by thick files of legal paperwork at the Newton District Court. Zohrab was also named in the Madarati conspiracy as frequenting Jack's shop, though he was never charged or accused of a crime in the case. In a 2023 call, Zohrab told me he had "nothing to do with their business," and by that, he meant drug trafficking.

Zohrab was, however, stopped by HSI with a large amount of cash and gold, crossing the border into Canada in 2010. HSI made this seizure with the help of the Woburn Police Department. The feds do this fairly regularly, especially when they are building cases. They can confiscate large quantities of cash and gold without making an arrest or accusing anyone of a crime, and the owner then has to provide provenance for the valuables to get them back. Zohrab was never charged or accused of any crime in connection with this seizure, but he was apparently unable (or too uninterested) to provide federal agents with a legitimate account of how he acquired the $13,000 in cash and fifteen gold bars worth $520,000. Zohrab withdrew his claim to the precious metal, and law enforcement pocketed the proceeds. When I asked Zohrab about the gold seizure, he told me he was "snitched on."

~

Jack also told me about Mark Cristofori, a man who owned a jewelry store in Nonantum. Cristofori was the guy Jack was charged with threatening in Operation Blackstone. During the course of the investigation, Cristofori also opened a sandwich and vitamin shop in Waltham named Beat Da' Wrap, registered under the corporate name Marc Restaurant Group INC, with Cristofori listed as the president, treasurer, secretary, and director of the corporation. He also listed himself as the founder of the restaurant on LinkedIn, and claimed to have received a PhD from the university of "Street Smarts." The Beat Da' Wrap logo featured a cartoon figure of a man wearing a suit and a fedora, holding a warrant with the words *Middlesex County* at the top of the document. The lime-green interior of the restaurant was decorated with framed posters from *The Godfather* and *Goodfellas*. Beat Da' Wrap later changed owners and was closed in 2015 by the Board of Health for failing to pay overdue taxes.

According to court documents, the opening statements of a federal prosecutor, federal agents, and Jack's own understanding, in early 2011, months after registering the restaurant, Cristofori and an associate robbed Jack's auto-shop associate of one hundred pounds of marijuana. Cristofori and his associate allegedly said they would pay for the weed, but they didn't, and then they stopped returning their phone calls, according to Assistant United States Attorney Neil J. Gallagher Jr.'s account. Madarati tried to get the money back on their behalf and was convicted of hiring the men to shoot up Cristofori's jewelry shop in a dramatic spectacle that took place in broad daylight on St. Patrick's Day, 2011. When Newton police officers arrived on the scene, Cristofori was pacing outside and talking on the phone. "Someone is going to pay for this," he said, according to the testimony of a Newton cop. Cristofori refused to cooperate with the Newton Police—a detective testified that an attorney advised Cristofori not to meet with Newton detectives and he was never charged with any crime in relation to Operation Blackstone.

After I tried to contact Cristofori at his home and at his jewelry store, I got a call from his attorney, Michael Kelly, telling me that Cristofori was glad the perpetrators of the jewelry store shooting were caught and requesting that I stay away from Cristofori's wife and place of business. When I asked for comment on the allegations that Cristofori stole one hundred pounds of marijuana, Kelly said that the allegations were false and Cristofori "had no dealings with any of those people in Watertown." When I told Kelly that Cristofori's dealings were clearly documented in the court papers and attested to by federal agents, Kelly told me he had no comment.

CHAPTER
FORTY-SIX

Roberto Velasquez-Johnson

Gail Miles's murder is an open case at the Boston Police Department. Her murder is mysterious and brutal, but it is also different from the Waltham crime in key ways. For one, I do not have information suggesting the crime scene was staged or that there was an ideological motive. And I found no indications this was a financially motivated killing either. While I learned that a gun was reported missing from Miles's home, it does not appear that anything else was taken. More to the point, Tamerlan Tsarnaev and Ibragim Todashev were behind the Waltham crime, and there is no indication that Gail Miles knew Tamerlan Tsarnaev or Ibragim Todashev or that they would have had any reason to kill her. It is unlikely that Ibragim Todashev returned to Massachusetts in early December 2011, when she was killed. Of course, there might be a direct connection between these two cases, as Masha Gessen has suggested. But an infinite number of possibilities could also be true, and I have found no evidence to support this particular claim. But not only was Miles murdered, she had also accused members of the Watertown Police Department of discrimination and abuse. I found the records of her allegations informative.

Gail Miles was the first Black person and only the second woman officer in the Watertown Police Department when she joined the force in 1984. According to her complaint, the harassment started on her first day. An officer allegedly went through her medical records and shared some highly personal information.

The Massachusetts Commission against Discrimination (MCAD) destroyed the records of her complaint pursuant to a statewide records retention schedule, but I obtained some of her personal papers. "My hair is breaking off and I am pulling out the rest from stress," she wrote. Miles said she was regularly subjected to racist and sexually charged jokes. But she never complained or took matters to her supervisor, until a male colleague allegedly groped her in the booking area. This incident was at least partially recorded on video. When the story reached Ed Deveau, who was then a captain and was chief at the time of the bombing, Deveau allegedly responded by accusing Miles of groping a male colleague. The officer who Deveau claimed Miles had groped would later deny under oath that Miles touched him. Miles's attorneys said that Deveau retaliated against Miles for coming forward instead of investigating her complaint. "This story is a complete fabrication by the very person who supposedly is in charge of the investigation, Captain Deveau," Miles's attorneys claimed.

After Miles filed an official complaint, another officer allegedly pulled a gun on her and aimed the laser at her torso. Four officers claimed that this never happened. But officials at MCAD found that Miles's reaction to this incident was captured on audio and video. Miles's attorneys wrote in an MCAD report filing that the coordinated cover-up was even more disturbing than an officer pulling a gun on Miles in the first place.

I was not able to obtain all the documents from Miles's civil claim. The case was settled and never went to trial. But Kathleen E. Donahue, Watertown's first female detective, watched how Gail Miles was treated, according to Donahue's own civil complaint. Miles's experience had a lasting impact on Donahue. She said Miles's fate was part of the reason Donahue was initially hesitant to advocate and come forward about her own experience at the department. But eventually, it seems, Donahue couldn't take it anymore, and she brought forth a claim.

In 2022 Donahue won a $4 million discrimination suit against the department. She alleged that Michael Lawn, who became chief after Deveau stepped down, used his power and position to isolate her and to invite her to engage in intimate relations over the course of four years, from 2009 to 2013. She also claimed to have been one of the first officers to arrive at the scene when Dzhokhar Tsarnaev was discovered hiding in the boat and that officers fired without orders, setting off a cascade of bullets, one of which passed inches from her head. When she reported this to Deveau, he berated her for her report and isolated her as a form of retaliation, and according to her complaint, Deveau told her to "let it go."

~

The indictment against Madarati alleged that he had infiltrated the Watertown Police Department and accused him of having "connections" with "members" of the Watertown Police Department. This implied that he was friendly with more than one officer. But Velasquez-Johnson, who is Black and Latino, was the only officer named and charged. At the time of his arrest, he was in the process of filing a complaint with MCAD against the Watertown Police Department for racial discrimination. In the complaint, Velasquez-Johnson argued that he was routinely punished for actions other officers got away with and detailed more than a decade of racial discrimination and harassment he said he experienced. After Velasquez-Johnson was arrested in the federal sting, MCAD dismissed his case without finding, in part because Velasquez-Johnson did not have sufficient documentation to support his claims.

In a filing submitted before Velasquez-Johnson's federal sentencing hearing, his attorney, Melinda Thompson, wrote, "The Government indicated that prior to the wiretaps of Mr. Madarati's phone, various members of the Watertown Police Department who were friends with Mr. Madarati were warned not to speak to him. Mr. Velasquez-Johnson was not involved in this meeting, and was never warned not to speak to Mr. Madarati." So, the other local officers were tipped off, except for the Black and Latino cops? A local drug dealer was allegedly communicating with multiple members of law enforcement, but Roberto Velasquez-Johnson was the only one named and charged?

It took me more than seven years to convince Roberto Velasquez-Johnson to agree to an interview. We finally sat down together at a pizza shop at a strip mall in 2021 and then continued to talk on the phone. He let his soggy slice of cheese pizza go cold while we sipped on sodas. He said reliving his experience at the Watertown Police Department made him too anxious to eat.

Velasquez-Johnson tried to fit in, but he said the "the good old boys' club" was not just a metaphor for the insular group of mostly white cops, many of whom grew up in the neighborhoods they patrolled and some of whom were related. He described a basement speakeasy in a private home on Main Street with Ping-Pong tables, a giant TV, and stripper poles where he said officers hung out when they were off duty.

Roberto said officers made racist jokes in front of him his first day of the job. His wife, Christine Creach-Velasquez, also submitted a letter before his sentencing hearing. She said when her husband came back from his first day, he looked scared. "I don't want to go back there," he told her. She told him he had to.

"You can't let them get to you," she said. "Telling him to stay in a place that breeds imposters, hate, discrimination, envy, and unknown enemies was the worst advice I ever gave my husband," she wrote. Christine passed away due to a long-standing illness over the course of my phone interviews with Roberto.

Back at the department, when Roberto vocalized his discomfort about the racist jokes, he said the other officers began to call out to watch out, "here comes the sensitive guy," every time he entered the room.

There were unwritten rules at the Watertown Police Department, Velasquez-Johnson told me. People who he should and should not pull over. He said his supervisors would often step in for a friend, or he would get chastised for ticketing the wrong actors.

~

Velasquez-Johnson said other detectives and officers were friends with Safwan Madarati, and they were warned not to speak to Madarati after the agents set up wiretaps. He also said several colleagues actually encouraged him to contact Madarati during this period. They told him that they were "supposed to go out drinking somewhere" with Madarati, but they couldn't get ahold of him, which is why they asked Velasquez-Johnson to call.

Roberto thought he was doing his colleagues a favor by giving Madarati a call. "I just, you know, went along with it, thinking that these people were, you know, my friends." Despite all the years of alleged abuse, he says he still wanted to fit in. In retrospect, Roberto said he feels like a "dumbass." He was embarrassed. "How could I have let them fucking set me up like that?" he said.

In an interview, former chief Deveau admitted that he may have discussed Roberto Velasquez-Johnson's reputation at the department with agents but said he was sharing valid concerns. Deveau said there was an investigation into the allegations against St. Onge and Connors, and the allegations were "unfounded."

He knew of no other officers who were in communication with Safwan Madarati. He said he did not warn officers not to communicate with Safwan Madarati.

Neither the Watertown Police Department nor the Waltham Police Department, which also oversees the Suburban Middlesex County Drug Task Force, responded to requests for information regarding the investigation into Madarati's initial allegation about the robbery and home invasion. Neither department answered queries or provided comment or clarification in response to a detailed list of the reporting that appears in this book pertaining to Waltham detective Joe Connors and St. Onge—who is apparently no longer working as a detective. St. Onge is currently listed as a patrol officer on the department website. Neither Connors nor St. Onge responded to requests for comment sent to them directly.

When I first spoke to Roberto Velasquez-Johnson, through a crack in the front door of his home, he told me he was scared. He told me that it didn't matter what he said, no one would believe him. His reputation was in ruins. Over the course of multiple interviews, Roberto did eventually bear witness to several other incidents of apparent corruption at the Watertown Police Department. The thing is, although there is precedent for Roberto's allegations of racism and abuse, he is also a convicted liar and an ex-cop who was friends with a known drug dealer. His allegations of racism may well be true, but he might have an axe to grind, or a reason to spread stories about the people he felt he was wronged by. I did not find any evidence to support many of his accounts of corruption.

Except for one claim. It seems as though Roberto Velasquez-Johnson was not the only member of law enforcement who was friendly with Madarati. In addition to the allegations laid out in court documents, another officer spoke to me and backed up this account.

Officer James Brown now works in the Cambridge Police Department, but he was assigned to the Watertown Police Department during the period in question. Brown said he went with the other Watertown officers to a nightclub and was introduced to Madarati through his colleagues in this way on one or two occasions. "I didn't feel quite comfortable," Brown said of the social arrangement. Around this time Brown heard rumors of "nefarious" activities among his colleagues. It was part of the reason he left the Watertown Police Department. "As soon as it started to smell fishy to me, I stepped away," he told me. (The

Watertown Police Department did not respond to allegations that multiple officers socialized with Safwan Madarati.)

Thus, it seems very likely that one of the Waltham murder victims, Raphael Teken, and multiple members of local law enforcement were all associates of the same local marijuana dealer. I am not at all certain that this overlap between the criminal milieu of the victims and the members of law enforcement tasked with investigating their death impacted the way the Waltham murder case was handled in 2011. There may be other explanations for why Tamerlan Tsarnaev slipped through their fingers. Investigators may have been incompetent or lazy. Admittedly, this is a complicated murder case. Perhaps the investigators' skill sets simply were not a good match for the job. It's also possible that, as in the Sean Ellis case, one or several investigators involved in the Waltham murder investigation may have been reluctant to aggressively pursue certain leads, for fear of what a thorough investigation might reveal about their own shady endeavors, or the endeavors of their friends and colleagues. Officials claim they cannot release information about the Waltham murders to protect the ongoing investigation. This may be so. But they are asking for the public's trust, and it's not clear that trust is warranted.

CHAPTER
FORTY-SEVEN

Delivery

In January 2014, I went to see Safwan Madarati at his sentencing hearing at the Moakley Courthouse. His case did not go to trial. He pleaded guilty to drug charges, money laundering, and extortion. The hearing did not attract the same throng of spectators and journalists as the bombing trial. The woman who I would later learn was Madarati's wife, Kim Dickert, was there. And while I was taking in the view outside the courtroom, I noticed a pair of men in work boots, jeans, and fleece vests. Thinking they might be Madarati's friends or family, I cautiously introduced myself to see what I could learn. As it turned out, they were not Madarati's allies. They were HSI agents and lead investigators P. J. Lavoie and Mike Kroll, who I would interview later.

I followed the agents into the courtroom. Moments later, Madarati was escorted in with his hands in shackles. Kim was seated in the back left of the courtroom, as far away from Lavoie and Kroll as possible. Madarati turned around and gave her a wink, and she promptly broke down in sobs.

Madarati was a man who "at least in his own mind, took over part of Watertown," Assistant United States Attorney Neil J. Gallagher Jr. told Judge Rya Zobel when the sentencing hearing began. I thought it was interesting; Gallagher was not arguing that Madarati had taken over Watertown, only that he believed he had done so. Gallagher asked the judge for a fifteen-year sentence.

Then Madarati's attorney, Thomas Butters, made his argument to the court for a lower sentence. Butters began by jokingly referring to his client as "Mr. Macho." The hired hit on a jewelry store was to help a friend, Butters explained. The final incident, in which he claimed Madarati was "casing the cops," was a big misunderstanding, Butters said. Madarati's belief that two local detectives had beaten and robbed a drug dealer was "I don't want to say *psychotic*," Butters said, implying it was exactly that. Butters said that Madarati had become extremely paranoid from his increasing use of steroids, cocaine, and OxyContin, and he completely discredited Madarati's allegations about Waltham detective Joe Connors and Watertown detective John St. Onge.

When Butters was finished, Madarati stood and addressed the court in a rolling accent. He was full of remorse, he claimed. It wasn't until the drugs left his system that he was able to see the consequences of what he had done. Madarati told Zobel how he had had the great opportunity to come to this country from Syria and he had "met a great woman." Kim let out another loud sob from the back of the court.

Zobel sentenced Madarati to 144 months in prison. After the ruling, Butters turned around and thanked the agents twice.

Strategically, Butters's argument was smart. The agents would later tell me that the stated focus of their investigation was not police corruption and that corruption was not part of the wider case they were trying to build, nor did it fall under HSI's stated mission and wheelhouse: transnational crime. Their job was to target narcotics crossing an international border. If the government was not trying to build a case against the local cops, Madarati stood to gain nothing by insisting that his allegation was true. (According to HSI agent P. J. Lavoie, after the bombing, Madarati did agree to speak with agents about a different matter. Lavoie, accompanied by federal prosecutors in the bombing trial, met with Madarati behind bars and asked him about the Waltham murders, due to his connection to Rafi Teken. According to Lavoie, Madarati said he did not know anything about Rafi's murder and that he didn't even know Rafi was dead, and that was the end of the conversation.) If Madarati was going to plead guilty, it was better to play ball, go along with the government's story, cooperate and try to gain their good favor. By claiming his client was delusional and dismissing his allegations about detectives Joe Connors and John St. Onge, Butters also served to soften Madarati's more threatening statements caught on wiretap. His client was all talk, a lot of bark but no bite, Butters argued.

~

But how did this mix-up happen? Peppered throughout the indictments against Madarati and his associates are indications of further crossovers between the lives of the defendants and local police. Another defendant, Victor Loukas, was a trainer at a now-defunct gym called Super Fitness, where Madarati worked out. Kroll also noted that part of the reason Madarati came to believe Connors and St. Onge beat up Bobby was because the officers did, in fact, know Madarati's friend-turned-enemy, Loukas. "Mr. Loukas had a relationship with Joe Connors and John St. Onge," said Kroll in a court hearing, and the relationship between the pair of detectives and the bodybuilding smuggler was "friendly" in nature.

I asked the agents about the allegations that Madarati "had frequent calls with several police officers from the Watertown Police Department." Kroll told me it was a small town. And anyway, Madarati called *them*, not the other way around. "Some of the police officers that Safwan was talking to, you know, even if Safwan called him, who knows if the guy wanted to talk to him? Maybe the guy was, like, *Why is this guy calling me?*" he said.

Lavoie said the relationships spoke to Madarati's "social skills." Madarati, he said, was "a very, very adept manipulator." He knows how to draw people in.

In court, attorney Gallagher officially accounted for Madarati's misunderstanding of an incident in 2006 when Madarati was arrested on drug charges in a case that Connors and St. Onge had helped build. Madarati and his associate, Karapet Dzhanikyan, were arrested by the Suburban Middlesex County Drug Task Force for possession with intent to distribute in a school zone after a warrant was issued at Dzhanikyan's home.

~

On a warm summer day, I went to the Waltham District Courthouse to pull up the 2006 case, vying for the clerks' attention with the producer of a reality court show, whom they unquestionably preferred, paid for my copies, and looked through the documents at home. I would return to this case many times over the years. The significance of this case was not immediately clear to me, and to this day this case raises questions I am unable to answer.

On the afternoon of November 9, 2006, Madarati was arrested with Dzhanikyan—who was also convicted in Operation Blackstone. They were sitting in Madarati's car parked outside Dzhanikyan's Watertown home when the officers came. This sting was led by Detective John St. Onge from Watertown. According to the initial police report, the focus of the arrest was actually Dzhanikyan. The report said that detectives were tipped off by a confidential informant identified only as "Mercedes" to the fact that Dzhanikyan sold OxyContin and used marijuana and steroids. Mercedes had provided information to task force officers in the past. After a brief surveillance campaign, conducted with surveillance assistance from the local mailman, the task force made the arrest.

But the 2006 arrest was not exactly as it appeared or how investigators categorized it in the initial report. St. Onge would later admit that his stated reason for the sting, the tip from Mercedes, was not the whole story. Detectives were not interested in Dzhanikyan; they were actually looking into Madarati's potential ties to an attempted shooting of a pizza delivery boy at a small redbrick two-family home at 68 and 70 Carroll Street in Watertown. Investigators were apparently trying to determine if Madarati was behind the shooting, which they believed was a hired hit. The questionable pretense of their investigation was a point of ire for Madarati's attorney, Barry Wilson.

St. Onge, while being questioned by Wilson, testified that during a meeting with members of the Suburban Middlesex County Drug Task Force and the Watertown Police Department, Madarati's name was "developed" as being behind the Carroll Street shooting. *Developed* is vague cop lingo that indicates nothing about how they arrived at that suspicion or how much evidence they had. Also, according to a motion filed by Wilson, no one except St. Onge—not even his fellow task force members or Watertown PD officers—had any recollection of the meeting ever taking place. (Gallagher stated that Connors was involved in the case, but Connors's name does not appear on the court documents I obtained.) St. Onge could not produce a single page of documentation of the meeting having taken place or evidence of how Madarati's name was linked to the shooting. The drug charges were later dropped.

~

One must be careful mapping any path paved with coincidences and coincidences alone. One need not account for every errant fact, and not every coincidence is significant. But some are. And in this instance, I found certain overlaps between this address, Ibragim Todashev, Madarati, and the Waltham murder investigation worthy of note.

One of Ibragim's many residences in the Greater Boston area listed in his immigration file and other official documents was this very same small, square brick two-family home in Watertown with the addresses 68 and 70 Carroll Street. These documents list Ibragim as having lived there in 2008 and 2009. In addition, in a brief interview in 2014, Angelos Davos, the current owner of 68 and 70 Carroll Street, informed me that Ibragim also lived at this address for three weeks in early 2013, sometime before the bombing. The only other account I've found of Ibragim Todashev returning to Boston to visit Tamerlan comes from John Miller, an FBI agent turned journalist, who reported this detail in the days after the shooting. John Allan of the Wai Kru gym told the *Boston Globe* that Ibragim Todashev returned to Boston. Unfortunately, I do not know anything else about Todashev's return to Boston in 2013 because after briefly speaking to Davos outside his home where he was working on his motorcycle, he apparently thought better of granting me an interview, went inside, and shut the door. Also of note: the Carroll Street home was once owned by Zohrab Sarkissian. Zohrab sold the residence in 2004 to another individual, who sold it to Angelos Davos in 2011, a week after the arrests in Safwan Madarati's case. Zohrab told me it was a "forty-year-old address," and ended the call.

These crossovers, unlike others I have found elsewhere in my investigation, I have deemed significant enough to note. One likely explanation for the connection between this address, the investigation by Connors and St. Onge into Madarati, and the hit on the unnamed pizza boy is simply that Watertown is a small town.

Yet I also found a direct connection between one of Ibragim's roommates at this Carroll Street home, Wagdy Gad, and the Waltham triple murder that appears to hold more weight. Unfortunately, I did not get the opportunity to interview Wagdy Gad before he died in 2019, at the age of forty-one, from what his boss Suhail "Sal" Oweis, the owner of Gerry's Italian Kitchen in Watertown, told me was cancer. However, I have police reports and tax records that show Gad lived in and listed this Carroll Street address as his residence from 2004 to 2016, at which point it appears he spent the last few years of his life in Quincy. Thus, he would have crossed paths with Ibragim Todashev before and after the Waltham murders.

Gerry's Italian Kitchen is a popular pizza and sub spot with a green awning. They mostly do delivery and takeout.

After the bombing, the *Boston Globe* spoke to another manager, Mina Askander, who said that someone called in an order to Gerry's from Brendan's apartment around 8:30 or 9:00 p.m. on the evening of the murders, and when a delivery woman arrived with the food, no one answered the door. The timing was curious. From all the accounts of people I've spoken to close to the case, the victims stopped answering their phones around 7:30 p.m. Who called in that order?

Matt Cook flew to Boston from Texas for a few frigid days in January 2022 to help me get to the bottom of the Gerry's mystery, among other questions. I looked skeptically at his light fleece pullover and Longhorns baseball cap, but he didn't complain about the cold as we made our rounds going door to door. Mina Askander wouldn't talk to us. But we did speak to Sal, the owner, briefly outside his home.

After the bombing there was reporting, later contested by Sal, that Tamerlan Tsarnaev worked at Gerry's doing delivery. This reporting was allegedly based on accounts of unnamed law enforcement officials who allegedly claimed to recognize Tamerlan as their delivery guy. Sal said that Tamerlan never worked there.

But Sal did say that it was Wagdy Gad, Ibragim's roommate, who took the call requesting a delivery to 12 Harding Avenue the night of the murders. Wagdy Gad sent the order out with a delivery woman, but no one answered when she arrived at the door. First Sal told us that Wagdy Gad had told the delivery woman to leave the food outside. Then Sal said he wasn't sure if the food was left outside. The caller would have had to pay for the order if Wagdy Gad gave instructions to leave the food outside, he said, and he was not sure if that happened.

Investigators never called the restaurant, Sal said, which is curious if the order did come in from one of the victims' phones. Instead, said Sal, Wagdy Gad called the police three days later, after he saw the news about a murder at that address. Sal said he did not know what came of this conversation between Gad and law enforcement.

Sal said law enforcement did not contact Gad or the restaurant in any official capacity after the bombing. Though he did say that then–Watertown Police chief Ed Deveau called. Sal described the call as more like a friendly chat and declined to elaborate more on his relationship with Deveau other than to say that Deveau is a patron of the restaurant and that Deveau called him when he saw reporting about Tamerlan in connection to the restaurant. Sal is a fairly well-connected guy, it turns out.

According to documents filed with the Secretary of the Commonwealth's Corporate Division, Sal was registered as the manager of a company called Natick Mercantile Building, LLC, for which Massachusetts State Representative John J. Lawn was registered as the agent. The Lawn family happens to be renowned in Watertown. Lawn's father was a Watertown police officer, and the state rep's brother, Michael Lawn, was a lieutenant with the Watertown Police Department at the time of the murders and was promoted to chief in 2016 after Deveau stepped down.

Representative John J. Lawn, who is the brother of former police chief Michael Lawn, and Sal's apparent former business partner, was quoted in the *New York Times* as living close to the murder scene, having talked to neighbors the day the bodies were found, and closely following the case. Lawn spoke to the *Times* in defense of law enforcement, claiming the investigation was "thoroughly done." Representative Lawn did not respond to questions regarding his business relationship with Suhail "Sal" Oweis sent over phone, mail, email, and social media. Oweis also declined to comment.

CHAPTER
FORTY-EIGHT

Another Bad Omen

Investigators found Jay's body in the living room of his Richmond apartment beside an overturned chessboard and his father's black leather Bible. Inside the Bible, on a page that begins with Psalm 34, Jay had apparently tucked nine pages of his own writing. On three of these pages, Jay accounted for his communications with Hiba the weekend of September 11, 2011. On six of these pages, Jay described his last meeting with Hiba. He appears to accuse her of trying to frame or implicate him in the Waltham murders. He also accuses Hiba of being involved in the murders herself. The final page is a to-do list in which Jay detailed plans to break his lease, move out, and "find new holy spirit filled friends."

I obtained Jay's writing from the Richmond Police Department after filing a records request in January 2022. I returned to Richmond in May 2023, to settle the matter in court. The Richmond Police Department turned over the documents one month later. Detective Jeffrey Crewell was the lead investigator on the case, and I also obtained redacted copies of Crewell's notes and records, as well as photos of the crime scene. It was satisfying to read through Crewell's work.

Jay was found dead in a secure apartment with a single shotgun wound to the right side of his head, according to the medical examiner's report. An investigator found a match to one of the socks on the second floor. The examiner later concluded that the blood was likely transferred when the decedent's pants were removed—it is not clear when or how—but the circumstances were not immediately deemed suspicious. Investigators took photos of a 12-gauge shot-gun they found near Jay's body. It was loaded with a single spent shell. In the days and weeks after the death, Crewell examined the shotgun in comparison with Jay's tall stature and determined it was feasible for Jay to turn this weapon on himself. He had forensic technicians test Jay's hands for gunshot residue, and the results came back positive. He pulled police records from other police departments, consulted with other detectives, interviewed Jay's family, Jay's roommate, and Hiba, and pursued leads as a result of these interviews.

Jay's writing is less clear. I can't confirm Jay's entire account of his communi-cations with Hiba or his characterizations of their relationship. Jay claimed they were often in touch. But Jay also said that this was because Hiba manipulated him. He stated that others could attest to Hiba's attempts to contact him "sexu-ally and emotionally." In the weeks before his death, Jay reported to police that Hiba sent him threatening and unsolicited messages.

Jay does not explain why he wrote these pages or clearly articulate plans to take his own life. Instead, he wrote that he intended to contact detectives the next morning and tell them everything he knew about Hiba, drugs, and selling marijuana. He also instructed investigators to "follow her," as if he might not be around to convey the message himself.

In the weeks leading up to his death, Jay established a narrative. In multiple instances, he sought to provide records of his relationship and communications with Hiba that cast her in an unflattering light and him as the victim of her schemes and influence. I cannot confirm the entirety of his account. Why would Jay lie about his communications with Hiba before and after the Waltham mur-ders? I'm not sure. It's also possible that the events unfolded as Jay described. There is a lot about Hiba and Jay I will never understand.

In addition to chess, Jay appears to have had an interest in art. He hung colorful oil paintings on his walls—abstract designs, men on street corners, a bejeweled sword. By the back door of his kitchen, he also hung a black-and-white print of a couple in a romantic embrace. The man and the woman in this image are brandishing pistols in a scene evoking the notorious us-against-the-world bank-robbing duo Bonnie and Clyde, together until the end, taken down side-by-side in a hail of bullets. Perhaps Jay and Hiba emulated the couple at one point in time. They wouldn't have been the first. Although their story certainly ended differently.

~

Jay wrote out a bullet-point timeline of his interactions with Hiba the weekend of the murders in blue ink on white, lined paper. He began by stating that Hiba came to visit "2 weeks ago." It's not clear if this meeting took place in late August, though that's what he suggests by including this point at the top of his timeline. He could also have meant two weeks from when he wrote the list, apparently in the last hours of his life, when she returned to Richmond after the murders. In any case, it seems that in addition to their meeting in early October, shortly before his death, Jay and Hiba also got together on at least one occasion in late August or late September 2011, according to Jay's account.

In the following line Jay wrote that he sent Hiba $300 via MoneyGram. He said Hiba asked for the money, she was frantic, and that the "NEXT DAY" Hiba texted him about her fight with Brendan. "I'm leaving him he embarrassed me in front of my friends," Hiba wrote, according to Jay's account. Jay noted that Hiba slashed Brendan's tires, and the landlord was involved.

Then Hiba texted Jay and asked for a plane ticket. "Asking to fly to Ft. Lauderdale with friend," she wrote, according to Jay. It was also Ian's understanding that Jay did, in fact, pay for Hiba's flight to Florida. Jay's roommate also said that Jay purchased the plane ticket, according to a police report. While she was in Florida, Jay said that Hiba sent him a disturbing text. "I have something to get off my chest that may impact the rest of our lives," she wrote, according to Jay. Jay stated that when he called Hiba, she could "not stop crying." When she calmed down, Hiba allegedly told Jay she was upset because she watched a movie called *The Encounter*. The movie in question appears to be a Christian film that came out in 2011, about a modern-day Jesus who frequents a diner. Jay does not provide the exact date and time of these communications. Hiba told me she was watching a movie with a friend on Sunday night, the night of the murders. But it is possible she watched a film on Saturday evening as well. Jay wrote that, on his call, Hiba said that she loved him and "seemed very sad." The next thing Jay knew, Hiba sent him another frantic text, asking for an early return ticket. Jay wrote that he obliged, as the situation "seemed serious."

On the Monday Hiba found the bodies, Jay wrote that she called and gave him the news and asked him for "money & phone bill." Jay wrote that he wired her $50 and told her to call her parents. Hiba called again, according to Jay, and asked him to log on to her T-Mobile account. She said people had taken her phone. Then she again asked for money, and according to Jay, he wired her another $50.

Jay concluded this timeline with one word, *Tool*, underlined in black ink.

While it is unclear to whom Jay's writing is addressed, it appears Jay was writing in reaction to a Wednesday, October 5, 2011, police interview and his last meeting with Hiba, although parts of his writings appear to contain a to-do list, potentially written prior to that day. According to police records, that Wednesday, Massachusetts state trooper Erik P. Gagnon traveled to Richmond to question Jay about his relationship with Hiba in connection to the Waltham murders. Later that evening, Jay invited Hiba into his home. Investigators were called to Jay's apartment by his roommate Friday evening. Gagnon, who was still in Richmond, arrived on the scene and identified his body.

While he was in town, Gagnon also questioned Hiba. I do not know what Gagnon discussed with Hiba. Those records are not available to me. But Gagnon's name has come up on multiple occasions over the course of my own investigation. Notably, he is the trooper whom Aria, Erik's sister, said threatened to sue her. Historically, Gagnon has opted for confrontational interview techniques.

On sheets of unlined paper in red ink, Jay begins a long, rambling account by stating that he was "100% innocent." Innocent of what? He is not clear. But again, he appears to be writing in response to the police interview with Gagnon. He claimed that Hiba was "plotting and scheming 110%" but that he withheld embarrassing information about her from the detectives. Jay said he wanted to meet her in person before he said anything incriminating. But apparently, that Wednesday, Hiba proved him terribly wrong. Hiba "is weaving a web of lies and bullshit," he wrote. "Please continue to follow her. She has woven an intricate scheme."

Jay wrote that Hiba was trying to implicate him in the Waltham killings as "payback for cheating on her and leaving her." He ruminated on karma and claimed she was out for revenge. But it's not clear that Jay had substantial evidence to support this allegation. And yet, as Hiba wrote to Ian in May 2013—"I[']m just gla[d] to know that Jay isn[']t involved as I originally thought"—it seems she previously vocalized a suspicion that Jay was involved in the murders at one point in time. The reports on Jay's death included a photo of a plastic hotel key card with information for a Waltham taxi company on the back. According to documents in the case file and my own interviews, Hiba obtained the key card more than three weeks earlier, from the hotel where investigators put her up after finding the bodies. Hiba apparently left the card in Jay's apartment after her visit on Wednesday. According to his account, after observing Hiba's behavior that night and "the planting of this card," Jay became convinced that Hiba was "involved deep."

But Jay's fears that Hiba was cooking up some sort of scheme predated his writings by several weeks. According to Jay's roommate, Hiba began "making threats" after the murders when she returned to Richmond, and had been contacting Jay via phone, text, and email. In the following weeks, Jay filed two police reports about Hiba's behavior. On September 28, 2011, Jay filed a report with Fairfax City Police, near his family home, regarding "obscene phone calls." He said Hiba was threatening to hurt herself and frame him for her injuries. "You are going to be the first suspect," Hiba said, according to Jay's account in the police report. He brought a witness, whose name is redacted, with him to the police station to support his account. Allegedly, Hiba also indirectly made threats to someone else in her messages to Jay. This name is also redacted, so it is unclear whether Jay is referring to this same witness. Jay filed a similar report with the Fairfax County Police the next day. He noted that Hiba was contacting him from blocked numbers. Jay's roommate told investigators he had copies of threatening emails Hiba allegedly sent and would provide these records to police. Those records are not included in the documents I obtained. Matt Cook and I reached out to the roommate on multiple occasions. He never got back to us.

Investigators heard from Jay's father, who believed that Hiba was regularly in and out of Jay's apartment and had her own key. But the roommate stated that he did not know of any other keys to the apartment and that Jay had installed alarms in the home a week before his death in response to Hiba's alleged threats. The roommate did not want Hiba in the house and moved out on Thursday, the day after Jay invited her in. Jay was distraught after seeing Hiba, the roommate said. He "looked like he had seen a ghost."

In their last meeting, Jay said Hiba asked him to "run away" with her to New Zealand—"another wild statement." He also wrote that the two of them used cocaine. It should be noted that it is very possible that this is why Hiba pulled out a plastic key card in the first place—to cut lines. Others have noted that Hiba's holding on to this key card in particular was somewhat odd; it is a somber token.

But maybe she was thinking of other things and had other priorities—priorities that may not have been healthy or legal but had nothing to do with her trying to frame Jay or her having any involvement in the Waltham murders. One could well understand why Hiba might want to numb her pain at this time or why she was not thinking clearly in wake of her shock and grief. Jay said he only used coke to ask Hiba questions without raising alarms and that she knows it's hard for him to say no. "She pushed and I obliged to appease," he wrote. Again, I cannot confirm Jay's characterization of this exchange. In her email to me, Hiba denied engaging in criminal activities in response to statements regarding her use of cocaine and other allegations.

At times Jay's writing veers into paranoia. He described a man at a sandwich shop with a tattoo of a snake wrapped around a naked woman and notes that Hiba arrived at his apartment at 4:44 p.m., "another bad omen."

"The detectives must have been listening and heard all these things," he claimed.

~

Jay wrote that investigators retained his emails and phones and that these devices "will show the truth." It's not clear that investigators did take a phone from Jay before his death. But they took two of them after he died. Investigators would likely be able to obtain records of who Jay communicated with and when on those devices. They might be able to use these records to confirm that Hiba and Jay communicated, when these communications took place, and digital financial transactions—if Jay's communications were limited to those devices. But it's unclear if investigators were able to read Jay's actual text messages. Richmond investigators made several attempts to unlock Jay's cell phones, according to police reports, and were unsuccessful. They called in Jay's associates to see if they knew his passcode. No luck. The detectives also contacted T-Mobile and AT&T and were informed that they would not be able to retrieve Jay's text messages if the phone was locked. On January 27, 2012, Richmond Police turned Jay's phones over to the Massachusetts State Police, and I haven't been able to obtain their records.

Crewell noted that he left a card at an address associated with Hiba, a day after Jay died. Hiba called him back. According to Crewell, Hiba said she did not want to talk to the police. The police had been to her house, "talking about a triple murder in Boston," and she said she was a victim but the police were still not treating her right. Crewell advised Hiba that he only wanted to talk about a phone issue pertaining to Jay. Hiba said she could maybe talk to Crewell the next week. It's not clear whether Hiba knew Jay was dead at this time.

Crewell interviewed Hiba ten days later, on October 18, 2011, in the back of a residential home. According to Crewell, Hiba said that she was aware that Jay was dead and that the last time she saw him they did powder cocaine. She reportedly said she left his apartment between 2:00 and 3:00 a.m. on October 6, 2011, and she said she never went back to his home. Though Hiba did mention that Jay texted her on Thursday morning to say that she had left a hotel room key.

Hiba also allegedly told Crewell that Jay once assaulted a white male because he owed Jay a few thousand dollars. It's unclear why Hiba shared this anecdote.

The detectives called Hiba again on Valentine's Day, 2012. According to Crewell's notes, she came to the department the next day and asked about Jay's note, and the detectives read it to her in its entirety. She also told Crewell that Jay paid for her plane ticket to Miami so she could see a friend. It was not unusual for Jay to buy her things and take care of her, she told the detective. Crewell asked if she was with anyone when she returned to Richmond, and she said she flew back with a male friend and a female friend who came to assist her after the "incident."

In regards to her communications with Jay in the weeks leading up to his death, according to Crewell, Hiba said Jay offered to pay her $50,000 for a divorce settlement. She said she sent him a text message suggesting that he pay her more. "Instead of 50,000 why not 500,000 dollars," Hiba texted, according to her own account, as recorded by Crewell.

∼

A couple weeks after the bombing, on May 3, 2013, the Richmond detectives were contacted by Massachusetts state trooper Jeff Saunders. The state trooper had a few basic questions. He wanted to know if Hiba and Jay were actually married—later Crewell would pull up their marriage license confirming that they had been. The trooper also wanted to know where Jay's writing had been in relation to his body—Crewell said that Jay died only a few feet away from the Bible with his writing tucked inside. The trooper also wanted to know Jay's religious affiliations. Crewell said he was Christian and again mentioned the Bible. Then Crewell wrote that he emailed the trooper five crime scene photos. On May 16, 2013, Crewell sent crime scene photos to the Middlesex office.

On June 5, 2013, Crewell met with Patrick Hart from the Waltham Police Department and FBI agents Darwin Suelen and Vince Chambers. In Crewell's records, he noted that he shared information about the case and identified individuals who were connected to the decedent. At the meeting the investigators made a to-do list, which included testing swabs from the shotgun, getting a copy of Jay's marriage license, and completing research on a woman (whose name is redacted) to determine if she was still living in the area. In addition to adding Hiba and Jay's marriage license to the file, Crewell later noted that the shotgun swabs did not produce DNA samples of value.

The next day, Crewell, Hart, and Suelen interviewed a man whose name was redacted. Crewell noted that this individual was "initially nervous" but spoke to the three investigators on the porch. The unidentified man said Jay had stored things at his place, but they never lived together. He described Jay as a "jealous type that was sarcastic," and "a schemer but most likely not a robber." The individual said that one time his apartment was burglarized, and he thought Jay had been involved, but he learned later that "two females did it." Crewell noted that this individual was evasive at times but clearly stated that he was never in the decedent's apartment.

On July 16, 2014, Crewell met with Katherine Boyd, a federal agent from Financial Crimes Enforcement after she sent him an email. She wrote that she did not know if there was anything "suspicious" about his death, but that he was "linked to someone murdered the month before he died." She also believed Jay was charged with marijuana possession in Fairfax County in 2009 but the charge was dropped. Officials redacted most of these email exchanges before releasing them to me. I was not able to contact Boyd. Crewell let Boyd read Jay's writing and view crime scene photos.

According to Crewell's records, the next time he was contacted about Jay's death was on November 20, 2021, when he received an email from me. He included the email in his files. "I think we would have a good conversation," I wrote. He never got back to me.

~

Evidently, in Hiba's account to me, she left things out. Apparently, Hiba's last encounter with Jay may not have been as "out of the blue" as she claimed, and it may not have been such a "long time" since they last met. Hiba and Jay characterized their relationship in different ways to different people at different times. Ian was under the impression that Hiba and Jay still spoke regularly while Hiba was in Massachusetts and that Hiba would turn to Jay when she and Brendan fought. Barbie was also under the impression that the two were in regular communication after the murders. "When she came back to Virginia, she did talk to him several times. [I] think they had a really solid relationship and were able to later continue their bond," Barbie told me. How does one reconcile those accounts with Jay's assertion to police that Hiba was making obscene phone calls and sending him threatening emails and texts? Or Hiba's account to Crewell that she was texting him about paying her a larger divorce settlement? Or Hiba's other account to Crewell that it was not unusual for Jay to take care of her? Or her account to me that they were "not often" in touch?

Hiba also told me that she did not *read* Jay's note. While that is technically true—investigators read "the entire" note to her—she was aware of the main themes of his writing. Barbie picked up Hiba from Jay's apartment after their last meeting, and Barbie remembered Jay calling Hiba as they were driving away. His voice sounded angry but she could not hear him clearly. Barbie wasn't sure if Hiba told her in the car that Jay was upset about her leaving the Waltham hotel key at his apartment or if Barbie learned about the key after Hiba was made aware of the contents of his note. But Hiba apparently told Barbie that Jay accused her of "attempting to frame him for the murders." Barbie didn't think there was anything obviously nefarious about leaving the hotel key behind. She told me she assumed Hiba went to visit Jay "because they still had a good connection and hung out." Later Hiba categorized Jay's note to Barbie and another one of Hiba's associates as "the ramblings of a madman." She apparently told Ian it was "gibberish." Hiba's categorization to me that she was unaware of the contents of the note is inconsistent with the facts, but I can understand why Hiba might not want to share that information, even if Jay's allegations about her are false. Even if the ease in which she came up with an alternative story is somewhat unnerving.

In December 2012, Hiba emailed Crewell that one of Jay's friends sent her a Facebook message and accused her "quite wrongly" of having involvement in his death. Apparently, the friend insisted that Jay was found with three gunshot wounds—according to Crewell's records there was only one. "[H]ow is it possible that you deem this as a suicide? [H]ow would he be able to shoot himself 3 times?" Hiba wrote. Hiba also asserted that Crewell only read her part of the note when she was "still in a state of complete shock" and could not ask all the questions she needed to. She was still Jay's wife and now she wanted all the information. She also wanted to know if Crewell confirmed the handwriting was in fact Jay's, and if so, she needed Crewell to provide her with the "credentials" of the handwriting testing facility. Finally, she wrote that she would like Crewell to release a statement "verifying" that he did not consider her to be involved in Jay's death. "It is not right for me to be harassed or my name to be slandered in such a manner. I think [I] have been through enough tragedy and turmoil to not also be accused in such a manner. [It's] extremely frustrating for me to think that as the detective on this case you did not make that clear," she wrote. Crewell advised that the case remained ruled a suicide and that if she wanted more information she would have to meet with him in person. Hiba stated that she might return to Richmond for just that purpose and provided him with a phone number so he could reach her in England. Perhaps Hiba remembered different things at different times.

Hiba told me she had a respectful relationship with law enforcement. Yet Barbie claimed she had to go so far as to call a psychic to coax Hiba into speaking once more to Massachusetts investigators, and this was before the alleged hot-and-cold interview Hiba mentioned, in which investigators questioned her about Brendan's other phone. Later she complained to Crewell that investigators were not treating her like a victim. But again, I can understand why Hiba would not want to mention that she was scrutinized by law enforcement to me. Especially in the wake of anonymously sourced reporting suggesting she had radical beliefs.

Hiba did not tell me that Jay paid for her trip to Miami. Given Jay's account that he bought her plane tickets, as supported by others, including her own account to Crewell, Hiba's story about the Wachovia ATMs not working is confusing. But perhaps that's why she needed Jay's help. Jay did not provide the precise dates and times of his alleged communications with Hiba. It seems likely that Hiba texted him about something she wanted to get off her chest on

Sunday, according to Jay's account. Yet, Hiba's accounts of her communications the night of the murders (that Brendan called and told her he loved her) and Jay's story of that night (that Hiba called him crying and said that she loved him) could both be true. Hiba's account that she planned to return to Boston on Sunday evening seems less compatible with Jay's apparent account that on the night of the murders Hiba texted him that she had life-changing news, spoke to him in tears about a Christian film, and then sent him a frantic text requesting a plane ticket. But they could be slightly more compatible if these communications occurred on Saturday—a possibility, given that Jay did not explicitly state when this exchange occurred. Jay's account that before the trip Hiba texted she was "leaving" Brendan and requested a one-way ticket seems somewhat at odds with Hiba's assertion that Brendan always expected her to return home. But it seems that during that period, Hiba's relationship with Brendan was very much in flux.

I can also understand why Hiba would not want to delve into accounts of Brendan's alleged infidelities or how these affairs may have also aggravated her relationship with Rafi. Yet the fact that this specific contention allegedly enraged her to the point of violence on multiple occasions is concerning. Telling me that she did not know about the affairs, and essentially putting me to task for questioning Brendan's character, goes beyond protecting one's private life and seems more akin to misdirection. She declined to answer other questions. She could have declined again in this instance or others, rather than provide a misleading account. The fact that suspected infidelities in her previous relationship also allegedly infuriated Hiba to the point of violence may be reason for further pause. Then again, Hiba was trying to maintain her public image in the aftermath of an international news event, apparently without counsel or media training and had every reason to fear that racism and Islamophobia could impact how she was portrayed in the press.

Hiba volunteered to me that she could not even imagine orchestrating a crime like what happened in Waltham, and that she did not have the ability, means, or connections. I did not ask her this question, which made it all the more startling when I later heard from three separate accounts that Hiba allegedly played a role in the plotting and execution of a vengeful, elaborate robbery of a roommate, as well as another robbery in which an accomplice was recruited, and another in which a victim was pistol-whipped. But Hiba has not been arrested or convicted in any of these crimes. Perhaps Hiba simply told the story that she felt best suited her in the moment so that she could move on with her life, start a new chapter, and devote her energy to giving back to society, teaching students, and taking care of orphans.

~

The Middlesex County District Attorney's Office did not answer questions or provide comment in response to a detailed list of reporting. Perhaps the office will soon issue a report debunking the overarching thesis of this book: a call for increased oversight, transparency, and accountability on every level. I don't know their side of the story. The office has not released a public account of what happened. Was Hiba involved in the Waltham murders, as others have alleged? I cannot resolve that question. I asked Hiba if she had prior knowledge of a robbery plan at Rafi or Brendan's apartment. She denied it. Are lingering questions about the role that Hiba, or anyone else, may have played in the Waltham murders cause enough to let the fundamental truth of the matter—Tamerlan Tsarnaev and Ibragim Todashev's guilt—go to rot? More than a decade later, that question still feels urgent.

A NOTE ON SOURCES

This is a work of narrative nonfiction. Every detail is as told to me, derived from firsthand experience or sourced from documentation. That is not to say everyone I spoke to told the truth. And some may have misremembered the past. That is why I also sought to corroborate reporting, highlight points of potential discrepancy, and identify the sources thereof within the text. The opinions and accounts of others, as detailed in this book, are not my own. Incidents in my childhood, teens, and early twenties, before I began reporting on this story, are supported by journal entries, news stories, and the accounts of others. I have sought to be accurate on these points of the story as well, and they are recounted to the best of my ability. In regard to the progression of my own thoughts and feelings, more often than not, I thought and felt many things at once at all times. I have simplified my perspective for the sake of clarity.

This book is the culmination of more than a decade of reporting, hundreds of interviews, trials, court documents, public records, reviews, records requests, and archives. Some of the interviews I conducted and the documents I obtained are sensitive. The names in this book are all real, except when noted otherwise in the text. This is a work of original journalism. I have included a table of some of the court cases I reported on in this book. Notably, *United States v. Tsarnaev* induced the sworn testimony of the Tsarnaev family's neighbors, friends, family, doctors, and trainers. I relied on this material extensively throughout the book. I also attribute the work of other reporters in this text, much of it excellent, and have included additional references to others' reporting, as well as historical references, in the endnotes. The endnotes do not account for my original reporting, which is attributed whenever possible in the text.

NOTES

Chapter One

"America's safest cities" *Reality Times.* "Safest, Most Dangerous Cities 2005." November 24, 2005.

"The Charles River, like the Boston Marathon, begins in Hopkinton" Hall, Max. *The Charles: The People's River.* Boston: D.R. Godine, 1986.

"Newton and Watertown argued" Thompson, Roger. Divided We Stand: Watertown, Massachusetts 1630-1680. Amherst, MA. University of Massachusetts Press, 2001.

"tidal estuary" Haglund, Karl. *Inventing the Charles River.* Cambridge, MA: MIT Press, 2003.

"heaving in and out like a lung" Rawson, Michael. *Eden on the Charles: The Making of Boston.* Cambridge, MA: Harvard University Press, 2014.

"like veins" Young, Alexander (Ed.) Chronicles of the First Planters. Boston, MA: Charles C. Little and James Brown, 1846.

"initially considered" Winthrop, John. *Winthrop's Journal, "History of New England," 1630–1649.* Vol. 1. New York, NY: C. Scribner's Sons, 1908. *December 21, 1630: "We met again at Watertown, and there, upon view of a place a mile beneath the town, all agreed it a fit place for a fortified town, and we took time to consider further about it."*

"'city upon a hill'" idea" Van Engen, Abram. A History of American Exceptionalism. New Haven, CT: Yale University Press, 2020

"romanticized rural life" Rawson, Michael. *Eden on the Charles: The Making of Boston.*

"built factories" Gitelman, Howard. Working Men of Waltham. Baltimore, MD: John Hopkins University Press, 1974.

"a weapons arsenal" "History of Watertown Arsenal." Historical Society of Watertown, 1928.

"6,000 years" Dinacuze, Dena F. "A Preliminary Report on the Charles River Archaeological Survey." Cambridge, MA: National Park Service, 1968.

"centered around estuaries" Bragdon, Kathleen J. *Native People of Southern New England: 1500–1650.* Norman, OK: University of Oklahoma Press, 1999.

"controlled burning" Cronon, William. Changes in the Land. New York, NY: Hill and Wang, 2003.

"take the land without asking" Shurtleff, Nathaniel B. (Ed.) Records of the Governor and Company of Massachusetts Bay, Vol. I. Boston, MA: William White, 1853. pp. 394.

"law forbidding the English to trade with Indians using actual money" Noble, John (Ed.) Records of the Court of Assistants of the Colony of the Massachusetts Bay 1630-1692, Vol. II. Boston, MA: Suffolk County, 1904. pp. 10.

"That which is common to all is proper to none" "General Observations: Autograph Draft." *Papers of the Winthrop Family, Volume 2.* 1629.

"let their animals wreak havoc" Morrison, Dane. *A Praying People, Massachusett Acculturation and the Failure of the Puritan Mission, 1600-1690.* New York, NY: Peter Lang Publishing, 1995.

"a myth that has been reiterated" Bond, Henry. Genealogies of the Families and Descendants of the Early Settlers of Watertown, Massachusetts, Waltham and Weston, Vol. I. Boston, MA: Little, Brown & Company, 1855.

"over and over again in local history books" O'Brien, Jean M. Firsting and Lasting: Writing Indians Out of Existence in New England. Minneapolis, MN: University of Minnesota Press, 2010.

"arranging to buy land from the Indians for Watertown" Shurtleff, Nathaniel B. (Ed.) *Records of the Governor and Company of Massachusetts Bay, Vol. I.* Boston, MA: William White, 1853. pp. 254, 292, 438.

"Gibbons set up several similar deals . . . a camp there . . . cleared a throughway" Krim, Arthur J. *Survey of Architectural History in Cambridge: Northwest Cambridge.* Cambridge, MA: MIT Press, 1977.

"In 1671, Indians tried to buy back the rights of the weir." Historical Society. *Watertown Records Compromising the First and Second Books of Town Proceedings.* Watertown, MA: Fred G. Barker, 1894. pp. 106.

"In 1738, a native community complained when Watertown set up a new damn" O'Brien, Jean M. *Dispossession by Degrees.* First Nebraska paperback printing: 2003.

"use the mystery surrounding Oldham's death to justify a brutal war" Cave, Alfred A. *The Pequot War.* Amherst, MA: The University of Massachusetts Press, 1996.

"Massachusetts colonists enslaved thousands of people" Newell, Margaret Ellen. Brethren by Nature: New England Indians, Colonists, and the Origins of American Slavery. Ithica, NY: Cornell University Press, 2015.

"Waban asked about securing land and protection for his people." Ress, David. "Autonomy, Not Assimilation." Australian Journal of American Studies, Vol. 41, July 2022.

"Chestnut Hill for a long time" Dinacuze, Dena F. "A Preliminary Report on the Charles River Archaeological Survey." Cambridge, MA: National Park Service, 1968.

"they were marched" "An historical account of the doings and sufferings of the Christian Indians in New England in the years 1675, 1676, 1677." Daniel Gookin.

"survivors returned" O'Brien, Jean M. *Community Dynamics in the Indian-English Town of Natick, Massachusetts, 1650–1790*, Vol. 2. Chicago: The University of Chicago, 1990.

"the Lake" "Nonantum, the New England Town with Its Own Special Language." New England Historical Society, 2022.

"Lake Talk is a cant" Noonan, Erica. "In Newton, They Still Speak the Language of the Lake." *Boston Globe*, September 13, 2001.

"*The Cannabible*" King, Jason. *The Cannabible*. Berkeley: Ten Speed Press, 2001.

Chapter Six

"boxed for Harvard" Rick, Spencer. "Crunch Time at the Gloves." *Lowell Sun*, February 13, 1985.

"refereed Golden Gloves tournament games" Hannan, Ed. "DA Tells Nashoba Grads: Exceed Your Potential." *Lowell Sun*, June 3, 2012.

"expert witness would later cast doubt" Cullen, Kevin. "Nanny's Case Could Have Broad Effects on Child Abuse Prosecutions." *The Boston Globe*, September 12, 2015.

"Jackie Delaire told Waltham *Newswatch*" Wangler, Chris. "Waltham Murder Victims' Throats Slit?" *Waltham Newswatch*, September 15, 2011.

"The murders were 'drug related,' police told the neighbors" Anderson, Travis. "Official Says 3 Slain Men Had Throats Cut." *Boston Globe*, September 16, 2011.

"it did not appear to be random" Jordan, Abby. "After Harding Ave. Murders, Neighborhood 'Will Never Be the Same.'" *Waltham Patch*, September 16, 2011.

"I don't think people need to worry" Ibid.

"provided no details" Anderson, "Official Says 3 Slain Men Had Throats Cut."

Chapter Seven

"three-day haul from LaGuardia to Boise" Ronnow, Karin. "Picking Up the Pieces: Family of Murdered Woman Struggles to Go On." *Bozeman Daily Chronicle*, October 21, 2000.

"She left the house on September 24 at 3:00 a.m." Ibid.

"around 7:00 p.m., she paid her bill" Jensen, Bill. "Long Island's Lost Girls: A Walk by the River." *Long Island Press*, March 2003.

"they found her cargo shorts" Ibid.

"fisherman found her naked" Kelly, Tina. "Victim in Idaho River Appears to Be Missing Flight Attendant, Police Say." *New York Times*, October 10, 2000.

"a boy walking his dog" Associated Press. "Idaho Murder Defendant Given Second Death Sentence." October 26, 2007.

"strangled with her own belt" Ibid.

"matched DNA" Ibid.

Chapter Ten

"War on Drugs" Edwards, Ezekiel, Will Bunting, and Lynda Garcia. *The War on Marijuana in Black and White*. ACLU Foundation, 2013.

Chapter Eleven

"the military ruler's mythic legacy" Manz, Beatrice Forbes. "Tamerlane and the Symbolism of Sovereignty." *Iranian Studies* 21, no. 1/2 (1988).

"2009 photo essay" Hirn, Johannes. "Will Box for Passport." Way Back Machine. Accessed April 19, 2013.

"Tamerlan's grandfather was one of hundreds of thousands" Williams, Brian Glyn. *Inferno in Chechnya: The Russian-Chechen Wars, the Al Qaeda Myth, and the Boston Marathon Bombings*. Lebanon, NH: ForeEdge, 2015.

"zombie" Shuster, Simon. "Exclusive: Relatives of Boston Marathon Bomber Break Their Silence." *Time*, April 15, 2015.

"sign up for a correspondence course" Gessen, Masha. *The Brothers: The Road to an American Tragedy*. New York: Riverhead Books, 2015.

"he was never actually an attorney" Jacobs, Sally, David Filipov, and Patricia Wen. "The Fall of the House of Tsarnaev." *Boston Globe*, December 15, 2013.

"an image of Islamic defiance" David Remnick. "In Stalin's Wake." *The New Yorker*, July 24, 1995.

"bowing to no ruler" Williams, *Inferno in Chechnya*.

Galeotti, Mark. "The Making of a Chechen Hitman." *Foreign Policy*, May 24, 2018.

"Islam to distinguish the Chechens" Williams, *Inferno in Chechnya*; Hellesøy, Kjersti. "Civil War and the Radicalization of Islam in Chechnya." *Journal of Religion and Violence* 1, no. 1 (2013).

"hub for organized crime" Cornell, Svante E. "The 'Afghanization' of the North Caucasus: Causes and Implications of a Changing Conflict." Strategic Studies Institute, US Army War College, 2012.

Hoffman, David. "Banditry Threatens the New Russia." *The Washington Post*, May 12, 1997.

"opening for Wahhabi extremists" Williams, *Inferno in Chechnya*; Hellesøy, "Civil War and the Radicalization of Islam in Chechnya."

"blamed the attacks on the 'Chechen terrorist nation,'" Williams, *Inferno in Chechnya*; Cornell, "The 'Afghanization' of the North Caucasus."

"theory that Putin orchestrated the apartment bombs" Knight, Amy. "Finally, We Know About the Moscow Bombings." *New York Review of Books*, November 22, 2012.

"Russia closed the apartment bombing" Myers, Steven Lee. "Russia Closes File on Three 1999 Bombings." *The New York Times*, May 1, 2003.

"especially popular among the Avar ethnic group" Williams, *Inferno in Chechnya*; Roshchin, Mikhail. "Sufism and Fundamentalism in Dagestan and Chechnya." *Insight Turkey* 6, no. 2 (Spring 2004); Cornell, "The 'Afghanization' of the North Caucasus."

Chapter Twelve

"working full-time to buy a house" Cullison, Alan. "A Family Terror: The Tsarnaevs and the Boston Bombing." *The Wall Street Journal*, December 13, 2013.

"Russian translations of Sherlock Holmes" Gessen, *The Brothers*.

"his pockets stuffed with merchandise" Davis, Aaron C., Jenna Johnson, Carol D. Leonnig, Tara Bahrampour, Will England, Stephanie McCrummen, and Mark Fisher. "The Tsarnaev Family: A Faded Portrait of an Immigrant's American Dream." *The Washington Post*, April 27, 2013.

"The Arbat Banquet Hall" Gaffin, Adam. "Russian Restaurant Gets One-Day Suspension for Bottle Service without City Permission." *Universal Hub*, April 12, 2013.

"whispering to her clients" Kilzer, Alyssa Lindley. "I've Met the Boston Bombers." Tumblr, April 19, 2013.

"filed for divorce" Jacobs, Filipov, and Wen. "The Fall of the House of Tsarnaev."

Chapter Thirteen

"sought out a copy of *The Protocols of the Elders of Zion*" Goldman, Adam, Eric Tucker, and Matt Apuzzo. "Bomb Suspect Influenced by Mysterious Radical." Associated Press, April 23, 2013.

"marked up the book with Russian translations of words" Cullison, Alan. "Boston Bombing Suspect Was Steeped in Conspiracies." *The Wall Street Journal*, August 6, 2013.

"stopped talking to Tamerlan when he moved to Rhode Island" Caryl, Christian. "'Misha' Speaks: An Interview with the Alleged Boston Bomber's 'Svengali.'" *New York Review*, April 28, 2013.

"felt there were two people living inside of him" Jacobs, Filipov, and Wen. "The Fall of the House of Tsarnaev."

"Tamerlan had his own subscription to *American Free Press*" Cullison, "Boston Bombing Suspect Was Steeped in Conspiracies." The Wall Street Journal, August 6, 2013.

"these publications were especially fixated" Meserlian, Donald "Pogo." "Domestic Terrorism: The Required Response to Tyranny?" *The Sovereign: The World's Only Truth Newspaper!*, no. 19 (January 2011); Griffin, David Ray. "9/11 Commission Omits Known Facts." *The Sovereign: 9/11 Was an Inside Job*, no. 27 (September 2011); Meserlian, Donald "Pogo." "Explosive Evidence = 9/11 Justice." *The Sovereign: Newspaper of the Resistance!*, no. 37 (July 2012); Gahary, Dave. "9-11 Cop Breaks Silence: Police Hero Who Busted 'Dancing Israelis' Talks to AFP." *American Free Press* XI, no. 40 (October 3, 2011).

"went to Phillips Exeter Academy and Yale" Cooper, Michael, Serge F. Kovaleski, Richard A. Oppel, and John Eligon. "Path from 'Social Butterfly' to Boston Suspect's Widow." *The New York Times*, May 3, 2013.

"she talked very slowly" Hesse, Monica. "Katherine Russell: Boston Bombing Suspect Widow's Enigmatic Life Journey." *The Washington Post*, May 5, 2013.

Chapter Fourteen

"compared their vision to the video games *Mortal Kombat* and *Street Fighter*" Plotz, David. "Fight Clubbed." *Slate*, November 17, 1999; Snowden, Jonathan. "UFC 1, 25 Years Later: The Story Behind the Event That Started an Industry." *Bleacher Report*, November 12, 2018.

Chapter Fifteen

"'the Coast,' a neighborhood in Cambridge" Maycock, Susan E., and Charles M. Sullivan. *Building Old Cambridge*. Cambridge, MA: MIT Press Cambridge, 2016; Cambridge Historical Commission. *Survey of Architectural History in Cambridge*. Vol. 3. Cambridge, MA: MIT Press, 1971; Boyer, Sarah, Kathleen L. Rawlins, and Kathleen Walcott. *We Are the Port: Stories of Place, Perseverance,* *and Pride in the Port/Area 4 Cambridge, Massachusetts 1845–2005*. Cambridge, MA: City of Cambridge, 2015.

"potentially where they cured fish" Krim, Arthur J. *Survey of Architectural History in Cambridge: Northwest Cambridge*. Cambridge, MA: MIT Press, 1977.

"W. E. B. Du Bois" City of Cambridge. "The Cambridge African American History Trail." City of Cambridge, February 9, 2022.

Chapter Sixteen

"stormed into the locker room" Sontag, Deborah, David M. Herszenhorn, and Serge F. Kovaleski. "A Battered Dream, Then a Violent Path." *The New York Times*, April 27, 2013.

Chapter Seventeen

"Russian intelligence agency secretly" Associated Press. "Russia Caught Bomb Suspect on Wiretap." April 26, 2013.

"My sons are innocent!" *Russia Today*. "'They Were Set Up, FBI Followed Them for Years'—Tsarnaevs' Mother to *RT*." April 19, 2013.

"I got more information from Russia" Ruzicka, Abbie. "Rep. Keating on Boston Marathon Bombing: 'I Got More Info from Russia than the FBI.'" *GBH News*, August 1, 2013.

"Tamerlan also complained about corruption in Watertown and Waltham" Gessen, *The Brothers*.

"Russia Didn't Share All Details on Boston Bombing Suspect, Report Says." Schmidt, Michael S., and Eric Schmitt. "Russia Didn't Share All Details on Boston Bombing Suspect, Report Says." *The New York Times*, April 9, 2014.

Chapter Nineteen

"Investigators believe that she knows more than she's let on." Martin, Phillip. "Is the Waltham Triple Murder Investigation at a Dead End?" *GBH News*, April 13, 2018.

"The anonymous associate said that Hiba and Tamerlan grew close" Rezendes, Michael, and Bob Hohler. "Stark Overtones in '11 Waltham Killings." *The Boston Globe*, May 24, 2013.

"Christopher Medeiros and Elizabeth Jason" Andersen, Travis. "Official Says 3 Slain Men Had Throats Cut." *The Boston Globe*, September 15, 2011.

"I love you." Hohler, Bob. "Waltham Victim's Girlfriend Says Tsarnaev Visited." *The Boston Globe*, May 25, 2013.

Chapter Twenty-One

"he hoped the murders could serve as a lesson" Grannan-Doll, Ryan. "One Year Later: Neighbors Moving on from Waltham Triple Murder." *Waltham Patch*, August 31, 2012.

Chapter Twenty-Four

"Solving this case remains a priority" Laguarda, Ignacio. "One Year Later, Few Answers in Murder of Cambridge Trio." *Wicked Local: Cambridge*, September 17, 2012.

"The police have done a great job," Ibid.

Chapter Twenty-Eight

"best friends" Rezendes, Michael, and Bob Hohler. "Police Probe Possible Link between Marathon Bomber and Unsolved Triple Homicide in Waltham." *The Boston Globe*, April 22, 2013.

"Police and prosecutors are stepping up their investigation" Ibid.

"He wasn't radical at all." *WESH 2 News*. "Interview: Friend Says Todashev Knew Boston Bombing Suspect." May 22, 2013.

"leave you alone" *Orlando Sentinel*. "Khusen Taramov Talks about Deceased Friend Ibragim Todashev." May 22, 2012.

"Ibragim had implicated himself" WESH.com. "Sources: Ibragim Todashev, Tamerlan Tsarnaev Are Responsible for 2011 Triple Murder in Mass." May 22, 2013.

"armed with a knife" Abad-Santos, Alexander. "The Killing of Tamerlan Tsarnaev's Would-Be Accomplice Wasn't So Simple." *The Atlantic*, May 23, 2013.

"tried to grab the agent's gun" Horwitz, Sari, and Jenna Johnson. "Man Tied to Boston Bombing Suspect Killed in Confrontation with FBI, Other Law Enforcement." *The Washington Post*, May 22, 2013.

"armed with a pipe." Schmidt, Michael S., William K. Rashbaum, and Richard A. Oppel. "Deadly End to F.B.I. Queries on Tsarnaev and a Triple Killing." *The New York Times*, March 22, 2013.

"pushed a table and thrown a chair." Friedersdorf, Conor. "Why Did the FBI Kill an Unarmed Man and Clam Up?: Law Enforcement Can't Get Its Story Straight in the Worrisome Case of Ibragim Todashev." *The Atlantic*, May 30, 2013.

"Ibragim was unarmed" Horwitz, Sari, and Peter Finn. "Officials: Man Who Knew Boston Bombing Suspect Was Unarmed When Shot," *The Washington Post*, May 29, 2013.

"FBI had cleared their own agents" Savage, Charlie, and Michael S. Schmidt. "The F.B.I. Deemed Agents Faultless in 150 Shootings." *The New York Times*, June 19, 2013.

"in other fatal FBI shootings" Sacchetti, Maria. "FBI Tight-Lipped on Todashev Killing." *The Boston Globe*, June 6, 2013.

"Maria Sacchetti wrote another report" Sacchetti, Maria. "Potential Witness Must Be Jailed until Leaving US." *The Boston Globe*, June 29, 2013.

Chapter Twenty-Nine

"cloaked in secrecy," Sacchetti, Maria. "Fla. Prosecutor to Investigate Todashev Shooting." *The Boston Globe*, August 10, 2013.

"McFarlane pleaded the Fifth" Sacchetti, Maria. "Ibragim Todashev Shooter Had Stormy Record as Officer." *The Boston Globe*, May 14, 2014.

Chapter Thirty

"her seminal book" Olmsted, Kathryn S. *Real Enemies: Conspiracy Theories and American Democracy, World War I to 9/11*. New York: Oxford University Press, 2009.

"In his 1999 paper 'Of Conspiracy Theories,'" Keeley, Brian L. "Of Conspiracy Theories." *The Journal of Philosophy* 96, no. 3 (March 1999).

"did not think Tamerlan killed him." Associated Press. "Boston Suspect under Scrutiny in Unsolved Killings." May 23, 2013.

"pointed reporters to Hiba." Anderson, "Official Says 3 Slain Men Had Throats Cut."

"Safwan Madarati was connected to a prominent businessman" Blackburn, Mark. "Name of Fugitive Businessman Who Once Traveled in Federal Conservative Circles Emerged during U.S. Drug Probe." *APTN News*, October 1, 2012.

Chapter Thirty-Four

"You always have to worry about false confessions," *This American Life*. "Update: 'Dead Men Tell No Tales.'" April 3, 2014.

Chapter Thirty-Six

"Bill and Denise Richard wrote an op-ed" Richards, Bill, and Denise Richards. "To End the Anguish, Drop the Death Penalty." *The Boston Globe*, April 17, 2015.

Chapter Thirty-Seven

"reporting and memoirs in Texas Monthly" Cook, Matt. "Soldier." *Texas Monthly*, January 21, 2013; Cook, Matt. "The Call of Battle." *Texas Monthly*, June 10, 2013.

Chapter Thirty-Eight

"pointed to as the first original work of true crime" Schulz, Kathryn. "Dead Certainty, How 'Making a Murderer' Goes Wrong." *The New Yorker*, January 17, 2016.

Chapter Forty-Two

"paid a visit to the department the day before she was killed" Horan, Kelly, and Bruce Gellerman. "Who Killed Gail Miles?: The Unsolved Murder of a Retired Watertown Cop." *WBUR News*, May 4, 2015.

"In 1935 Italian immigrants formed the St. Mary of Carmen Society" *The History of the Festival of St. Mary of Carmen in Newton*. Newton, MA: St. Mary of Carmen Society.

"1929 bank robbery that was dressed up" *The Newton Graphic*. "Nonantum Bank's Assets Gone." May 1, 1931.

"Some families lost a lot, some families lost everything" Pasquariello, Michael John. The Growth and Development of an Italian Community: Nonantum 1895-1940, A Masters Essay Presented to Professor Andrew Buni. Boston, MA: Boston College, 1978.

"allusion in a *Boston Herald* story" Carr, Howie. "Carr: Final Chapter in Winter Hill Gang History." *Boston Herald*, April 17, 2016.

Chapter Forty-Five

"stopped by HSI with a large amount of cash and gold" *WCVB*. "Local Police Dept. Getting $520K for Helping Feds Foil Gold Smuggler." October 7, 2017; *Boston.com*. "More than $500k Shared with Woburn Police Department after Precious Metals Probe." August 10, 2013.

"Beat Da' Wrap later changed owners and was closed in 2015" Grannan-Doll, Ryan. "Waltham Sandwich Shop Pays Overdue Taxes, Closes." *Waltham News Tribune*, March 25, 2015.

Chapter Forty-Seven

"someone called in an order to Gerry's" Rezendes, Michael. "Bombing Case Casts Shadow Over Waltham Triple Murder." *The Boston Globe*, June 8, 2013.

"returning to Boston to visit Tamerlan" *CBS News*. "Boston Bombing Suspect's Friend Ibragim Todashev Killed in FBI Shootout." May 22, 2013.

"thoroughly done." Kovaleski, Serge F., and Richard A. Oppel Jr. "In 2011 Murder Inquiry, Hints of Missed Chance to Avert Boston Bombing." *New York Times*, July 10, 2013.

SELECTED BIBLIOGRAPHY

COURT CASES

Bar Counsel, Petitioner v. Kris C. Foster, ESQ., Anne K. Kaczmarek, ESQ., and John C. Verner, ESQ. (Massachusetts, Board of Bar Overseers of the Supreme Judicial Court 2019).

Commonwealth of Massachusetts v. Erik Weissman (Norfolk, Brookline District Court 2008).

Commonwealth of Massachusetts v. Erik Weissman (Suffolk, Brighton Court 2008).

Commonwealth of Massachusetts v. Erik Weissman (Suffolk, West Roxbury District Court 2011).

Commonwealth of Massachusetts v. Ibragim Todashev (Suffolk, Boston Municipal Court 2010).

Commonwealth of Massachusetts v. Karapet Dzhanikyan (Middlesex, Waltham District Court 2006).

Commonwealth of Massachusetts v. Safwan Madarati (Middlesex, Waltham District Court 2006).

Commonwealth of Massachusetts v. Sean K. Ellis (Suffolk, Supreme Judicial Court 2016).

Commonwealth of Virginia v. Jeffrey Richard Runion (Henrico, Circuit Court 2011).

Dominion Creekwood & Dominion Olde West Apts v. Jay Edosomwan (Richmond-Civil General District Court 2011).

Estate of Ibragim Todashev, Plaintiff v. United States of America, Aaron McFarlane, Christopher John Savard, Curtis Cinelli and Joel Gagne, Defendants (United States District Court of the Middle District of Florida, Orlando 2017).

Hibatalla Kamal Eltilib, Plaintiff v. Aimee Johnson Edosomwan, Defendant (Henrico County Circuit, Civil Division 2011).

Hot Spot One, LLC v. Noble Resource MGT., LLC, Plaintiff and Jay Edosomwan, Defendant (Richmond, Circuit Court 2011).

Kathleen E. Donohue, Plaintiff v. The Town of Watertown and The Watertown Police Association, Defendants (Middlesex, Superior Court 2019).

Pyramid Investment Management, LLC, Plaintiff v. Umar A. Khasan and Khusen Taramov, Defendant (Osceola County, Ninth Judicial Circuit 2013).

State of Florida v. Ashurmamad Miraliev (Osceola County, Ninth Judicial Circuit 2013).

State of Florida v. Ibragim Todashev (Orange County, Ninth Judicial Circuit 2013).

United States v. Dzhokhar A. Tsarnaev (United States District Court of Massachusetts, Boston 2013).

United States v. John Analetto (United States District Court of Massachusetts, Boston 2012).

United States v. Safwan Madarati et al (United States District Court of Massachusetts, Boston 2011).

United States v. Steve F. Dunn (United States District Court of Massachusetts, Boston 2013).

United States v. Thomas Bailey (United States District Court of Massachusetts, Boston 2011).

United States, Appellee v. Dzhokhar A. Tsarnaev, Defendant-Appellant (United States Court of Appeal for the First Circuit, 2016).

United States, Petitioner v. Dzhokhar A. Tsarnaev, Respondent (United States Supreme Court, 2021).

RULES, LAWS, AND REPORTS

DOJ: Civil Rights Division. Rep. *Report On The Death of Ibragim Todashev.* March 25, 2014.

Inspectors General of the Intelligence Community, CIA, DOJ, DHS. Rep. *Unclassified Summary of Information Handling and Sharing Prior to the April 15, 2013 Boston Marathon Bombings.* April 10, 2014.

Jeffrey L. Ashton and Eric Edwards: State Attorney's Office, Ninth Judicial Circuit of Florida. *Law Enforcement Use of Deadly Force SAO Review Case Number 48-2013-UF-000014.* March 17, 2014.

Massachusetts General Law, § 12:27 (2013).

Massachusetts Rules of Court, 1-State § 3:07 (2013, 2020).

ACKNOWLEDGMENTS

First and foremost, I want to thank the families of Brendan Mess, Raphael Teken, and Erik Weissman for all interviews, extensive and brief. These were not easy conversations. Thank you, Bellie Hacker. Thank you, to Aria Weissman, for offering countless hours of your time to share your thoughts and experiences over the last decade. It would be impossible to tell this story without your guidance and help. I am in awe of your grace, clarity, joy, and strength.

Thank you to everyone directly impacted by this case, especially those who took the time to talk. People spoke to me when they were grieving and scared. People relived old memories and told stories they had never told before, for good reason. Thank you.

Thank you to everyone who spoke to me at any point of time in this investigation, even if only briefly before shutting the door.

Thank you to courthouse clerks, public information officials, and members of law enforcement who actually provided information. Thank you to the librarians and archivists at the Watertown Free Public Library, the Cambridge Public Library, the Tozzer Library at Harvard, and the Morse Institute Library in Natick.

A special thanks to those I collaborated with along the way. Thank you to *Boston* magazine, especially my editors Carly Carioli and S. I. Rosenbaum. Thank you to everyone at *This American Life*, especially Ira Glass, Julie Snyder, and Brian Reed. I could not have done this without you. A huge thanks to my incredible agent, Bridget Wagner Matzie, and the team at Aevitas Creative Management. Thank you, Kate O'Brian and the Turkey Land Cove Foundation. Thank you, Errol Morris and Josh Kearney, for wise counsel and advice. Thank you, David Hoffman. Thank you, Joe Tardiff. Thank you, Matt and Lauren

Cook. Thank you to everyone I collaborated with on *The Murders before the Marathon* docuseries, the team at Anonymous Content, the team at Story Syndicate, and the team at ABC News Studios. That was a wild ride and had a huge impact on my reporting. Thank you to the whole team at Little A for supporting this project and your patience, especially my editor, Laura Van der Veer.

Thank you to my friends who held me together at various points in time over the years: old friends, painter friends, café friends, book-club friends, photographers, poets, journalists, dancers, weight lifters, neighbors, lawyers, lovers, historians, botanists, and birders. You know who you are. I couldn't have done it without you, either. Extraspecial thanks to my journalist friends.

Reporting on this story was emotional and dark at times. But it also connected me to those I love, especially my family. I had a lot of great conversations with my father. I bet you I'll have some more after he reads this book. I love you. Writing this book strengthened my relationship with my father, for which I am so grateful. He was always there to talk about the law and push me on, as I detailed in the book. Reporting on this case also brought me closer to my older sister, Ariel, who was raised with a similar nose for crime. She was the first person I turned to when I was scared, or struggling emotionally with the information I found. This book is dedicated to her for good reason. A huge thanks to my mother for getting us to talk about something else. Easier said than done and absolutely crucial. And thanks to my brother for introducing me to the language of the Lake.

Thank you again to Erik for always believing in the best in people. I have collected dozens of accounts of those who remember Rafi, Brendan, and Erik and their kind words and their generosity that I was not able to include in this book. The memories of these men live on in the lives they have touched.

ABOUT THE AUTHOR

Photo © 2023 Nafis Azad

Susan Clare Zalkind is an investigative journalist based in the Boston area. Her work has appeared in *This American Life*, the *Guardian*, CityLab, *VICE*, the *Daily Beast*, *The Irish Times*, and *Boston* magazine. She also wrote and produced the 2022 Hulu docuseries *The Murders Before the Marathon*, named one of the best shows of the year by *The Wall Street Journal*. She likes to swim in the ocean.